KU-472-603

The British Isles

Certificate Geography

by

John G. Wilson B.A.

Schofield & Sims Ltd Huddersfield

0 7217 1038 7
0 7217 1043 3 Net edition

First printed 1978
Reprinted 1978, 1980, 1981

Certificate Geography is a series of five books:

Landscape and Atmosphere	0 7217 1031 x
Man in his Environment	0 7217 1033 6
World of Man	0 7217 1032 8
Language of Maps	0 7217 1034 4
The British Isles	0 7217 1038 7

Printed in England by Henry Garnett & Co. Ltd.
Bound in Scotland

Acknowledgements

The author and publishers wish to thank the following for permission to use copyright material and photographs:
Aerofilms *15, 23, 53, 90, 144(2), 146*
Airviews *50, 52 (upper), 58 (upper), 79, 102, 112, 123, 152 (upper)*
Amey Roadstone Corporation *24 (lower)*
K. M. Andrew *8 (2)*
Peter Baker *1 (left), 58 (lower), 61, 63*
Barnaby's Picture Library *48 (upper)*
John Beecham *11 (right), 155 (2)*
Birds Eye Foods Ltd. *47*
Bord na Mona *19, 81*
British Airports Authority *94*
British Gas Corporation *73*
British Rail *86, 88 (2)*
British Steel Corporation *25, 107 (right), 108, 109*
British Tourist Authority *45, 55, 147 (lower), 152 (lower)*
British Waterways Board *95, 96*
Bruce Coleman Ltd. *51, 57*
Controller of Her Majesty's Stationery Office *33, 35, 138, 139 (2), 140*. Crown Copyright Reserved.
Courtaulds Ltd. *122*
Coutant Electronics Ltd. *128*
Crown Copyright photograph *91 (left)*
English Clays Lovering Pochin & Co. Ltd. *29*
Esso Petroleum Ltd. *97*
Felixstowe Dock and Railways Board *99 (lower), 100*
Stephen Gibson *92*
Greater Manchester Council Joint Reclamation Team *159 (2)*
Archie Handford *74 (upper), 103*
Harland & Wolff Ltd. *113 (lower), 114*
ICI Ltd. *26, 28, 48 (lower), 120 (2)*
Irish Base Metals Ltd. *30*
London Brick Co. Ltd. *160*
Manchester City Council *91 (right)*
Mersey Docks & Harbour Company *87, 99 (upper), 137*
National Coal Board *71 (3)*
National Coal Board Opencast Executive *70*
Northern Ireland Tourist Board *10*
North of Scotland Hydro-Electric Board *83*
North-West Water Authority *43*
Peak Park Joint Planning Board *156*
Potato Marketing Board *46*
Sanderson & Dixon Ltd. *9 (lower)*
Kenneth Scowen, F.I.I.P., F.R.P.S. *67*
Shell *20 (2), 22, 74 (lower), 147 (upper)*
Shrewsbury Information Centre *134*
Skelmersdale Development Corporation *150 (2)*
Spectrum Colour Library *9*
Studio Jon *77*
United Kingdom Atomic Energy Authority *82*
Vauxhall Motors Ltd. *116, 117 (2)*
Waverley Photographic Ltd. *113 (upper)*
Josiah Wedgwood & Sons Ltd. *107 (left)*
West Country Tourist Board *11 (left)*
Wiggins Teape Ltd. *64 and cover*
David and Jill Wright *12, 54*

Contents

Preface

The traditional regional approach which has served geography so well for so long declines in popularity. It gives way to broader, more systematic studies. This book conforms to the current trend with content appropriate to the lower level of public examinations. The geography of the British Isles is treated in bold outline, but specific examples are frequently included to add precision and reality to the overall picture. Change is as much a feature of geography as it is of life. This aspect receives particular emphasis. The present is given its historical perspective and current trends are stressed.

The book is furnished with abundant and varied illustration. Maps, diagrams, photographs, statistics and graphs reinforce the text with which they are closely integrated. They also serve to prepare the student for the more elaborate types of question now commonly set in examinations.

The terms used for political groupings within the British Isles are a possible source of confusion. In this book, Great Britain refers to England, Scotland and Wales. The addition of Northern Ireland gives us the United Kingdom, for which 'Britain' is used as a synonym. The island of Ireland is made up of the Republic of Ireland and Northern Ireland.

The collection of the up-to-date material needed for this book would have been impossible without the kind assistance of many companies, corporations, authorities, associations, boards, federations and departments of government, both national and local. Mention in the text is an indication of help received and appreciated. Many who are credited for photographs also supplied valuable and topical information. My thanks are also due to the following:

Aluminium Federation
Brick Development Association Limited
British Ceramic Manufacturers Federation
British Independent Steel Producers Association
British Man-made Fibres Federation
British Quarrying and Slag Federation
British Road Federation Limited
British Transport Docks Board
Cement Makers Federation
Central Electricity Generating Board
Central Statistical Office
Chemical Industries Association Limited
China Clay Association
Container Base Federation Limited
Cornish Chamber of Mining
Countryside Commission
Coventry Central Library
Department of Commerce for Northern Ireland
Department of the Environment
Dover Harbour Board
English Industrial Estates Corporation
Freightliners Limited
Freight Transport Association
Government Information Services, Dublin
Greater Manchester Council – Joint Reclamation Team
Hull Fishing Vessel Owners Association Limited
Inland Waterways Limited
Institute of Geological Sciences
Institute of Petroleum
Irish Base Metals Limited
Medway Ports Authority
Milford Docks Company
Milford Haven Conservancy Board
National Ports Council
New Towns Association
Office of Information Services, Belfast
Port of London Authority
Port of Manchester
RHM Foods Limited
Road Haulage Association Limited
Sand and Gravel Association
Scottish Industrial Estates Corporation
Shipbuilders and Repairers National Association
Society of Motor Manufacturers and Traders
South of Scotland Electricity Generating Board
Stevenage Development Corporation
Textile Statistics Bureau
Tunnel Cement Limited
Water Resources Board
Welsh Industrial Estates Corporation
White Fish Authority

This book is dedicated to Kenneth Vose.

J.G.W.

1 The Firm Foundation

Fig. 1

Fig. 1 shows part of the Isle of Harris in the Outer Hebrides. The rugged land surface has been moulded by ice and frayed by waves to give a scene of quiet charm and beauty. In contrast, a dreary foreground dominates Fig. 3 which looks across the Dee estuary to the hills of Wales.

Fig. 2

Era	*Period*	*Million years ago*	*Geological events*	*Important rocks*
Quaternary	Recent		Ice-Age	Alluvium Boulder clay
	Pleistocene	2		
Tertiary	Pliocene	7	Alpine Mountain Building Period	
	Miocene	25		
	Oligocene	35		London Clay
	Eocene	55		
	Paleocene	65		
Mesozoic	Cretaceous	135		Chalk
	Jurassic	195		Oolitic limestone Clay
	Triassic	225		Sandstone
Paleozoic	Permian	280	Hercynian Mountain Building Period	New Red Sandstone
	Carboniferous	350		Coal Measures Millstone Grit Limestone
	Devonian	400	Caledonian Mountain Building Period	Old Red Sandstone
	Silurian	425		
	Ordovician	500		
	Cambrian	600		Slate
	PRE-CAMBRIAN	4500		

Fig. 3

Look again at the photographs. In Fig. 1, the thin soil is pierced by Britain's most ancient rocks. They are more than 1 700 000 000 years old. The flat land in Fig. 3 was not there when the Romans built their town of Deva (now Chester) 10 kilometres to the south-east.

The British Isles has a variety in landscape and rock that is unequalled in any equivalent area of the earth's crust. It stems from a geological history that has been both long and eventful. Fig. 2 gives the names of the eras and periods which serve as milestones.

The changing crust

The earth's thin outer shell is split into a number of large sections or *plates*. These are not anchored in any way. Powered, it is thought, by deep-seated convection currents, they are in slow but constant movement in relation to one another. Plate movements have profound consequences. The crust is rifted and oceans are born as plates drift slowly apart. Coming together they squeeze rocks into mountain ranges. Plates may slip laterally past each other. Their boundaries are shaken by earthquakes and punctuated by volcanic outbursts.

Today, as Fig. 4 shows, Britain is far from the edge of its plate. It rides safe from the violent geological

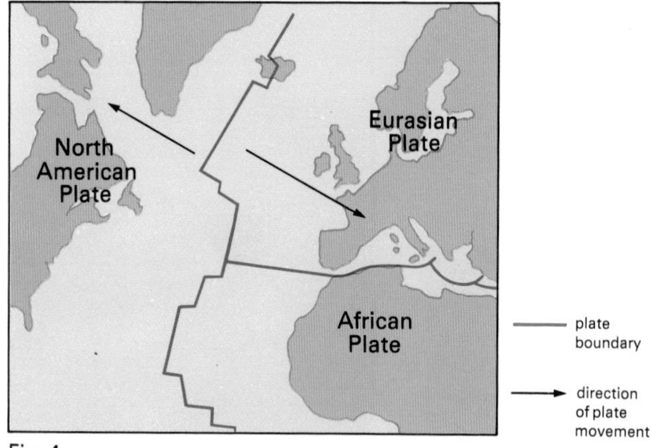

Fig. 4

Fig. 5

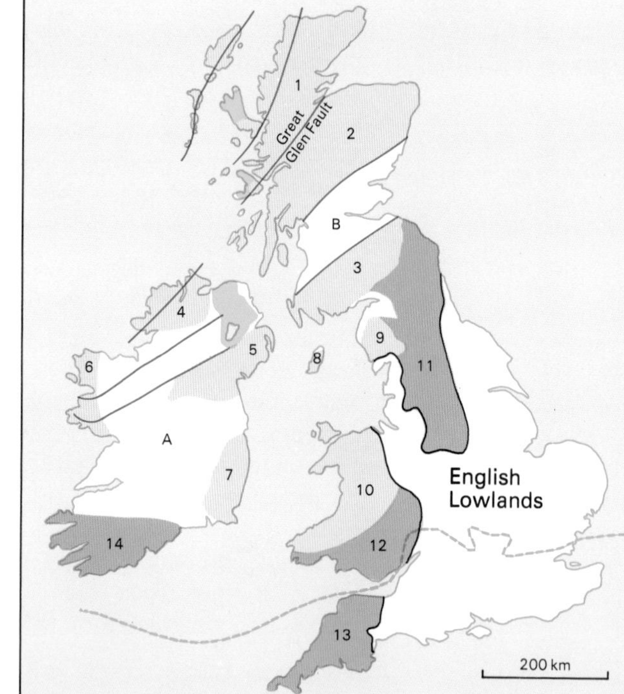

major fault line
Caledonian
Hercynian
Tertiary lava flow
edge of Highland Zone
most southerly extent of ice sheets

1 North West Highlands
2 Grampian Mountains
3 Southern Uplands
4 North-west Ireland
5 Mourne Mountains
6 West Connacht
7 Wicklow Mountains
8 Isle of Man
9 Lake District
10 North and Central Wales
11 Pennines
12 South-east Wales including Brecon Beacons
13 South-west Peninsula
14 South-west Ireland including Macgillycuddy's Reeks

A Central Plain of Ireland
B Central Lowlands of Scotland

disturbances which are common in other parts of the world. This has not always been the case.

Britain's oldest rocks, formed and distorted deep in Pre-Cambrian times, are found in small and widely separated areas. The ancient rocks of the Outer Hebrides are the visible remnants of an ancient plate. In England's midland counties, pin-points of Pre-Cambrian rocks pierce a thick cover of younger strata to form the minor hills of Malvern, Charnwood and Long Mynd. This again is an echo of a former plate. These two plates were once separated by wide seas which received thick sediments eroded from the bounding land masses. Slowly, over a period of many millions of years, they came together. As the seas narrowed, sedimentary rocks were compressed and contorted. Great volcanoes added a quota of volcanic material to the growing thickness of rock which eventually became a mountain range of alpine proportions. This range of mountains, known as the *Caledonian*, welded the two plates together. Little remains of its former lofty grandeur. Buffeted by crustal movements and attacked by denudation, it has been reduced to the series of worn-down discontinuous remnants located on Fig. 5.

On the flanks of these new-born mountains, and in low-lying basins within the system, debris accumulated and, with the passage of time, was turned into rock. Old Red Sandstones reflect the dry, arid deserts of Devonian times. Later, in the Carboniferous period, an advance of the sea led to the formation, in sequence, of limestone, Millstone Grit and Coal Measures. These great thicknesses of rock were destined not to be undisturbed for long, for a plate was arriving from the south. In a lengthy period of uplift, a new range of fold mountains was created. The British Isles were only on the fringe of this *Hercynian* mountain system, but eroded remnants are found in south-west Ireland and the South-west Peninsula. The most obvious relics are the great intrusions of granite which extend from the Scillies to Dartmoor (Fig. 47, page 30). The shuddering impact of plate collision had effects beyond the zone of rising mountains. Carboniferous strata were flexed into gentle folds. A long anticline produced the Pennines. Areas of Coal Measures were preserved in downfolded basins. Further north, the Caledonian mountains felt the impact and their brittle rocks moved along the lines of existing faults.

With the Caledonian and Hercynian systems, the British Isles gained the bare bones of its structure, but many details were still to be added. In the angle between these ranges, desert deposits have become the New Red Sandstone which underlies much of midland England. Evaporation of arms of the sea and inland lakes left a valuable legacy of beds of salt and other chemicals. Later, shallow seas spread over much of what is now south and east England. They received the sediments which are now the limestones, clays and chalk of this part of the country.

Britain bears minor scars of other plate movements. In late Tertiary times, for instance, far to the south, the plates of Europe and Africa were in collision. The impact created the Alps, but only the faintest tremors were felt in Britain. These were strong enough to flex the sedimentary rocks of south-east England.

Raw materials made available by crustal movements have been modified by natural processes. The agents of erosion have added fine detail to the landscape. Ice, for instance, has been a recent visitor. Four times it accumulated in the highlands and crept down to blanket the fringing lowlands. Uplands were carved into the sharp relief of glacial erosion, while eroded material was plastered over the lowlands. Fig. 5 reveals how small was the area which escaped its attentions.

Change continues. Rivers deepen their valleys and the seas nibble away at the coastline. Fig. 3 reminds us that in other moods the agents of erosion may create new land. Present processes are a living continuation of a long geological past.

Landscapes

Caledonian remnants

Compare Fig. 5 with the relief map in your atlas. The battered and broken remains of the Caledonian mountains correspond closely to the areas of elevated relief which dominate the north and west of the British Isles. These highland areas have a unity which stems from a common origin. All display the characteristic NE-SW trend of the former mountain system. This can be recognised in the direction of the principal folds within a complex geological structure. It is also seen in the line of major faulting. The Great Glen Fault, for example, can be identified in Donegal. The faults which bound the central lowlands of Scotland also extend into Northern Ireland, but are widely masked by outpourings of Tertiary lavas. The Caledonian remnants gain further unity from the nature of their rocks. These are predominantly ancient sedimentaries which have been transformed by metamorphism. Volcanic rocks are locally important, and, here and there, erosion has exposed masses of plutonic granite. All Caledonian areas have been harshly treated by time and the potent power of denudation. They retain little of their former lofty grandeur. They have been ground down to *dissected plateaus* of modest elevation. Rolling upland surfaces are a dominant feature; an aeroplane has landed on Helvellyn and a car has been driven to the top of Ben Nevis.

In spite of their common origin, the Caledonian areas show significant regional variations.

The Highlands of Scotland are the highest and most extensive of Britain's mountain remnants. Much of the land surface lies between 400 and 900 metres above sea-level and, in restricted areas, the Cairngorms, for instance, summits often exceed 1000 metres. In Ben Nevis, 1347 metres, Scotland claims the highest point in the United Kingdom. Fig. 6 was taken looking north from a Grampian summit.

Fig. 6

Fig. 7

The skyline is unbroken by sharp mountain peaks. High ridges of roughly uniform elevation extend to the distant misty horizon. Their uniformity of height reflects the former rolling plateau surface from which the present landscape has been carved. Rivers and ice have cut deeply down to create the greatest contrasts in relief. The highest summits usually correspond to areas of tough rock, such as granite, which have proved more resistant to denudation.

The plateau of highland Scotland is slightly tilted. The highest land, and hence the watershed, generally lies to the west. The streams which join the Atlantic tend to be short and sharp. In contrast, eastward drainage shows longer and larger rivers such as the Dee and the Spey. Before reaching the sea, these rivers flow over relatively wide coastal lowlands, a type of relief which is severely restricted on the west.

In the fine detail of its famed scenery, highland Scotland reveals the fresh imprint of the erosive work of ice (Fig. 7). Upland masses have been scoured into huge cirques kept apart by sharp arêtes. Glaciers have converted gentle valleys into straight steep-sided troughs which are deep enough to provide narrow strips of low relief. Local over-deepening produced the long, narrow basins now occupied by freshwater lochs. Powerful westward-flowing glaciers deepened their valleys below present sea-level to create the many sea lochs of a fjord coastline. This is in marked contrast to the smooth outlines of the North Sea coast.

The Southern Uplands rise as a barrier between England and Scotland. Caledonian in age, they are, however, more restricted in area and lower in altitude than the highlands to the north. Land above 600 metres is relatively rare, and the highest summit, Merrick, is 843 metres. The Southern Uplands are mainly composed of shales and grits which give rise to moorlands of gentle gradients, where the signs of glaciation are muted. Only locally, where igneous rocks intrude, does the scenery take on a sharp and rugged aspect. Drainage is mainly to the south and east. The valleys of rivers such as Nith and Tweed extend tapering lowland fingers deep into the upland masses.

The Lake District is England's small, compact share of the ancient Caledonians. Small it may be, but the charm of its varied scenery is appreciated by twentieth-century tourists as it was by nineteenth-century poets. Its scenic attractions have a geological origin. High mountains were worn down to a plateau which was submerged beneath the sea and thickly covered by sedimentary rocks. Earth movements arched the area into a dome, and a radial drainage system stripped away the cover of younger strata to expose the tougher rocks which now form the high core of the Cumbrian Mountains. A radial pattern of drainage was superimposed on these old rocks. Glaciers deepened the valleys and created numerous ribbon lakes.

Fig. 8 gives us a glimpse of lakeland beauty. Alluvial infilling at the head of Derwent Water is the setting for the village of Grange. Near, and to the right of the camera, volcanic lavas and ash have been chiselled into the craggy scenery that is typical of Borrowdale, once the home of a major glacier. In the left background,

Fig. 8

slates have been moulded into the more gentle outlines of the Skiddaw range.

In Scafell Pikes, volcanic rocks rise to 978 metres and so give England her greatest elevation.

Wales, north of the Brecon Beacons is dominated by Caledonian structure. Rocks are mainly sediments of lower Paleozoic age, but in Gwynedd, where folding was intense, mudstones have been metamorphosed into slate of commercial quality. Active exploitation, especially in

Fig. 9

the nineteenth century, has left its destructive mark on the present-day landscape. In Fig. 9, open pits and spoil heaps disfigure the area around Blaenau Ffestiniog.

The relief of upland Wales is dominated by rolling plateau surfaces trenched by deep valleys. These surfaces are generally more than 400 metres and often exceed 600 metres above sea-level. The highest elevations are found in the north-west where tough volcanic rocks have proved highly resistant. Sculpted by ice, they give the attractive scenery of Snowdonia where summits achieve 1000 metres. Extensive areas of high elevation leave little room for lowland. A narrow strip follows the coast, but it only widens significantly in Anglesey, in the Lleyn Peninsula, and where wide valleys, such as those of Conway, Clwyd and Dovey, extend inland.

Ireland reveals her Caledonian connections more clearly in the geological map than in that of relief. North-west Ireland shares its metamorphic rocks with the highlands of Scotland. To the east, the affinity is with Wales and the Southern Uplands. In Ireland the fragmented Caledonian remnants are relatively small in area and elevation. In the north-west, for instance, they consist of

Fig. 10

isolated hill masses or short ranges separated by wide lowland areas. These ranges, often glorified by the name of mountains, show the familiar NE–SW trend. Those of Blue Stack and Sperrin provide examples. The latter rises to the skyline above the peat-shrouded foreground of Fig. 10. Summits commonly lie within the range of 650 metres to 750 metres, and in this unity we have a faint shadow of a former plateau surface. In the east of Ireland it is only the presence of intrusive masses of tough granite that enables the Mourne and Wicklow areas to claim upland status. The surrounding slates and shales, which form high plateaus in Wales, are here reduced to rolling landscapes of modest elevation.

Hercynian folds

The British Isles lay on the outer fringe of the mountain-building activity of Hercynian times. Nevertheless, the shudderings of distant plate collision were sufficient to distort strata of Devonian and Carboniferous age into structures which are now the basis of upland areas of contrasting character.

In *south-west Ireland* the trend of Hercynian folding is well preserved. High ridges of resistant sandstone alternate with wide valleys excavated in weaker limestone. Towards the Atlantic, ridges rise to considerable heights, and the charmingly named Macgillycuddy's Reeks gives Ireland her maximum altitude of 1041 metres. The western ends of the ridges extend into the ocean like a hand of gnarled fingers, and submergence of intervening valleys has produced a pronounced ria coastline.

South Wales shows Hercynian folds which trend from west to east. Tough sandstones give rise to the high moorlands of the Brecon Beacons and Black Mountains. To the south, a synclinal trough preserves the full sequence of Carboniferous strata. This, levelled off to a plateau, has been deeply dissected by sets of parallel rivers. Their deep valleys give access to valuable coal-seams. Coastal areas of gentle relief give a southern fringe to the uplands of Wales. In the west, submergence has produced an indented coastline, the pride of which is the fine ria estuary of Milford Haven.

The South-west Peninsula is an area of varied relief. For the most part, sedimentary rocks support an undulating surface less than 200 metres above sea-level. Exmoor is an exception. Here, denuded folds of Old Red Sandstone form high, open moorland rising to 520 metres. The other upland areas in Devon and Cornwall are based on a line of granite intrusions which extends from the Isles of Scilly, through Bodmin Moor to Dartmoor (Fig. 47, page 30). They increase in size and altitude towards the east. The scattered Isles of Scilly are close to sea-level, but Dartmoor has a considerable area above 400 metres, and achieves a maximum of 621 metres. In Fig. 11, Bowerman's Nose, a *tor* of weathered granite, points to a typical Dartmoor landscape. Beyond a wide, open valley, the sides of which are patterned by cultivation, the land rises to the level skyline of a barren moorland plateau.

Fig. 11

The South-west Peninsula is unique among the uplands of the British Isles in that, thanks to its southerly position, it escaped the effects of ice. A varied coastline of cove, cliff, bay and beach helps to make this part of England highly attractive to the tourist.

The Pennines show the Hercynian mountain-building episode at its most restrained. A slight shiver of an earth movement was sufficient to arch Carboniferous strata into a long and gentle anticline. Trending N–S for more than 250 kilometres, it forms the dominant upland feature of northern England. Subsidiary folding has caused the westward extension of high relief in the major spurs of Bowland and Rossendale. Folding is asymmetrical with the more gentle dip towards the east. Major faults mark the western limb of the anticline, and it is here that the highest elevations occur. This is best seen in the north (Fig. 12) where Cross Fell (893 metres) towers above the wide down-faulted valley of the River Eden.

Fig. 12

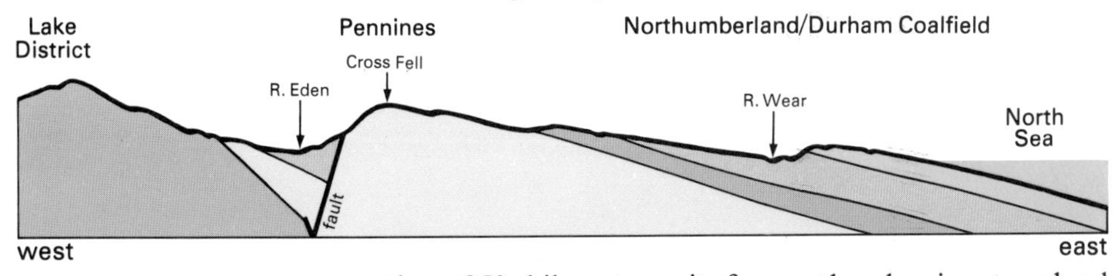

Fig. 13

The Pennine anticline has been stripped of its former cover of Coal Measures strata, remnants of which outcrop on the lowland flanks (Fig. 24, page 18). Millstone Grit persists in central districts and forms rolling moorland more than 400 metres above sea-level. Gentle surfaces are blanketed by thick layers of peat. In other areas, the Millstone Grit has been removed to expose the underlying limestone, which gives landscapes of great contrast. In north Derbyshire, for instance, inward facing gritstone scarps overlook a gently undulating limestone plateau of about 300 metres which displays the characteristic features of karst scenery. Fig. 13, looking west from Curbar Edge, provides illustration.

The nature of the surface rock has great influence on Pennine drainage. The wet Millstone Grit moorlands have a copious run-off and support an abundance of streams. The limestone is dry. Drainage is mainly underground. Only in the deepest valleys does water flow. The westerly position of the watershed sends the majority of major streams towards the North Sea. The charming valleys of Wharfe, Swale and Ure are among those which contribute to the natural beauty of the Yorkshire Dales National Park.

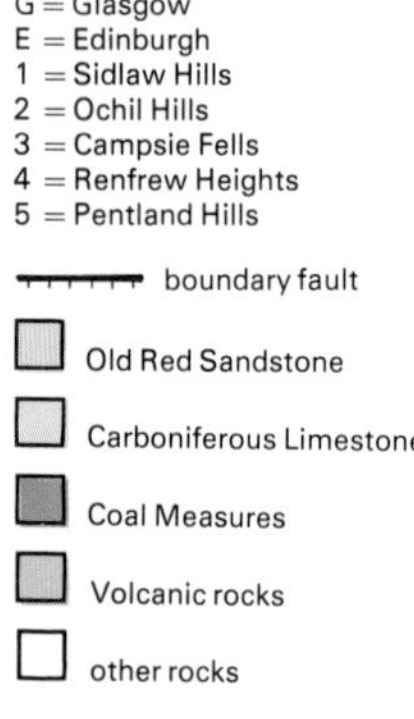

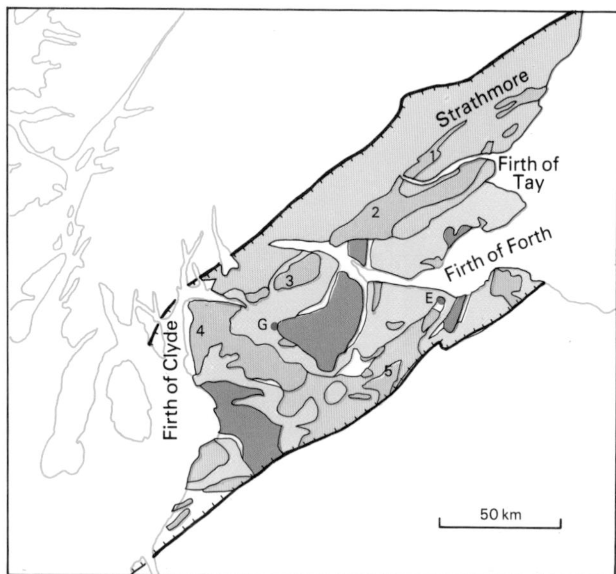

Fig. 14

Included lowlands

A glance at the relief map in your atlas reveals that the elevated parts of the British Isles are concentrated in the north and west. Highland Britain, however, is diversified by areas of low relief, two of which are large enough to merit special attention.

The Central Lowlands of Scotland (Fig. 14) is a tract of country up to 80 kilometres wide. It retains in its varied relief the evidence of an eventful history. Geologically its boundaries are precise. They correspond to major faults of Caledonian trend and age. The one to the north is marked by a scarp which rises steeply for over 300 metres. The southern boundary fault, though distinct in the rock, is not clearly seen in the relief. The land between the faults, having subsided to form a rift-valley, was submerged beneath Devonian and Carboniferous seas and received a thick sedimentary cover. Subsequent folding and erosion restrict the present coal-seams to small synclinal basins. Volcanoes poured out the rocks which now form the line of isolated upland masses which extends from the Sidlaw Hills to the Renfrew Heights. These volcanic fragments are separated from the Grampians by a wide vale, known in the north-east as Strathmore. On the southern margin of the Central Lowlands, relief features are less distinct. Volcanic rocks give rise to uplands such as the Pentland Hills, but they merge into the larger mass of the Southern Uplands. Small scale evidence of volcanic activity is frequently found within the lowlands. Resistant sills and dykes are common features. The castles of Edinburgh and Stirling sit neatly on top of eroded vents.

The sea makes great inroads into the lowlands, for the three great firths of Forth, Clyde and Tay extend far inland.

The Central Plain of Ireland shelters behind its broken upland rim but extends broad lowland avenues to the Atlantic Ocean and Irish Sea. Most of the surface is below 100 metres, but low plateaus of slightly higher elevation are found in restricted areas. The Central Plain is generally floored by Carboniferous rocks. These are mainly limestone, which in parts of the west have been weathered into the clints and grikes of stark limestone pavements (Fig. 15). Younger Carboniferous strata are also found but, sadly, the rare seams of coal are poor in quality. Here and there, anticlines bring older, tougher rocks to the surface and give rise to isolated hill masses such as Slieve Bloom.

Fig. 15

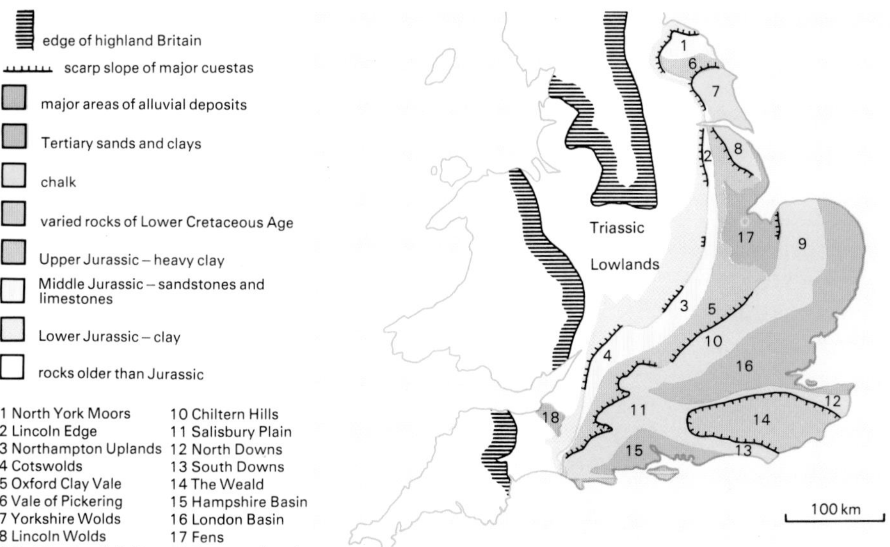

Fig. 16

Over much of the Central Plain, little is seen of the underlying rocks, for they have been thickly plastered with glacial debris. It is this that provides most of the small but significant contrasts which diversify the lowland surface. Boulder clay is widespread. In some areas, especially the north, it has been moulded into drumlin swarms. Elsewhere it rests in level sheets. Spreads of glacial sands and gravel provide dry areas in a generally ill-drained lowland. Moraines and eskers add further minor contrasts. Common in central districts are the extensive peatbogs which give a flat landscape of little charm, but which provide Ireland with a fuel resource of considerable importance (Fig. 26, page 19).

The lowlands of England

After the disturbances of the Hercynian mountain-building period, low-lying crustal areas to the north experienced a climate of great aridity. The reddish sandstone rocks which underlie much of central England are a memento of this period. Later, the wide advance of shallow seas was the prelude to the formation of a range of sedimentary strata. In Fig. 16, we see how they extend south-eastwards in bulging arcs from a line roughly joining the mouths of the rivers Tees and Exe. Limestone, clay and chalk are the dominant elements of the sequence. These young sedimentary rocks are the foundations of lowland England. But even here we see the characteristic diversity of the British landscape. The rocks differ in their resistance and are tilted and locally folded. Working on this varied raw material, denudation has created significant contrasts in relief. Steep-edged cuestas are separated by wide, open vales of clay. Illustration is provided by the simplified geological section given in Fig. 17.

A glance at Fig. 5 (page 6) reminds us that much of lowland England was swamped by ice in the recent geological past. Over wide areas, the bedrock is hidden beneath layers of boulder clay, sands and other glacial deposits.

The Triassic lowlands have their heart in the triangle bounded by the Pennines, the highlands of Wales, and the Jurassic cuesta. From this area, Triassic rocks extend in three directions to reach the coasts of the English Channel and North and Irish Seas. The link with the Channel is thin and tortuous, but in other directions Triassic rocks sweep round the southern Pennines to floor the broad lowlands of Lancashire, Cheshire and the Vale of York. These gentle plains are less than 100 metres above sea-level. Their slight surface undulations are mainly due to glacial deposits and the recent work of rivers. The midland triangle presents a greater variety of rocks and relief. Drift-plastered sand-

Fig. 17

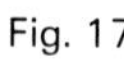

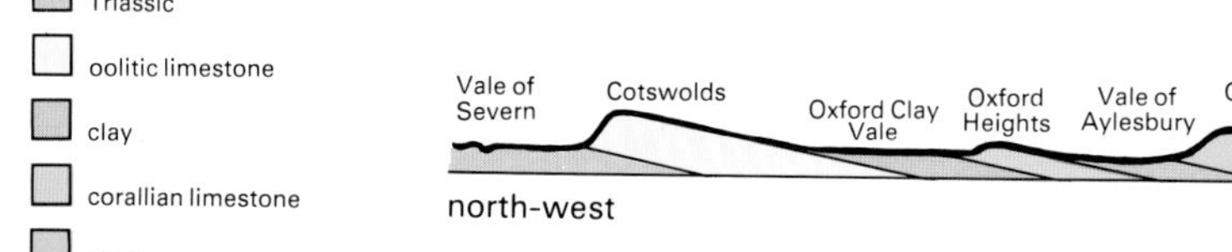

stones predominate, but here give low, undulating plateaus. Ancient rocks pierce younger strata and stand out as small islands of higher land. Charnwood Forest and The Wrekin are examples. Carboniferous rocks are also locally exposed, and give rise to a number of small but significant coalfields.

Jurassic hills and vales sweep south from the mouth of the Tees to the Dorset coast. They are developed on a variety of sedimentary strata among which weak clays and the more resistant sandstones and limestones are important. The tougher rocks give rise to landscapes of moderate elevation, the character of which varies from district to district. In the north, for instance, they give the rolling plateaus of the North York Moors and the Cleveland Hills. Much of the land is more than 250 metres above sea-level and the maximum is 454 metres. A steep scarp-face is presented to the lowlands of the Lower Tees. In Lincolnshire, Jurassic limestone gives rise to the low, narrow cuesta that is known as Lincoln Edge. To the south-west, Jurassic outcrops give the elevated but disorganised relief of the Northampton Uplands. It is in the Cotswolds that we see the Jurassic cuesta at its most majestic. From the Bristol Avon almost to the Avon of Warwickshire, they rise proudly from the lowlands bordering the River Severn. The fretted scarp-slope climbs to a maximum elevation of 330 metres. The gentle tilt of the oolitic limestone takes the dip-slope very gently away to the east. This slope carries the broad valleys of many small streams, most of which find their way into the Thames.

Fig. 18

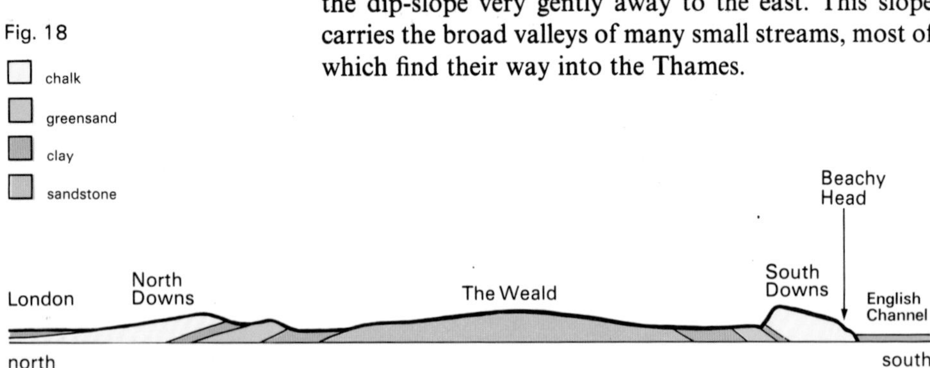

The disjointed arc of Jurassic hills is followed eastwards by plains of varying width which correspond to outcrops of weak and impermeable clays. In the south, a low ridge of limestone splits the claylands into gentle vales which bear the local names of Oxford, Aylesbury and White Horse. The rivers Thames and Thame handle the drainage of these low-lying areas. The lowland, now bearing glacial drift, widens as it swings northwards through the counties of Bedford and Cambridge. The clay disappears beneath the Wash but emerges in Lincolnshire to support the tapering vale which is finally pinched out just south of the Humber. Jurassic clays reappear once more to floor the Vale of Pickering. Here they have a veneer of alluvial deposits received when ice dammed both ends of the vale to create a large but temporary lake.

The chalklands have their focus on Salisbury Plain. From this area, a low rolling plateau rather than a plain, fingers of chalk point in several directions. To the north it mirrors the trend of the Jurassic outcrop. Starting strongly with the pronounced cuesta of the Chiltern Hills, it fades to more modest relief in Norfolk and Suffolk. After a break for the Wash, the chalk line is continued in the neat cuestas of the Lincolnshire and Yorkshire Wolds. The latter hides much of its dip-slope under the boulder-clay plain of Holderness. To the east of Salisbury Plain, the chalk has been affected by folding. The weakened crest of an elongated dome has been destroyed by denudation to reveal the sequence of rocks and relief indicated in Fig. 18. The chalk now forms the inward facing cuestas of North and South Downs. In a southerly direction, chalk reaches the Channel via the Dorset Downs, whence, with an eastward twist, it continues as a narrow ridge through the Isle of Wight.

Chalk gives rise to a distinctive landscape. A concave scarp-slope rises brave and bold, but rarely exceeds an altitude of 250 metres. The gentle dip-slope undulates with intricate valley systems which rarely hold water. A thin, dry soil characteristically carries a carpet of fine,

Fig. 19

springy turf. Part of the South Downs is viewed from the air in Fig. 19.

The Tertiary basins of London and Hampshire are the result of Alpine folding. The same crustal movements which arched up the Weald depressed these areas beneath the sea. They received deposits of clays and sands which were later elevated above sea-level. Relief is low and gentle.

The 'final touches' to the shape of the British Isles are provided by areas of new land formed by recent deposits. The Fens of eastern England is the largest area so created. The Wash is a lingering remnant of a wide, shallow bay which once extended over the clays of the Jurassic lowlands. Rivers and seas brought sediments, and created conditions favourable for the accumulation of peat. The new surface was made cultivable by elaborate schemes of man-made drainage. Except where former islands have been trapped in alluvium, the land is flat, low and monotonous. It generally lies but a metre or two above sea-level. In one or two districts, negative altitudes are recorded.

The Somerset Levels and the land which flanks the upper Humber estuary have been created in similar fashion.

2 Resources of the Rocks

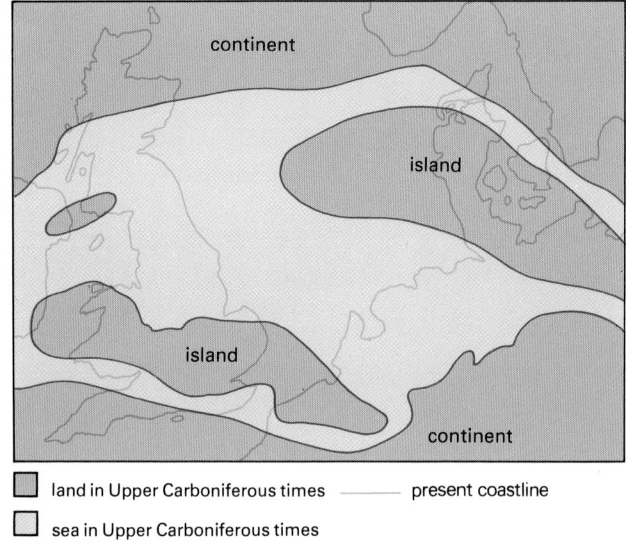

Fig. 20

Coal

Fig. 20 shows the distribution of land and sea in Upper Carboniferous times. A distant island-studded ancestor of the present North Sea was gripped between upland areas of continental proportions. Rivers draining these uplands built extensive interlocking deltas into the shallow waters. At intervals, this created conditions which nourished dense tropical forests. With the slow passage of time, sands became sandstones, muds became mudstones and, here and there in the sequence, forest remains were converted into seams of coal. These are geology's greatest contribution to the mineral wealth of the British Isles.

Fig. 21

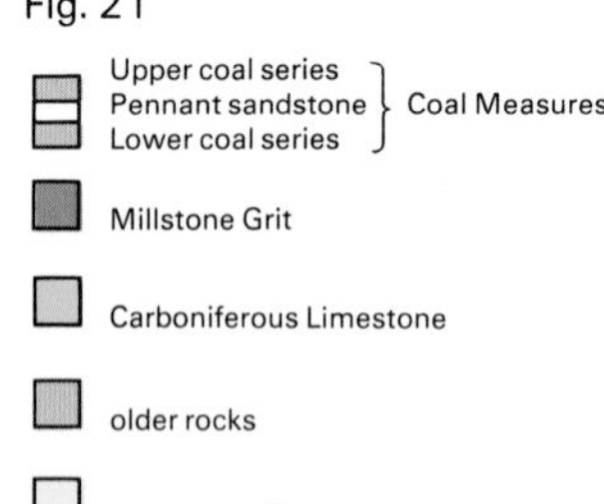

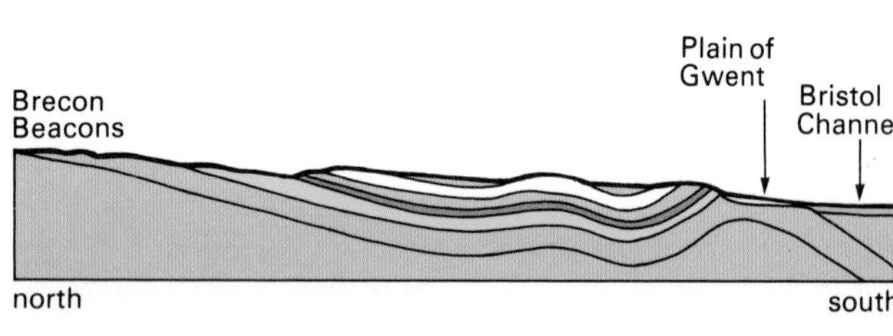

Nearly 300 million years have elapsed since the Carboniferous seas finally retreated. During this lengthy period much has happened to disturb the Coal Measures and restrict their workable occurrence to the areas indicated in Fig. 125 (page 70). Widespread earth movements have folded and flexed the strata. Uplifted areas have been stripped by denudation. Extensive deposits are now concealed beneath great thicknesses of younger rocks. In some districts, major faults have taken coal-seams well below the economic limit of present mining methods.

Britain's coalfields vary in size and structure. Those of Scotland, for instance, are preserved in small synclinal basins. South Wales (Fig. 21) has a similar structure, but is unique in its upland relief. The coalfields of northern England, which flank the denuded Pennine anticline, are but fragments of the former outcrop. Dipping beneath younger rocks, they sink to unworkable depths. In Cumbria and north-east England (Fig. 12, page 11) workings extend beneath the sea. The small coalfield of Kent is completely concealed and its existence was not proved until 1890.

Geological processes are responsible for further coalfield contrasts. Forest debris was converted into rock by the weight of overlying strata. Variations in the degree of compression have created different types of coal, each best suited to a particular use. Individual coalfields and even a single mine may yield a variety of coals. The emphasis varies from district to district. South Durham is noted for its high-quality coking coals. The production of anthracite is restricted to the western part of the South Wales coalfield.

Coalfields also show important contrasts in mining conditions. When a seam is faulted, folded, or varies in thickness, the extraction of coal is made more difficult and expensive. These unfortunate circumstances are common in Scotland and South Wales. In contrast, coalfields in the South Midlands commonly enjoy thick seams which have suffered little distortion. Mining is relatively easy and cheap, and output per man-shift is twice as high as it is in South Wales.

Consideration of coalfields which flank the southern Pennines will emphasise the contrasts outlined above.

Lancashire

The Carboniferous rocks of south-east Lancashire are arched up by the Rossendale anticline to form a westward extension of Pennine relief. Fig. 22 gives a simplified geological section of the exposures mapped in Fig. 23. On the northern flank, between Blackburn and Burnley, seams lie close to the surface but are thin and much disturbed. To the south, Coal Measures outcrop over a much wider area. Extending eastwards from St. Helens, they skirt Manchester before narrowing along the Pennine foothills into Cheshire. The strata dip to the south and pass beneath a cover of younger rocks. The dip is steep and depths too great for economic working are soon reached. Thus the concealed part of the coalfield is very narrow.

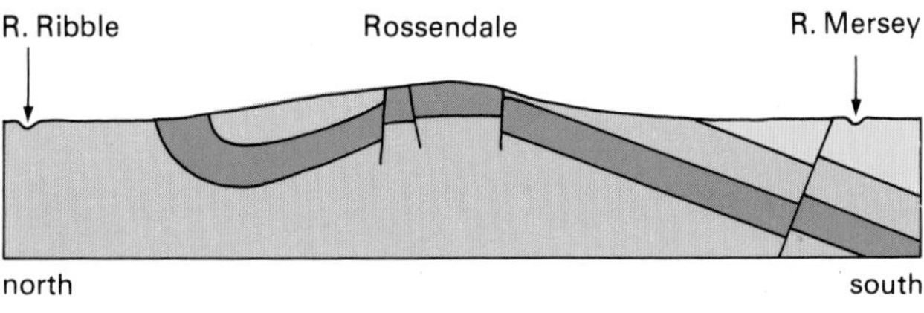

Fig. 22

major fault
younger rocks
Coal Measures
Millstone Grit
older rocks

Mining in Lancashire dates back at least to the thirteenth century, but only with the coming of the Industrial Revolution did it achieve any real significance. On an ever-increasing scale, coal was raised from small, primitive pits to power expanding industries and meet the domestic needs of growing urban populations. Production reached a peak in 1907 when, by pick, shovel and explosive charge, more than 26 million tonnes were mined. Since then the industry has suffered a long and steady decline. After a century of intense activity, the richest seams were exhausted. Costs of production rose

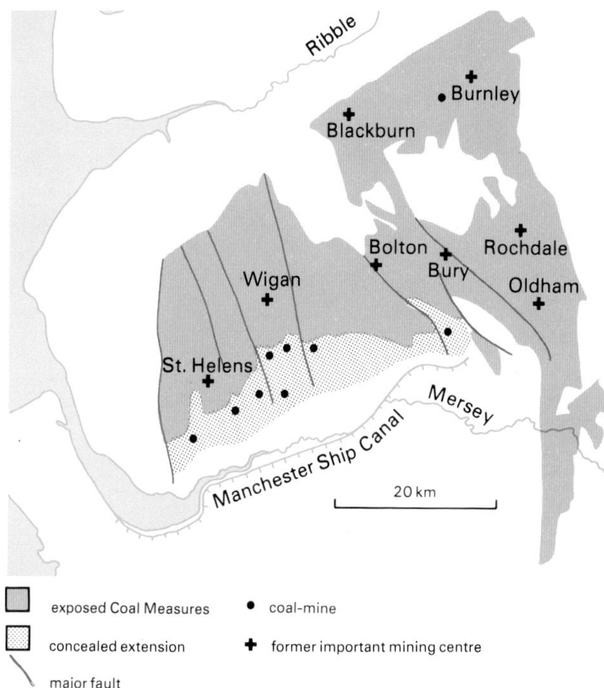

exposed Coal Measures
coal-mine
concealed extension
former important mining centre
major fault

Fig. 23

steeply. In all parts of the exposed coalfield, mines closed down in rapid succession. Over extensive areas, mining is now only a memory, but the scars are often still fresh on the landscape.

In 1975/6 total output was less than 4 million tonnes. Active mines are located on Fig. 23. Apart from a small and isolated exception near Burnley, they exploit the narrow strip of concealed resources on the southern fringe. Here, eight new or reconstructed mines contend with difficult geological conditions. The major faults, which give the coalfield its irregular outline, split the reserves into relatively small patches of workable coal. Seams are fractured by minor faulting. The steep angle of dip creates other difficulties, but these are partly overcome by new techniques which take mining down to depths of over 1000 metres.

Yorkshire, Derbyshire and Nottinghamshire

Only a narrow strip of bleak Pennine moorland separates two sharply contrasting coal-mining areas. To the west lies the difficult and declining coalfield of Lancashire. To the east is found the large coalfield shared by the counties of West and South Yorkshire, Derbyshire and Nottinghamshire. It has a history of exploitation as lengthy as that of Lancashire, but its present importance and future prospects are infinitely greater. It steadily increases its share of British production.

Fig. 24

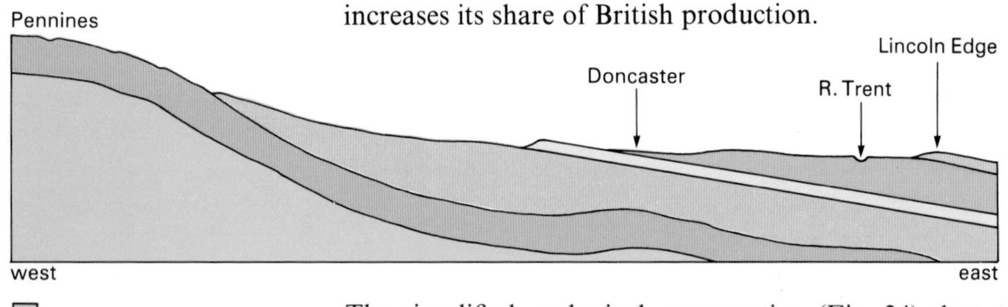

The simplified geological cross-section (Fig. 24) shows Coal Measures dipping off the Pennines in the wide outcrop of the exposed coalfield. Eastwards, the gentle dip takes them under younger strata to give a large concealed extension. The thickness of overlying strata increases steadily and coal lies deeper and deeper beneath the surface. The line of the Trent roughly marks the limit of profitable mining by present techniques. Fig. 25 indicates the great size of the coalfield. Coal Measures are exposed for a north–south distance of 100 kilometres. They widen northwards from 15 kilometres to 30 kilometres and cover an area of more than 2500 square kilometres. The concealed field is nearly twice as large.

Size is matched by richness of resources. More than 30 seams are of workable thickness, and together they offer a range of different types of coal, often of high quality. The strata are locally disturbed by folds and faults, but to a much lesser degree than is the case in Lancashire. Thick, gently dipping seams with good roof conditions facilitate mining operations.

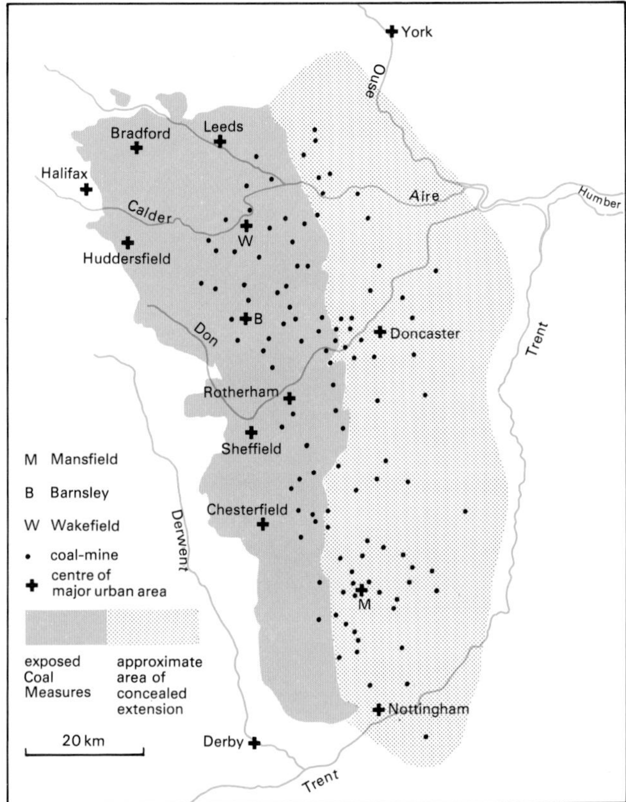

Fig. 25

As in other coalfields, it was the Industrial Revolution that stimulated large-scale mining activities. Early demand was met by active exploitation of the western edge of the exposed field. Over the years, mining has migrated further and further away from the Pennines. Old mines died, but new ones sprang up (or down!) to the east. The present distribution of mines is given in Fig. 25. The exposed coalfield is by no means exhausted, but the emphasis has shifted to the concealed extension. Here, rich reserves and good mining conditions have attracted much capital investment. New mines have been established and old ones deepened and reorganised. Most are now fully mechanised.

Peat

In watery environments, the remains of water-loving vegetation decay very slowly and accumulate as layers of peat, the poor relation of the coal family. Ill-drained upland surfaces are often covered to a depth of several metres. In lowland areas, peat has replaced many shallow lakes created by glacial action. Dug by hand and dried in the wind, peat still serves as domestic fuel, especially in remote parts of Ireland and Scotland, where alternative fuels are scarce and expensive.

It is Ireland that claims the most extensive deposits. The flat, dreary landscape of the peatbog covers wide areas, especially in the central lowlands to the west of Dublin. In recent years, great progress has been made in the mechanised exploitation of this resource. Annual output now exceeds 4 million tonnes. 25 per cent of this is in the form of 'machine turf', which resembles the hand-dug form, but is of better quality. Of even greater importance is the production of 'milled' peat. Work is in progress in Fig. 26. The peat has been exposed as far as the distant horizon. Deep drainage ditches divide the surface into wide strips. Powerful tractors draw triple milling-machines, which shave the bog to a depth of a centimetre and fray the peat into small strands. Other elaborate machines facilitate drying and gathering operations. A dozen harvests are taken in the average summer season, and the total yield is over 175 tonnes per hectare. Most milled peat is burned in power-stations. The remainder is compressed into briquettes for domestic and industrial fuel.

Fig. 26

Peat has other uses. Certain types are favoured in horticulture, as poultry litter and for packaging. Irish production for these purposes exceeds a million cubic metres, and 80 per cent is sold in overseas markets.

Petroleum

The remains of simple marine life were buried in the thick sediments which floored the seas and oceans of distant geological time. Long processes of decay, and complex chemical reactions, led to the formation of varied mixtures of hydrocarbons collectively known as petroleum. This, in the form of crude oil or natural gas, rose slowly through the pores and cracks of overlying strata until upward progress was checked by the occurrence of impermeable layers. Accumulating in huge anticlines and other structural traps, petroleum formed great reservoirs which awaited discovery by the modern techniques of oil exploration.

The rocks beneath the land surface of the British Isles have so far proved niggardly in their yield of petroleum. Oil is obtained from several fields, mainly in the east midlands, but total output is insignificant.

The rocks of the continental shelf have proved infinitely richer in resources of vital petroleum. Developments are recent, rapid and continuing. In 1959, enormous reserves of natural gas were discovered deep beneath the plains of the northern Netherlands. This stimulated interest in the strata that lay masked by the shallow but stormy waters of the North Sea. An international agreement, ratified in 1964, defined the rights of bounding countries to the submarine mineral resources.

Winning petroleum from beneath the sea is fraught with difficulty and only achieved at high cost. Seismic survey may reveal the structural arrangement of deep-seated strata, but only a well can prove the existence of petroleum. Many wells are drilled, but few strike oil or gas in commercial quantities. Drilling proceeds in a hostile environment. This is particularly so in deeper northern waters, where the weather is often unkind. Storms may bring gusts of 150 km/h and waves of 20 metres. Mighty mobile drilling-rigs are needed to withstand these conditions. An example is pictured in Fig. 27. This is the self-propelled 'Chris Chenery' at work in a strangely placid North Sea. It has a displacement of

Fig. 27

Fig. 28

27000 tonnes and its deck is the size of two football pitches. It is secured by eight anchors each weighing 20.5 tonnes.

The exploitation of successful strikes demands further great expense. A permanent production platform must be purchased and put in place. An example is seen in Fig. 28. It stands up to its neck in the deep waters above the Auk field. Oil from several wells is collected and delivered by pipeline to an 'Exposed Location Single Buoy Mooring' which rests at anchor 2 kilometres away. Visiting tankers are loaded while moored, then shuttle the oil to the Teesport refinery. From other North Sea fields, petroleum is brought ashore by submarine pipelines which may, in deep waters, cost a minimum of £1 million per kilometre to lay.

North Sea oil is not cheap oil, nor is it easily won. Production has demanded the development of a new and costly technology, and vast capital investment.

oilfield
gas field
oil terminal
gas terminal
oil pipeline
gas pipeline
sector boundary
water < 200 m deep
water > 200 m deep

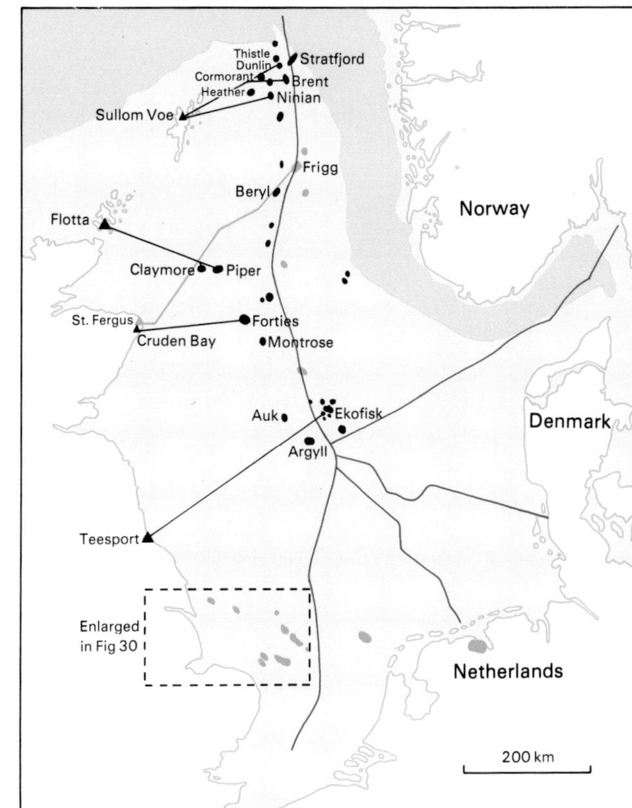

Fig. 29

major gas field
terminal
submarine pipeline

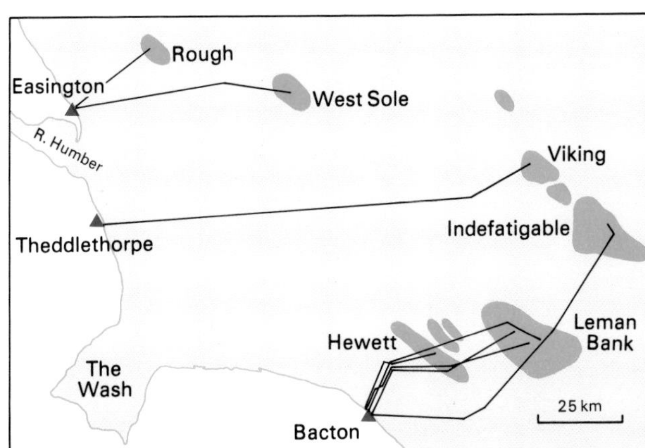

Fig. 30

The intense efforts of recent years have been well rewarded. Fig. 29 records the location and nature of important discoveries made up to 1976. Resources are seen to lie in three major provinces. It was in the most southerly of these that the first developments took place.

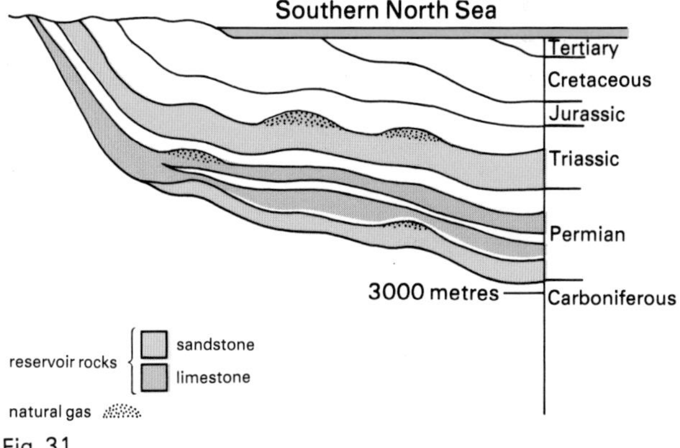

Fig. 31

Fig. 31 is a diagrammatic cross-section of the structure of this part of the North Sea. The varied deposition of over 300 million years is represented in the sedimentary sequence. Gas migrated slowly upwards, and accumulated within huge anticlines capped by impermeable strata.

The first successful strike was made in October 1965. This was the West Sole field, 65 kilometres east of the Humber. By 1968, four more major fields, and more than twenty of lesser significance, had been discovered. Within four more years major fields were piping gas to coastal terminals. Supplies from the Rough field began in 1976. Fig. 32 shows one of the six fixed unmanned production platforms which dot the sea above the Leman field – the largest yet discovered.

In the North Sea's central petroleum province, yield is dominated by high-quality crude oil. The Forties Field is the largest of several substantial finds. A submarine pipeline 136 kilometres long delivers oil to a terminal at Cruden Bay, north of Aberdeen.

Fig. 32

The third province lies between the Orkney and Shetland Islands and Norway. Large reserves of both oil and gas have been proved. The Frigg gas field lies mainly in Norwegian waters, but, because of a trough of deep water off the coast of Norway, it is more economic to lay a pipeline to mainland Scotland. After a journey of 320 kilometres, gas is received by a terminal at St. Fergus, near Peterhead. Flotta in the Orkneys is linked to the Piper and Claymore oilfields. The Shetland Islands serve the rich discoveries in the far north.

The dramatic story of Britain's oil and gas unfolds into the future. There are high hopes of new discoveries beneath the North Sea. Drilling rigs hold their station in the Irish Sea and in Atlantic waters west of the Shetlands. Exploration proceeds off the coasts of Devon and Cornwall. Successes may well be reported in tomorrow's newspapers.

Building materials

Geological outcrops have long provided man with convenient building materials. Often, the use of local resources has given a distinctive regional flavour to the human landscape. The charm of many Cotswold villages owes much to the use of oolitic limestones which weather to the warm and attractive colour of honey. Clays were moulded and fired into bricks which varied in colour and size from district to district. The textile towns of West Yorkshire grew out of quarries working the buff Pennine sandstones. With the development of efficient transport facilities, rocks of particular value could be transported far from their point of origin. Hillsides in North Wales (Fig. 9, page 9) were opened up to provide slate roofs for most of Britain's houses. Polished slabs of plutonic rock, such as the distinctive granite from Shap in Cumbria, came to grace the façade of many a public building. But taste and economic considerations change with time. Few of today's buildings are made of stone. The emphasis has shifted from natural to manufactured rock. Slate, for instance, has given way to tiles as the common roofing material. Reinforced concrete is favoured for public buildings, bridges, and towering blocks of flats and offices. Significantly, today's popular building materials have their origin in geological deposits. Cement, the adhesive of much modern construction, is a case in point. In its manufacture, calcium carbonate in the form of limestone or chalk, is mixed with silica and the oxides of iron and aluminium which are found together in rocks such as clay, shale and alluvium. In a rotating kiln, the mixture is fired by a third sedimentary rock – pulverised coal. Output now amounts to nearly 17 million tonnes a year.

Clay

Denudation of the land surface produces rock fragments ranging in size from large boulders to particles barely visible to the naked eye. Sorted by geological processes, they give deposits of distinctive texture. The finest particles accumulate to give clay which is of varied economic importance. It may, for instance, be used in the production of cement, and has an obvious significance in the pottery industry. It is, however, the manufacture of bricks and tiles which consumes most of Britain's annual clay output of over 30 million tonnes.

Clays suitable for brick manufacture are found in many parts of lowland Britain, but of prime importance is the outcrop of Oxford Clay which arcs southwards from the Humber to the English Channel (Fig. 16, page 13). This deposit of Jurassic age is thickest in the vicinity of Peterborough and Bedford. Here it is actively exploited to feed clusters of large works which account for the greater part of Britain's annual output of more than 5000 million standard building bricks. The dark grey Oxford Clay is particularly well suited to brick-making. It has a uniform texture and is cheaply excavated by large machines. It contains a proportion of combustible tar oil which burns during processing. This greatly reduces the amount of fuel required, and hence the costs of production.

5000 tonnes of clay are needed to make a million bricks, and excavation makes a major contribution to the distinctive landscape of brick production. Seen in Fig. 33, the works at Fletton in Bedfordshire are set amid abandoned and water-filled clay-pits.

Fig. 33

Sand and gravel

The distinction between sand and gravel is made purely on particle size. A diameter of 2 millimetres is the generally accepted dividing line. Sands of special quality are used in the manufacture of glass, and for moulding purposes in a variety of industries. The bulk of the output of both sand and gravel is delivered to the building industry. Recent decades have seen a sharp increase in the extraction of sand and gravel. In the last fifty years, annual production has risen from 2 million tonnes to well over 100 million tonnes. This increase is due largely to the growing popularity of concrete as a building material. Concrete is an aggregate of coarse rock particles bound together by cement, and it is geological deposits which provide the aggregate.

Sand and gravel are won from a variety of sources. In some areas they are obtained by crushing pebble-rich layers that occur within certain sandstones. A growing proportion of annual output is dredged to the surface in coastal waters such as those of the Bristol and English Channels. It is, however, deposits laid down during the Ice-Age which form the bulk of Britain's resources. These take two main forms. Melt-waters removed much fine material from the chaotic debris of glacial erosion to leave irregular deposits of *glacio-fluvial* sand and gravel, which are an important source of supply in the West Midlands and the north of England. In late-glacial times, flooded rivers floored their broad valleys with thick spreads of gravel which have since been carved into terraces by river action. These *terrace-gravels* are actively exploited, especially in southern England. The Thames Valley holds many large workings, for the gravel is of high quality and the great and growing market of London and south-east England is close at hand.

There are nearly 1000 active sand and gravel-pits in Great Britain. The small example pictured in Fig. 34 is located a few kilometres west of Scarborough. The

Fig. 34

deposit is of glacial origin, and includes pebbles from as far afield as the Lake District and Norway. The gravel is simply dug by mechanical excavators and taken to grading equipment by means of a lofty conveyor system. The exploitation of terrace deposits is often more difficult, for the gravel may lie below the water-table. In this case the gravel must be dredged or sucked from the bed of a flooded pit. This type of operation is pictured in Fig. 35. It leaves a water-filled blot on the landscape.

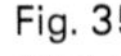

Fig. 35

The average house contains 50 tonnes of sand and gravel. A million tonnes are needed for 16 kilometres of motorway. With increased population and higher living standards, demand for aggregates will doubtless continue to rise. Even at present rates of production, extraction eats up land at a rate of more than 160 hectares a year. Happily, restoration of derelict land can provide valuable facilities for leisure activities. Examples will be found in Chapter 9.

Iron-ore

Britain's principal resources of iron-ore are bedded within the varied Jurassic rocks of eastern England. Fig. 36 reveals their patchy distribution. They occur in beds which range in thickness from 2 metres to as much as 9 metres. At their western edge, these beds lie close to the surface, but a gentle easterly dip takes them under a progressively thicker cover of younger strata and glacial deposits. The ore is of poor quality, for the iron content is only 25 per cent.

Apart from a small contribution made by drift (adit) mining, the ore is obtained by highly mechanised opencast methods. It is only the efficiency and low cost of

Fig. 36

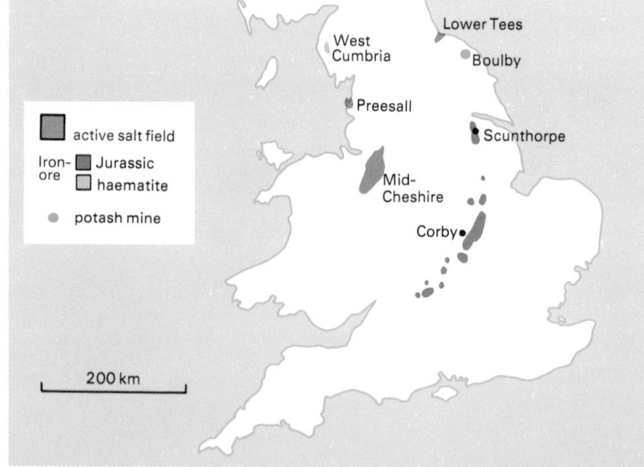

Fig. 37

this method of mining that makes it economically possible to exploit the ore. The scale of operations may be appreciated from Fig. 37.

Fig. 38 includes production figures for the principal Jurassic ore fields, and illustrates the significant changes of recent decades. The formerly important Cleveland district of North Yorkshire ceased production in 1964.

Fig. 38

Iron-ore production: British Isles *thousand tonnes*

Type	*Iron content %*	*Area*	*1913*	*1965*	*1975*
Jurassic	28	Cleveland	6137	—	—
	24	Scunthorpe	2683	7718	2490
	26	Other districts	3978	7529	1832
Haematite	49	Cumbria	1383	265	168
	50	Glamorgan	45	149	—
Blackband (Coal Measure)	33	Staffordshire	905	—	—
		Scotland	602	—	—
		Lancashire	413	—	—
		Total	16146	15661	4490

Mining in the vicinity of Banbury met a similar fate in 1967. Figures for the remaining ore fields record a marked decline. Annual production is now only 28 per cent of the 1965 level. Two major factors contribute to the continuing decline. Demand for lean Jurassic ores decreases as the British steel industry makes greater use of rich ores imported cheaply from overseas. The second factor is the growing expense of domestic ore production. The more accessible beds have been fully exploited. New development involves the costly removal of greater thicknesses of overburden. It is also more costly to replace rock, subsoil and soil in the correct sequence in order that the land may be restored to agricultural use.

Jurassic ores represent 96 per cent of domestic production. The balance comes from West Cumbria. Here the yield is of a different type. The ore occurs in irregular masses set within limestone strata, and has an iron content of 49 per cent. Today's output of some 168 000 tonnes is only a faint echo of former activity. The nineteenth century growth of the steel industry in Cumbria was fostered by the rich local ores, production of which rose as high as 3 million tonnes a year.

Coal Measure strata often include beds of low-quality iron-ore. Their occurrence, in close association with coal, was much appreciated by the nineteenth century iron and steel industry, especially in Staffordshire, South Wales and Scotland. Today, they are of historical interest only. After many years of decline, exploitation finally ceased in 1942. It is not that reserves are exhausted. Far from it. Many millions of tonnes remain, but the cost of mining thin seams at great depth is prohibitive.

Evaporites

During Permo-Triassic times, much of what is now lowland Britain experienced a climate of great aridity. Salt lakes were a common feature of the landscape and, at intervals, shallow arms of the sea extended over the lower parts of the land surface. These waters, rich in dissolved minerals, were exposed to fierce evaporation in the hot desert sunshine. Minerals were deposited thickly on the dried beds of lakes and oceans and are today preserved beneath younger sedimentary rocks. The most important of these *evaporites* are salt and potash.

Salt

Common salt, the chloride of sodium, adds flavour to food and melts snow on the road, but its most important use is as a raw material in the chemical industry. Britain is well endowed with this important natural resource. Known salt fields are indicated in Fig. 36. In addition, thick beds of salt underlie much of east Yorkshire and north Lincolnshire, but at unworkable depths. Today, salt is extracted in Northern Ireland, Lancashire, Teesside and Cheshire. The last named field, mapped in Fig. 39, accounts for more than 90 per cent of the United Kingdom's output which totalled 8 million tonnes in 1975.

The Meadowbank mine near Winsford exploits a rich bed of salt which occurs at the relatively shallow depth of 120 metres. Large cavities are excavated, but wide columns of salt are left to support the roof. Mining by this 'room and pillar' method yields approximately 2 million tonnes of rock-salt which is crushed for winter road maintenance. Elsewhere it is salt in solution which is brought to the surface. In some areas brine is formed naturally as underground water circulates in the strata. This 'wild' brine is obtained from wells near Sandbach and Middlewich in Cheshire. Of much greater importance is brine produced by solution mining methods. A steel pipe is drilled down to the salt. A narrower pipe is inserted within it. Water is forced down the outside and brine is drawn up through the inner pipe. Holford is the main centre of solution mining, and well-heads, such as the one seen in Fig. 40, are dotted over a wide area. Evaporation of the brine gives salt for domestic and industrial use. Most of the brine output, however, is moved by pipeline to large chemical works in Widnes and Runcorn.

Extractive industries leave their mark on the landscape, and salt is no exception. Nineteenth-century activity caused great damage through subsidence, especially in the Northwich area. Buildings tilted drunkenly and wide, shallow lakes or 'flashes' appeared in the surrounding countryside. Today, fortunately, the risk of subsidence is greatly reduced. Solution mining is tightly controlled to minimise the danger. Many large underground cavities are produced, but they are full of brine when abandoned. The large masses of salt left between the cavities provide additional support for the overlying strata.

Fig. 39

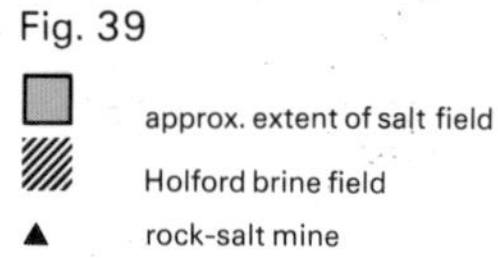

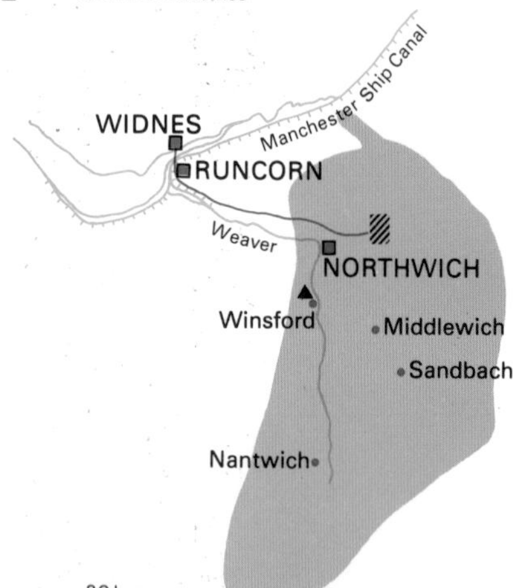

Fig. 40

Potash

Fig. 41 shows Britain's one and only potash mine. Set in the rural landscape of the North York Moors National Park, it lies near the village of Boulby, 25 kilometres east of Middlesbrough. Surface installations rise above twin shafts which reach down to a depth of 1100 metres. Fig. 42 charts their journey.

Fig. 41

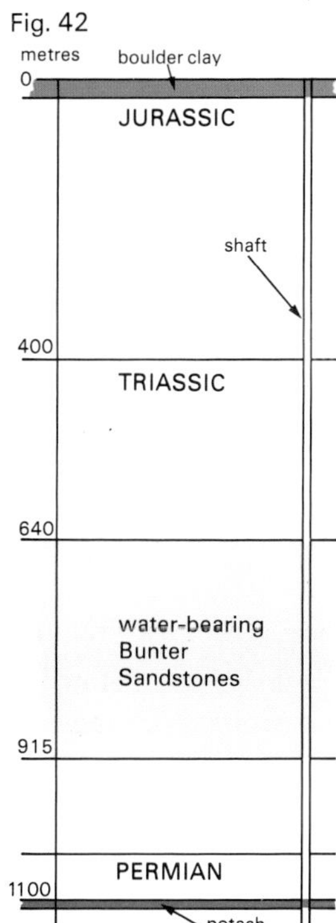

Fig. 42

The occurrence of potash in this area has been known since 1939. It was, however, only with renewed exploration in 1964 that the deposit was encountered at workable depths. It was a most valuable discovery. The ore is abundant and rich. It varies in thickness between 5 metres and 10 metres, and, with a potassium chloride content of 47 per cent, it is comparable with the best in the world.

Room and pillar mining methods are employed at Boulby. Blasted by explosives, the broken ore is conveyed to the foot of the shaft and lifted to the surface, where it is processed to remove impurities. Waste material, mainly common salt, is discharged off-shore by pipeline. Potash, much used in the manufacture of fertilizers, is produced at the rate of a million tonnes per year. This satisfies home demand and leaves a useful surplus for export. Some potash is despatched by road, directly to the customer, but most passes through a wharf on the south bank of the Tees estuary on its way to home and overseas markets.

Limestone

In many ancient seas, the remains of marine organisms rained down through clear waters to accumulate on the floor beneath. These deposits of calcium carbonate are now the varied limestones which are found in many parts of the British Isles.

Limestone is an economic resource of great importance. It is a vital raw material in many branches of the chemical industry, and the blast-furnace consumes large amounts as iron is freed from its ore. Ground to a powder or processed into lime, it is spread on the land to improve the quality of acid soils. Tough varieties, crushed to convenient size, are widely used in the construction of roads and railways. Its significance in cement manufacture was indicated on page 22.

Of Britain's several limestones, two are of major importance. These are the chalk which stands up as prominent cuestas in lowland England, and the massive limestones of Carboniferous age exposed in the Pennines, north and south Wales, the Mendips and elsewhere. 20 million tonnes of chalk are quarried annually. The figure for limestone is nearly five times as great.

In the Peak District of Derbyshire, rich resources of Carboniferous Limestone are exploited in twenty-six large quarries. Ten are clustered in the vicinity of Buxton (Fig. 43). By far the largest is the Tunstead quarry of I.C.I. Ltd., which is located on the western side of Great Rocks Dale. It is a highly favourable situation. The deep, steep-sided dale is flanked by high exposures of pale grey limestone. Bedding is thick and virtually horizontal, and the rock is of exceptional purity. Some horizons are more than 99 per cent calcium carbonate. The floor of the dale carries rail communications and large markets for limestone are close at hand.

Tunstead quarry is worked in two faces. The more important, part of which is seen in Fig. 44, is 2 kilometres long and rises as high as 60 metres above floor level. A thin overburden is scraped away, and holes are

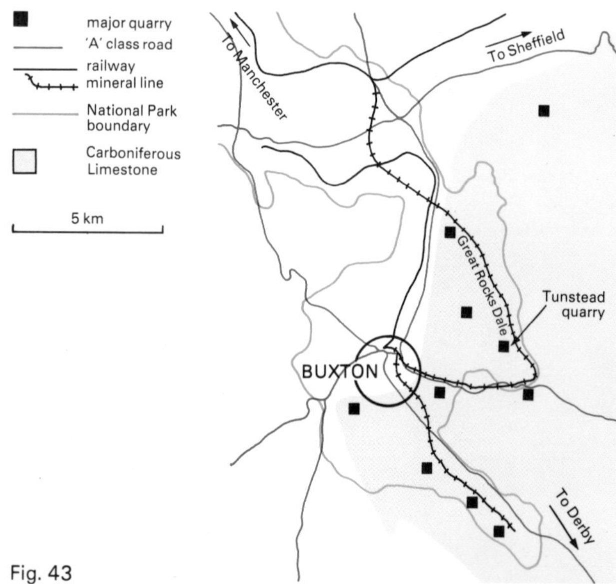

Fig. 43

Fig. 44

drilled deep into the rock from the top of the face. Slurry explosive is pumped into a set of holes and detonation can bring down as much as 100 000 tonnes of shattered rock. There is more to quarrying than blasting and shifting. 25 per cent of output is despatched direct to I.C.I.'s chemical works in mid-Cheshire, but the balance is processed on site. Much is crushed and graded for use as road-stone, some being coated with asphalt. Tunstead is the country's largest single producer of lime and hydrated lime. The processing of large quantities of rock is cheaply accomplished by elaborate large-scale equipment.

Kaolin

Granite, with its prominent crystals of feldspar, mica and quartz is, perhaps, the most familiar of all plutonic rocks. In parts of the South-west Peninsula, especially in the vicinity of St. Austell, granite has been affected by hot vapours rising from deep in the earth's crust. These vapours have changed the feldspar into a fine, white clay known as kaolin or china clay.

Kaolin is used as a raw material in a variety of industries. 80 per cent of production goes into the manufacture of paper and board. It is kaolin, for instance, that gives these pages the smooth, bright surface that is required for clear colour printing. A further 10 per cent is delivered to the ceramics industry, and the balance finds its way into such diverse products as paint, tyres, pills and fertilizers. The extremely high quality of Cornish kaolin is appreciated throughout the world and almost 75 per cent of output is exported through the small but busy ports of Fowey and Par.

Kaolin occurs in large masses set in areas of unaltered granite. Fig. 45 illustrates the quarrying method. A remotely controlled monitor directs a powerful jet of water at the pit face. The rock disintegrates and flows to the bottom of the pit. Coarse quartz sand is extracted, lifted to the surface and piled into tall, white spoil heaps.

Fig. 45

The clay-charged water is pumped from the pit and piped to nearby processing plants. Mica and other impurities are filtered out and most of the water is also removed. Finally, the clay is dried and prepared for shipment.

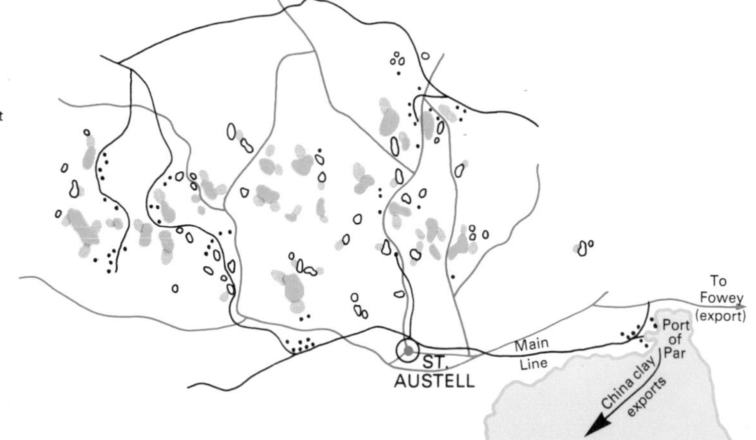

Fig. 46

It will be appreciated from Figs. 45 and 46 that the quarrying of kaolin has a damaging effect on the landscape. The unsightly pits are not obtrusive, but the spoil heaps, glistening in the Cornish sunshine, are visible for some distance. It is damage that is hard to control and virtually impossible to repair. For every tonne of clay extracted, 6 tonnes of sand are added to the spoil heaps. The sand cannot be returned to the pits for this would cover reserves which often go down to depths of over 100 metres. Efforts are made to find economic outlets for waste products. Sand is used in road-building and in the manufacture of pre-cast concrete products. Tiny flakes of mica, which once polluted local rivers, are now used to make Christmas 'glitter'. These activities dispose of only a small fraction of current waste production, and make no impact on the legacy of dereliction left by two centuries of exploitation. If pits and tips cannot be removed, at least they may be disguised. Active pits are now often hidden by growing trees. Recent experiments suggest that it is possible to terrace the spoil heaps and clothe them in vegetation. It will, however, take much time and effort to soften the stark outlines of the distinctive landscape of kaolin quarrying.

Non-ferrous metals

The ancient rocks of Britain's highlands and uplands contain the ores of a wide range of non-ferrous metals, including tin, lead, zinc, copper and gold. Exploitation has a long history and at times has been locally important. Roman miners were busy in the Peak District, Mendips and elsewhere. Cornwall has been worked for tin from even earlier times, and was, for many centuries, the world's chief source of supply. Mining declined drastically in the nineteenth century. Britain's deposits are generally small and scattered. When the more accessible ores had been removed, costs of production

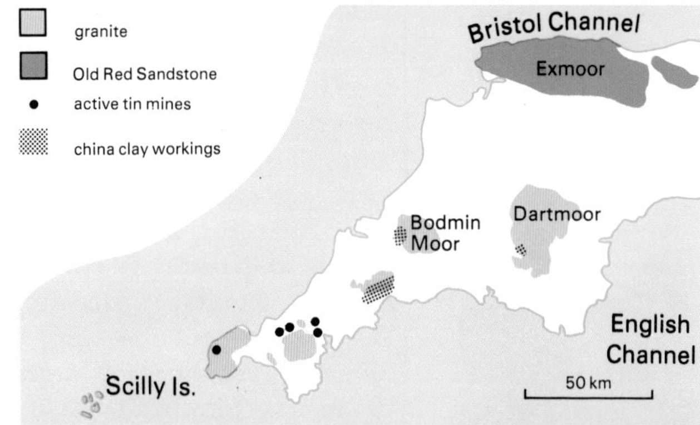

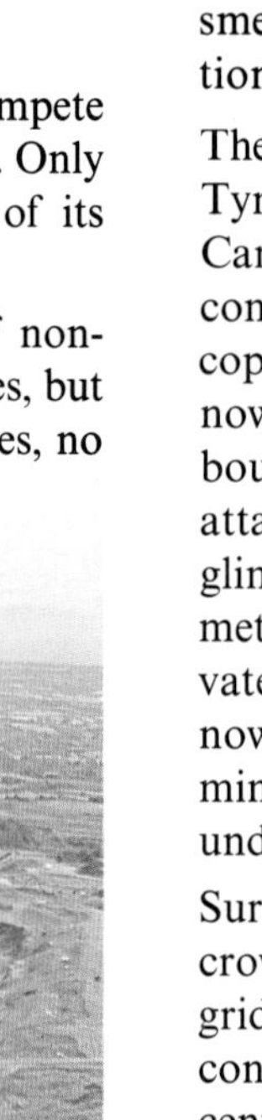

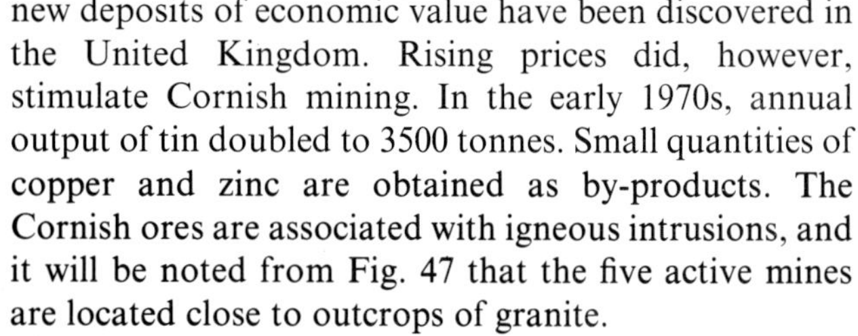

Fig. 48

Fig. 49

rose steeply, and domestic mines could not compete with a flood of cheap ores imported from overseas. Only in Cornwall does mining retain even a vestige of its former importance.

In the 1960s, a steep rise in the world price of non-ferrous metals stimulated interest in home resources, but in spite of active prospecting by modern techniques, no new deposits of economic value have been discovered in the United Kingdom. Rising prices did, however, stimulate Cornish mining. In the early 1970s, annual output of tin doubled to 3500 tonnes. Small quantities of copper and zinc are obtained as by-products. The Cornish ores are associated with igneous intrusions, and it will be noted from Fig. 47 that the five active mines are located close to outcrops of granite.

In the Republic of Ireland, recent exploration has met with considerable success. Fig. 48 locates important new mining developments. Further promising areas are under active investigation. All ores are exported for smelting and this item now makes a valuable contribution to the Republic's balance of trade.

The first of the modern discoveries was made at Tynagh, 30 kilometres ESE of Galway. Emplaced in Carboniferous Limestone, the deposit is large, rich and complex. Lead and zinc are the principal metals, but copper is also present. The mine was opened in 1965 and now has a work-force of 310. A thick overburden of boulder clay was stripped away and the ore body attacked by open-pit methods. The roughly oval pit, glimpsed in Fig. 49, has length and breadth of 732 metres and 213 metres respectively, and has been excavated to a depth of 100 metres. Open-pit working has now ceased. Deeper and richer ores are won by deep-mining techniques. A 230-metre shaft gives access to underground workings at several levels.

Surface installations are fed with water from the Kilcrow River and power is taken from the state electricity grid. Ores, which vary greatly in their richness, are concentrated to a metal content of between 50 and 65 per cent. Daily output can be as high as 450 tonnes. Concentrates are trucked to the port of Galway for shipment to smelters in Germany, Belgium and France.

Weather or not

The state of the atmosphere is the common concern of both weather and climate, which must therefore be carefully distinguished. Weather describes the state of the atmosphere at a particular time. Climate, on the other hand, is concerned with the conditions found by long observation to be typical for a much longer period – a month or a season, for instance. Both are of great importance. The farmer considers the climate in planning the use of his land, but his crop may be ruined by frosty or stormy weather. We prefer the climate of summer for our annual holiday which may be ruined by rainy weather.

Weather

Variability is the most distinctive characteristic of British weather. Everyday experience provides ample illustration. Washing, drying happily on the line, is suddenly soaked by a short, sharp shower. An umbrella, valuable in morning rain, becomes a superfluous burden after lunch. Weather varies not only from time to time but also from place to place. A Test Match in Birmingham can be ruined by rain when grounds in the south are fine and dry. When London lies under a blanket of fog, aircraft are diverted to sunny Manchester. Responsibility for the notorious variability of British weather can be laid at the door of *air masses*, and their interaction.

Air masses

In sub-tropical latitudes the broad Atlantic Ocean presents a vast extent of uniform surface conditions. The air which rests upon these warm waters responds to their warmth and is highly charged with moisture. In this area, which extends over many thousands of square kilometres, the lower atmosphere shows a marked uniformity of temperature and humidity. This is one of the air masses which so greatly influence the weather over the British Isles. From the location of its source area it is known as Tropical Maritime (or *Tm* for short).

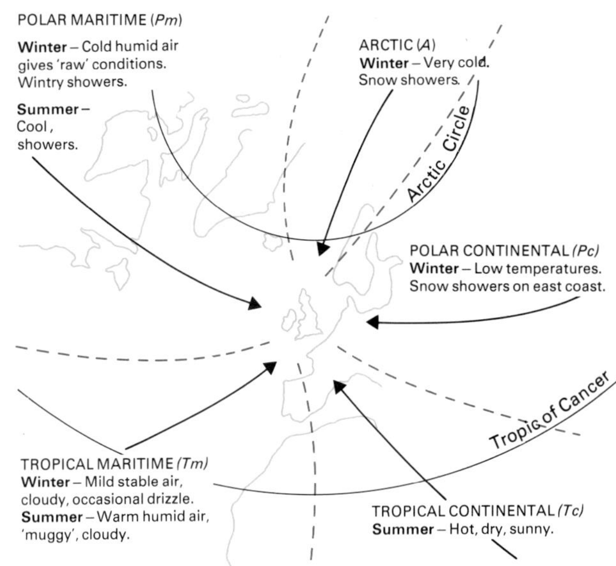

Fig. 50 shows that the *Tm* air mass is but one of five which contribute to British weather. They all take their differing characteristics from conditions prevailing in their source areas. The northern parts of North America, where land and sea intermingle, is the home of Polar Maritime *(Pm)*. Temperatures are low and the air is quite humid. In contrast, the Tropical Continental *(Tc)* air mass, centred on North Africa, is hot and dry.

Air masses do not rest content in their source areas. Prompted by pressure changes within the atmosphere, they expand and contract in conflict with their rivals. One air mass advances to envelop the British Isles. It holds sway for a short spell, but is then displaced by the advance of another. Each air mass brings to Britain conditions which reflect their widely contrasted source areas. They are, however, considerably modified in the course of their long journey. Temperatures in particular are greatly moderated, and thus the British Isles are spared the extremes of polar cold and desert heat.

Each air mass brings its own particular pattern of weather. The Polar Maritime, our most frequent visitor, is a good example. In winter, the air in its source area is exceedingly cold. It moves across the North Atlantic and approaches these shores as a north-westerly air stream. In passing over the relatively warm ocean, it picks up additional moisture and its temperature is raised. The warming is greatest in the lower levels of the atmosphere which therefore have a tendency to rise. Unstable air gives frequent showers, perhaps of snow or sleet. Skies are often bright between the showers, but the cold, humid, briskly moving air is not generally appreciated. In summer, *Pm* air brings fewer showers and the air is cool rather than cold.

Britain's most extreme winter temperatures are recorded when the Polar Continental *(Pc)* air mass is in charge of our weather. Cold winds sweep in from the icy plains of Eurasia. This easterly air stream is slightly warmed by passage over the North Sea. It also gains a little moisture which may be precipitated as showers of snow on eastern coasts. Inland, the skies are usually clear and bright, but weak winter sunshine can do little to raise the temperature. At night, terrestrial radiation takes temperatures well below freezing-point.

Conditions typically associated with these and other air masses are summarised in Fig. 50. It should be noted that air mass frontiers may lie across the British Isles, thus giving pronounced contrasts in the weather experienced in different areas.

Low and high

Air masses are always in touch with their neighbours. They come together in a narrow zone known as a *front*. Here, air of different physical properties is in contact. Interaction between them produces localised pressure differences. Areas of low pressure are shaped into troughs and depressions ('lows'). High pressure commonly takes the form of ridges and anticyclones ('highs'). Prompted by the power of the prevailing westerly circulation, these pressure systems generally track eastwards from the Atlantic to the British Isles and beyond. As they jostle along in procession they display their differing characteristics, and add detailed variety to our weather.

Depressions

Fig. 51 is taken from the Daily Weather Report published by the Meteorological Office. It provides a detailed picture of the weather conditions recorded over the British Isles at 06 hours on the 25th of November 1975. The key (Fig. 52) enables us to interpret the abundant information mapped in the form of symbols. A well-developed depression dominates the weather situation.

A depression is dynamic. Things are happening. Consider the warm front which is shown in diagrammatic section in Fig. 53. This front is a gently inclined plane extending high into the atmosphere. To the east is a wedge of relatively cold air, usually of *Pm* origin. West of the front is a segment of the *Tm* air mass. This warmer air rises steadily over the cold. As it rises it expands, and as it expands its temperature is reduced. Cooling below saturation point leads to precipitation. Thus, the passage of the warm front over the observer on the ground is preceded by thickening cloud and a period of rain. Look again at the weather-map (Fig. 51). The round symbol for rain is dotted about the warm front.

The cold front (Fig. 54) rises more steeply from its surface position. Of the two types of air here in contact, the colder moves the more quickly. It bustles into the lighter, warmer air, forcing it upwards. Ascent may produce a narrow belt of rain, or showery conditions. On Fig. 51, rain is recorded as the cold front moves over Ireland.

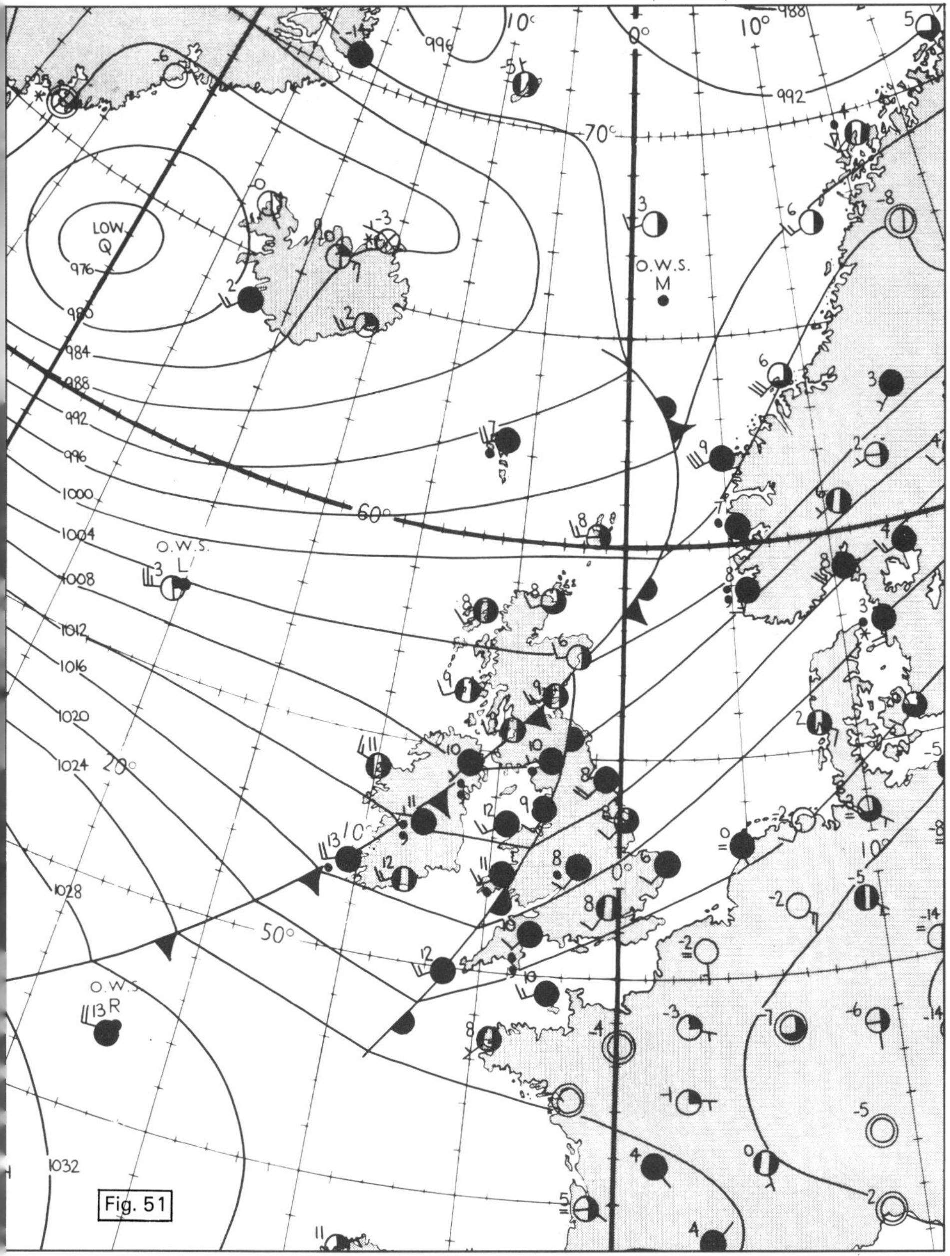

Fig. 51

Fig. 52

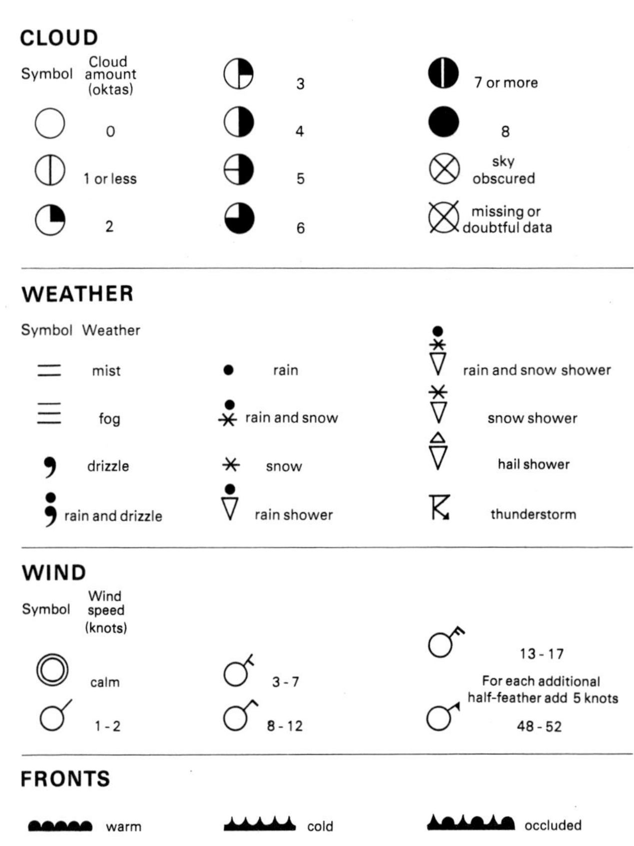

Fig. 53

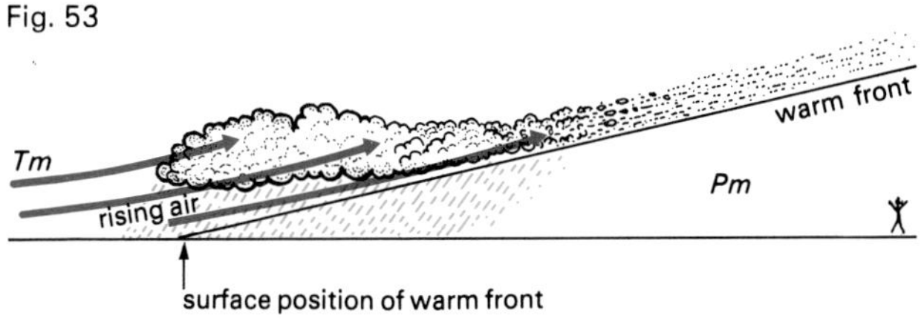

Tm
rising air
warm front
Pm
surface position of warm front

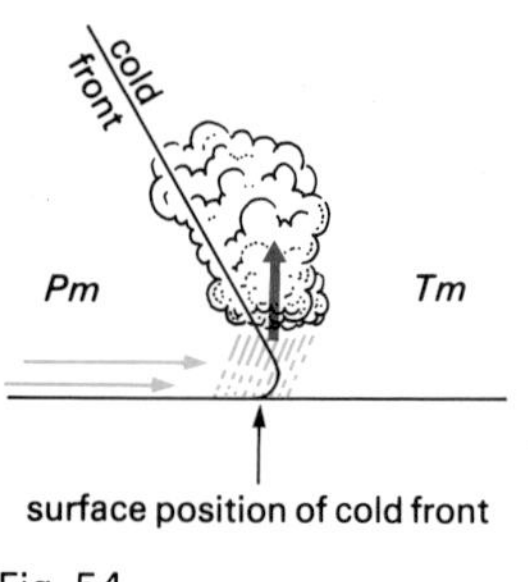

Fig. 54

Weather conditions are again different where fronts have been *occluded*, a situation simplified in Fig. 55. The greater speed of the cold front has brought it up to the warm. The two arms of *Pm* air, now differing slightly in temperature, are in contact. One rises over the other. The sector of *Tm* air is lifted above the surface. Cloud persists and rain may continue to fall. Eventually, warm air disperses high in the atmosphere. On the weather-map rain is falling, indicating that the battered remnant of *Tm* is still being driven upwards. (There is a further description of *occlusion* in *Landscape and Atmosphere*, Book 1 in this series.)

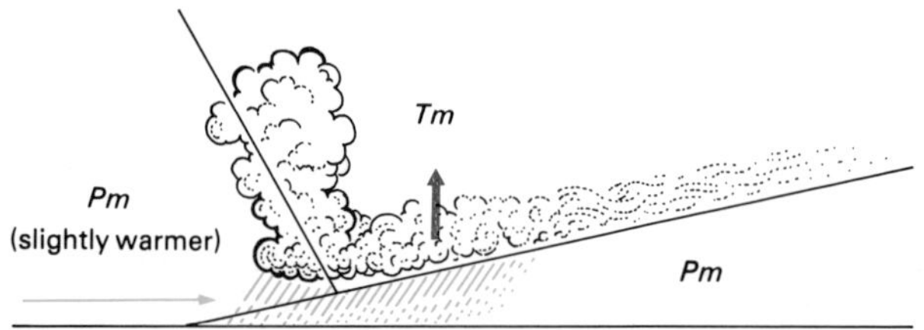

Fig. 55

The different parts of a depression are united in a huge circulating mass of air. The sequence of weather recorded at a particular station will depend on its position in relation to the depression's line of movement. A generalised sequence is sketched in Fig. 56. This would be appropriate to, say, East Anglia as the depression in Fig. 51 drifts slowly eastwards.

Fig. 56

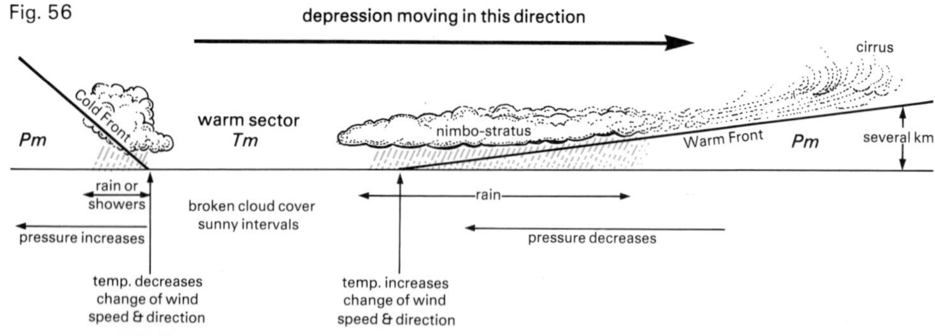

It will be appreciated that the passage of a depression produces complex weather patterns which vary from place to place. Further complexity stems from the fact that no two depressions are identical. They share the same basic features but differ greatly in detail. Some are larger than others. Speed and direction of movement may differ. A 'deep' depression shows a steep pressure gradient and may give gale-force winds. Upland relief may squeeze rain from a front when nearby lowlands are dry. The meteorologist, faced with such uncertainties, deserves our sympathy as he prepares his daily forecast.

Anticyclones

When, after a period of turbulent, rainy weather, the barometer shows a rise in atmospheric pressure, there are good prospects of more settled conditions. When pressure is high, the atmosphere is in placid mood. Rain is rare and winds are weak. These conditions are often experienced when a *ridge* of high pressure, separating a pair of depressions, drifts along in the westerly air movement. They are more pronounced and longer lasting when an *anticyclone* controls the weather. This was the situation when the weather-map included as Fig. 57 was prepared.

At dawn on 2nd March, 1976, an anticyclone was centred over East Anglia and the Netherlands where pressure was more than 1032 millibars. Over the whole of the British Isles, light and variable winds showed a generally clockwise circulation. Under high pressure conditions air descends rather than rises and conditions therefore are unfavourable for precipitation. We search the map in vain for signs of rain. Stray Atlantic fronts brought cloud to western districts, but over England and Wales the skies were clear. Strong overnight cooling had lowered the temperatures to freezing-point and below, and mist and fog were locally recorded.

Summer anticyclones share dry, stable conditions and gentle breezes with their colleagues of cooler months.

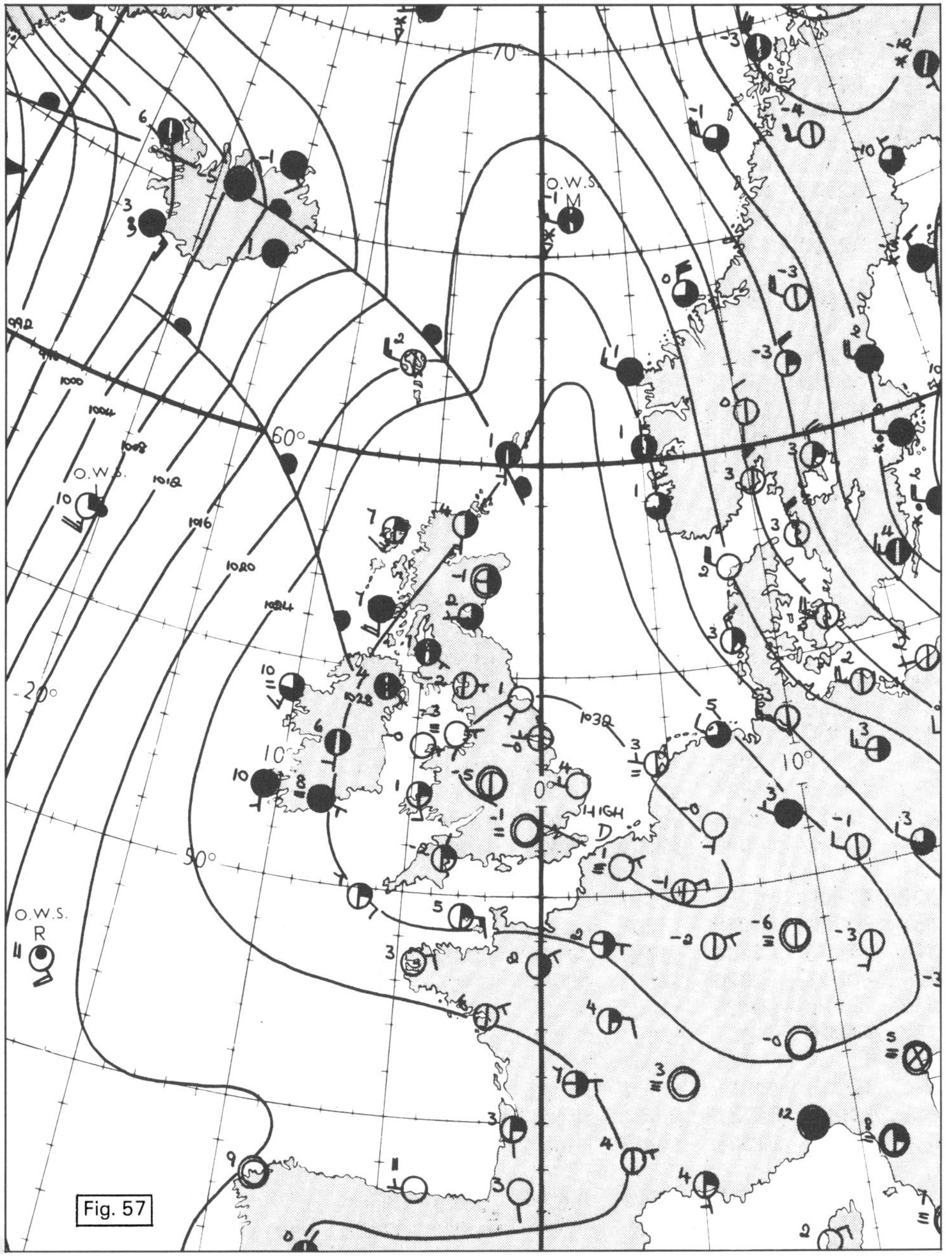

Fig. 57

Temperatures respond to clear skies and more powerful insolation, and the warm sunny days of summer high pressure are much appreciated in the holiday season.

Anticyclones are not invariably associated with clear skies. Sometimes, due to temperature conditions within the atmosphere, a thick, dense layer of cloud forms 1000 metres or so above the ground. It is an effective barrier to sunlight and days are dark. Cloud persists and the air is still. This dreary, monotonous weather, when nothing meteorological seems to happen, is described as *anti-cyclonic gloom.*

Climate

General considerations

Fig. 58 indicates the several aspects of position which together help to shape the climate of the British Isles. If the island outposts of Shetland and Scilly be excluded, the British Isles lie between 50°N and 60°N. These are cool-temperate latitudes. The angle of the noonday sun varies greatly throughout the year. On the latitude of London it ranges from 15° in December to 62° in June. The power of insolation keeps in step and steady seasonal change is experienced. Latitude fixes the British Isles firmly within the great planetary circulation known

Fig. 58

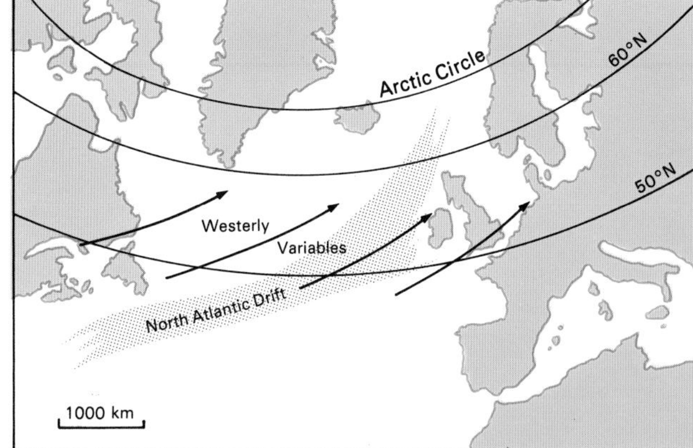

as the 'Westerly Variables'. Winds are not, of course, exclusively from the west. As we saw in the last section, air masses arrive from all points of the compass. The frequent passage of depressions adds further complications. So, too, does local relief. Wind direction everywhere is highly variable. It is, however, air moving in from directions between S.W. and N.W. which is dominant. The significance of this is greatly enhanced by the position of the British Isles in relation to the contrasting surfaces of land and sea. Fig. 58 emphasises that the British Isles lie on the Atlantic edge of the Eurasian land mass. Prevailing winds come in from over the ocean. Even when, relatively rarely, air approaches from the east, it still has water to cross. Thus the maritime influence, extended well inland by channels and estuaries, pervades the climate of the British Isles.

Position provides a set of general climatic characteristics which are shared by all parts of the British Isles. This is not to say that climate is everywhere the same. Indeed, there are many regional differences which, though often small, are nevertheless highly important. These will be reserved for later consideration, for they must not be allowed to obscure the essential unity of the British climate.

The broad pattern of climate and its local variations are identified by climate statistics. These are derived from precise observation over a lengthy period. Take rainfall for instance. Totals for a particular month are averaged out over thirty-five years to give a figure for the mean (average) monthly rainfall. Figures for mean monthly temperatures are produced in similar fashion. Fig. 59 uses Birmingham as an example. Statistics and graphs such as these are valuable but must be used with care. The fact that they are averages must always be borne in mind. They give a good indication of climate, but hide the exceptional but significant conditions which occur from time to time. 1976 provided graphic illustration. In June, July and August, southern England received only 18 per cent of its average summer rainfall, but the month that followed proved to be the wettest September for 60 years.

Let Birmingham illustrate the main features of the lowland climate of the British Isles. Look again at Fig. 59. The January mean temperature of 3.2°C reflects the characteristic mildness of British winters. With a mean of 16.7°C for the warmest month, summers are relatively cool. The annual range of temperature is a modest 13.5°C. The British Isles enjoy temperature conditions which are pleasingly free from extremes. Not often does 'winter snow lay round about' and the frost is seldom 'cruel'. The British summer rarely suggests a siesta and a healthy tan is hard to achieve.

In equable temperature conditions we see the power of the maritime influence. Air is heated from the surface

Fig. 59

Birmingham

	J	F	M	A	M	J	Jy	A	S	O	N	D	
Average temp. (°C)	3.2	3.7	5.8	8.7	11.5	15.0	16.7	16.4	13.9	10.0	6.6	4.4	Annual range 13.5°C
Average rainfall (mm)	76	54	48	54	63	48	46	69	59	70	77	67	Total 731 mm

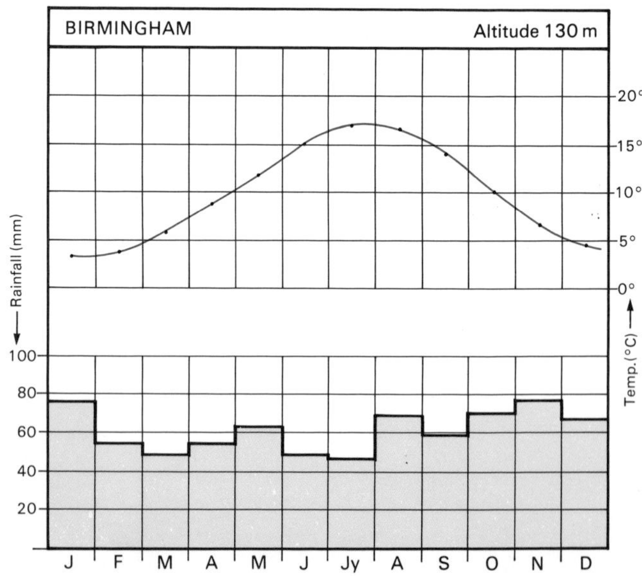

above which it lies. Water is slow to respond to insolation and is cooler than the land in summer. Thus the prevailing winds from over the Atlantic moderate the summer temperatures recorded over the British Isles. In winter, the ocean is reluctant to give up its heat to the atmosphere and remains relatively warm. The north Atlantic has an additional asset, for the Gulf Stream, and its extension the North Atlantic Drift, transfer masses of warm water from tropical areas to high latitudes. Air masses, originating or tracking over the Atlantic, bring welcome winter warmth to the British Isles.

The maritime influence affects other climatic elements. Air coming in from the ocean is well charged with water vapour. Much is precipitated as rain, especially when carried by travelling depressions. Total annual rainfall varies greatly from place to place, but is nowhere less than adequate for agriculture. It is well distributed throughout the year and occurs at frequent intervals. Indeed, a dry spell of twenty days or so is often headline news. Maritime air brings abundant cloud which effectively masks the sun.

Regional variations

TEMPERATURE

As the crow flies, Manchester and Buxton are only 30 kilometres apart, but, as Fig. 60 reveals, there are significant differences in mean monthly temperatures. These differences are due to the effect of altitude. Manchester is 38 metres above sea-level, whereas Buxton, high in the Pennines, has an altitude of 307 metres. This difference is sufficient to give Manchester an advantage of more than 2°C in almost every month. Altitude obviously has a great influence on recorded temperatures. If these were plotted, the result would resemble a relief map in its complexity. To eliminate the effect of altitude, and so facilitate comparisons, temperatures may be reduced to sea-level values and plotted as isotherms. This has been done in Fig. 61, which gives a bold, generalised impression of the variation in mean July temperatures throughout the British Isles. In summer, insolation is the dominant influence, and temperature decreases from south to north. The lower Thames valley enjoys the highest temperatures with a mean figure of over 17°C. The northern tip of Scotland is more than 4°C cooler. Note how the isotherms arc northwards over the mainland areas. Here we have evidence of maritime influence, for cool air from over the seas moderates the temperature of coastal districts.

Mean Monthly Temperatures (°C)

	altitude \ *month*	J	F	M	A	M	J	Jy	A	S	O	N	D
Manchester	38 m	4.0	4.3	6.5	8.9	12.0	15.0	16.5	16.3	14.1	10.5	7.2	5.1
Buxton	307 m	1.9	2.0	4.0	6.5	9.4	12.6	14.3	14.0	11.8	8.4	5.3	3.3

Fig. 60

Fig. 62 paints the January picture. Isotherms, again based on sea-level values, trend roughly north to south. Temperatures decrease from west to east. In winter, insolation is weak and air from over the Atlantic is the major source of warmth. It is western districts which enjoy the greatest benefits. The Outer Hebrides are as warm as the coast of Sussex. The south-west tips of England and Ireland record mean temperatures in excess of 7°C. Look again at Fig. 62 and note how the influence of the Irish Sea bulges the 6°C isotherm beyond the Isle of Anglesey. The length of the growing season, so important to the farmer, responds to the winter warmth of the south and west. It is mapped in Fig. 63. Eastern Britain, being further from the Atlantic and more exposed to cold easterly air masses, experiences winters of less pronounced mildness.

Comparison of Figs. 61 and 62 reveals regional contrasts in the annual range of temperature. It is highest in the south-east of England. The London area, with averages of over 17°C in July and less than 5°C in January, shows a range of more than 12°C. For the western coastlands of Ireland and Scotland the figure is about 4°C lower.

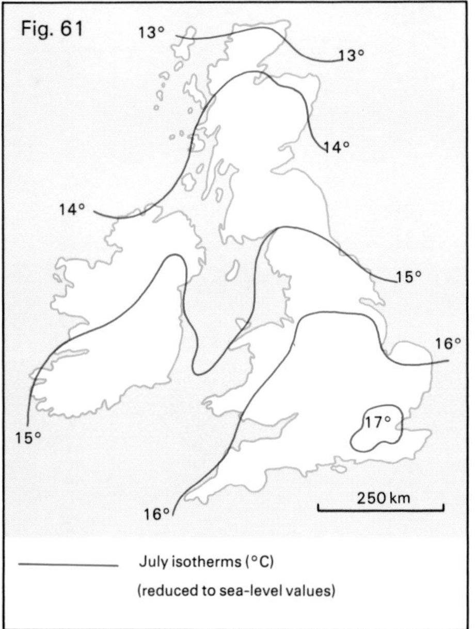

July isotherms (°C)
(reduced to sea-level values)

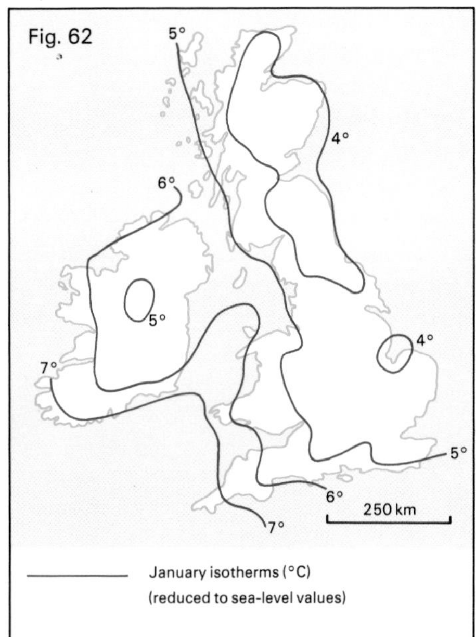

January isotherms (°C)
(reduced to sea-level values)

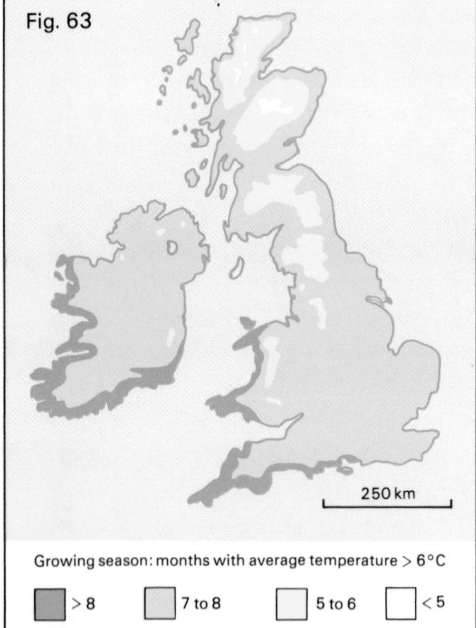

Growing season: months with average temperature > 6°C

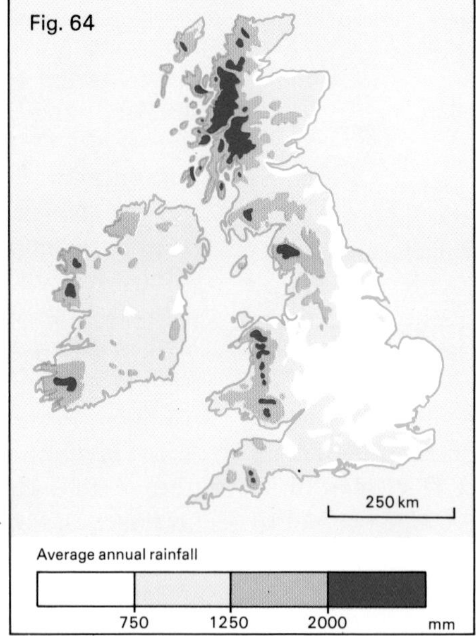

Average annual rainfall

RAINFALL

It is in mean annual rainfall that climate shows its greatest regional variations. This important element of climate is mapped, in a generalised way, in Fig. 64. Major contrasts are immediately apparent. Western districts stand out as areas of heavy rainfall. Virtually everywhere, mean annual totals are in excess of 750 millimetres. For much of north Wales and western Scotland the figure is more than twice as high. These western districts suffer from close proximity to the ocean. They are fully exposed to moist air sweeping in from the Atlantic. Depressions, many of which track north-eastwards, are numerous. There is an additional factor which greatly swells the rainfall totals. Highland dominates the western flank of the British Isles. Moist incoming air is forced to rise, and copious relief rain is the result.

Eastern districts are distinctly drier. This is evident in Ireland, but is much more pronounced in Great Britain. After an eventful journey over high Atlantic coasts, maritime air has little moisture to spare for the east. Winds which blow in from over the North Sea are relatively dry, and give little precipitation. Fig. 64 shows that wide areas of lowland England, sheltering in the rain-shadow of western highlands, experience an average rainfall of less than 750 millimetres. Relief rain is of little consequence, but cuestas often squeeze a few extra millimetres of rain from the passing air.

Rainfall varies not only in amount but also in distribution throughout the year. Fig. 65 gives graphs for selected stations. Those for western districts show a distinct winter maximum. This is the result of full exposure to powerful depressions which are particularly common at this season. In eastern districts, where totals are lower, the distribution is much more uniform. Spring tends to be dry and a slight maximum is recorded in the second half of the year. The holiday month of August is usually prominent.

Fig. 65

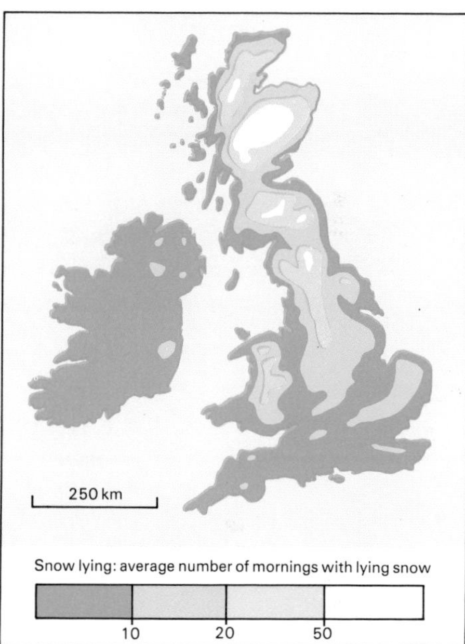

Fig. 66

Fig. 67

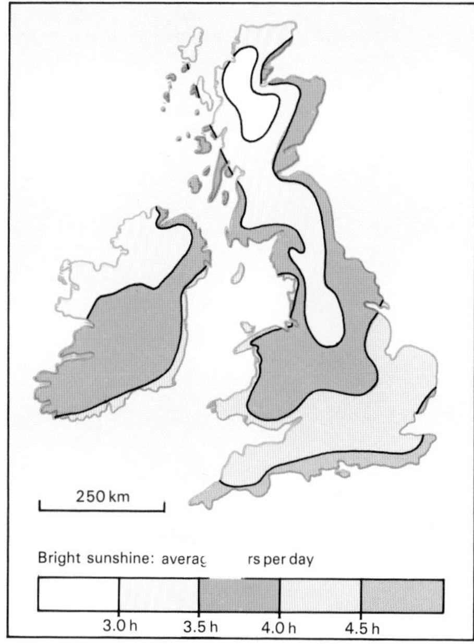

SNOWFALL

Snow represents only a tiny fraction of total precipitation experienced over the British Isles. Its occurrence varies greatly from year to year, but a general indication of the average number of mornings when snow lies on the ground is given in Fig. 66. It is over the northern highlands that snow lies deepest and longest. The map gives one very good reason why the Cairngorms are Britain's chief centre for winter sports.

SUNSHINE

Fig. 67 maps the mean hours of bright sunshine recorded over the British Isles. Sunshine decreases from south to north and from coasts to higher elevations. The Channel coast of England is particularly well favoured, and this fact is stressed in the brochures published by the many holiday resorts in the area.

STATISTICS

We have seen that the main features of the climate of a particular station are neatly summarised in its statistics. From evidence contained in such statistics, it is possible to identify the general area where the station is located. This is a skill which is frequently demanded of examination candidates, and a little practice is therefore suggested. Fig. 68 may prove useful, for it emphasises significant climatic values.

Fig. 68

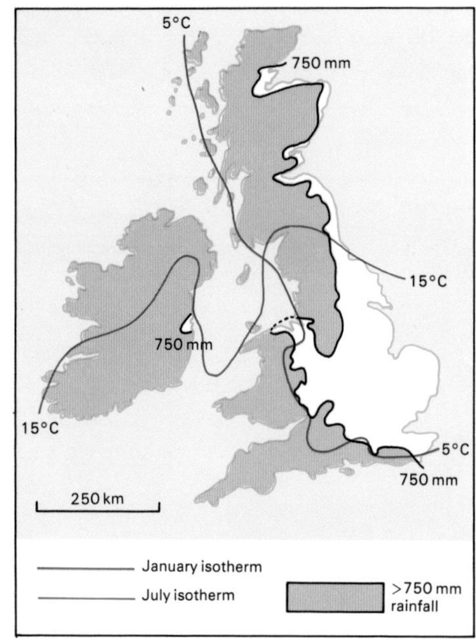

Consider the following statistics:

		J	F	M	A	M	J	Jy	A	S	O	N	D	
Altitude 17 m	Temp. (°C)	7.2	6.8	8.3	9.9	12.2	14.9	16.4	16.6	15.1	12.4	9.7	8.0	range 9.8°C
	Rainfall (mm)	130	89	81	64	61	51	69	76	81	111	124	122	total 1059 mm

The low altitude of the station is noted. A July average of more than 15°C suggests a location in the southern half of the British Isles. A rainfall total of more than 750 millimetres, and its winter maximum, turn our attention to the west. This is supported by a mean January temperature of more than 5°C. The fact that the January figure is as high as 7°C indicates a position far to the south-west – in Cornwall, perhaps, or the south-west tip of Ireland. In fact the statistics belong to Penzance.

Similarly:

		J	F	M	A	M	J	Jy	A	S	O	N	D	
Altitude 74 m	Temp. (°C)	3.0	3.2	5.0	7.0	9.7	12.4	14.2	14.0	12.0	8.0	5.8	4.2	range 11.2°C
	Rainfall (mm)	69	48	38	45	54	50	75	78	67	95	63	59	total 741 mm

Here, the evidence of total rainfall and distribution points to a location on the eastern side of the British Isles. A July mean temperature only slightly higher than 14°C gives the statistics a Scottish flavour which is supported by the low temperature figures for January. Inverness is the town in question.

Now, suggest a possible location for the sets of statistics in Fig. 69.

Fig. 69

	J	F	M	A	M	J	Jy	A	S	O	N	D
1.	*Altitude 58 m*											
Temp. (°C)	2.4	2.9	4.5	6.6	9.0	12.0	14.0	13.6	11.7	8.8	5.6	3.7
Rainfall (mm)	76	56	51	56	69	54	84	71	69	89	86	78
2.	*Altitude 6 m*											
Temp. (°C)	4.3	4.6	6.7	9.4	12.5	15.9	17.6	17.3	14.9	11.1	7.7	5.4
Rainfall (mm)	54	39	37	46	46	44	62	57	50	57	63	52
3.	*Altitude 3 m*											
Temp. (°C)	5.3	5.2	6.3	7.8	10.1	12.2	13.7	13.8	12.6	10.4	7.9	6.4
Rainfall (mm)	122	79	68	66	53	71	89	91	114	142	124	119
4.	*Altitude 50 m*											
Temp. (°C)	7.7	7.3	8.5	9.7	11.7	14.3	16.0	16.5	15.2	12.7	10.3	8.6
Rainfall (mm)	91	69	61	56	56	43	56	61	61	89	94	89
5.	*Altitude 33 m*											
Temp. (°C)	4.0	4.4	5.7	7.7	9.7	12.9	15.1	14.9	13.2	10.4	7.3	5.4
Rainfall (mm)	61	43	41	43	54	46	78	78	59	64	66	59
6.	*Altitude 340 m*											
Temp. (°C)	0.6	1.0	2.8	5.2	8.3	11.4	13.1	12.6	10.2	7.0	3.8	2.0
Rainfall (mm)	107	69	54	59	66	48	74	78	78	104	91	97

Water

A sure supply of pure, clean water is commonly taken for granted. It flows unchecked at the turn of a tap. In addition to its obvious significance in the home, water has an important role to play in many aspects of economic life. Channelled in canals it serves for inland navigation. Falling water may be harnessed to generate electricity. A piped supply is a great asset to the farmer. In rivers and lakes it contributes to the natural beauty of landscapes which attract the tourist. Industry values water as raw material, coolant or solvent, and rivers often enable bank-side factories to dispose of waste products.

As will be appreciated from Fig. 70, water resources are a reflection of climate and rock. Precipitation is the original source, but some is lost by evaporation which is influenced by temperature and wind. More is returned to the atmosphere through transpiration by plants. Impermeable rocks give a high rate of surface flow, but where strata are permeable, rain is readily absorbed to accumulate as underground water.

Differences of climate and rock lead to great regional contrasts in water supply and resources. The major contrast is between lowland Britain and the elevated areas which lie to the west.

Over lowland Britain, mean annual rainfall is generally below 750 millimetres. This relative dryness is accentuated by a high rate of evaporation. Indeed, in the summer months, most of south-east England loses more by evaporation than it receives by precipitation. Rainfall is readily absorbed by extensive outcrops of highly permeable rocks. Chalk and the coarse sandstones of Permo-Triassic age are examples mapped in Fig. 71. The large resources of underground water stored in these *aquifers* are often tapped by deep wells and powerful pumps. Cambridge and Luton are two of the many towns which obtain water in this way.

In other lowland areas, where rocks are impermeable, surface flow is abundant. Highland tributaries often contribute to the numerous large rivers – the Severn for instance – which cross the lowlands on their way to the sea. On their journey, they lose water to the needs of nearby towns.

Many towns exploit both surface and underground resources. London is a case in point. About 10 per cent of consumption is drawn from wells driven deep into the underlying chalk. The balance is derived from the flow of the rivers Thames and Lea.

The water resources of lowland areas are greatly exceeded by those of highland Britain. Here, rainfall is abundant everywhere and evaporation is low. Impermeable rocks support numerous streams which often flow in deep, steep-sided valleys. Highland areas support few people and little industry, and thus make little demand on their ample resources. Large towns on the flanking lowlands have looked to the hills to meet their ever-growing need for water. The example of Liverpool illustrates the growth and present scale of these undertakings.

Liverpool's first public water supply was obtained from wells sunk in the underlying Bunter Sandstone. The two wells marked on Fig. 72 are still in use but their contribution to present consumption is of little significance. The search for increased supplies began in the middle of the nineteenth century. Dams were built to impound the flow of several small moorland streams which drain the

Fig. 70

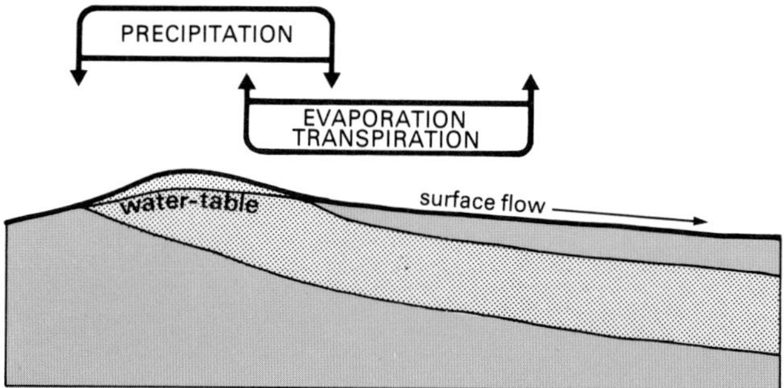

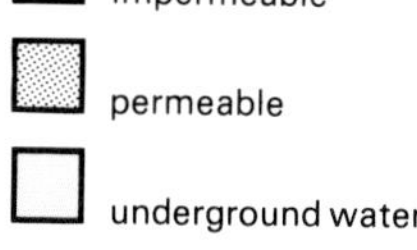

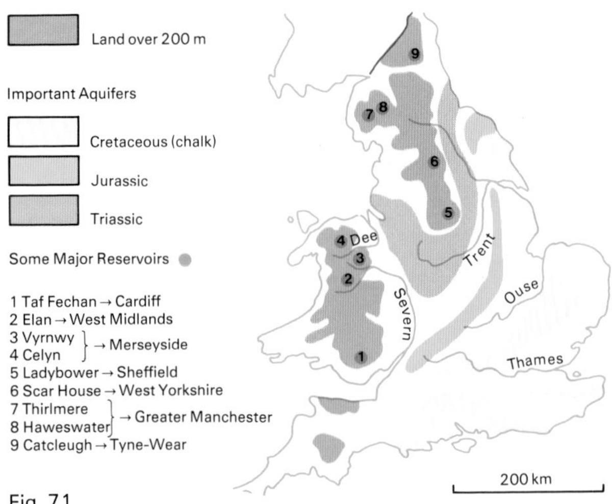

Fig. 71

western edge of Rossendale. The Rivington reservoirs are linked to storage facilities at Prescot by a 28-kilometre pipeline along which water moves by gravity.

Well before the end of the century, the combined resources of wells and Rivington were to prove inadequate, and Liverpool was forced to seek a further source of supply. It was found in the highlands of Wales. The headwaters of the River Vyrnwy drain an area which enjoys an average annual precipitation of 1280 millimetres. A high masonry dam created what was, at the time, the largest artificial reservoir in Europe (Fig. 73). The natural flow of the River Vyrnwy is maintained at a rate of 49 million litres per day. Water for Liverpool moves along a 109-kilometre aqueduct which tunnels under the Manchester Ship Canal and the River Mersey on its way to Prescot. The first delivery was made in 1891 and yield has been steadily increased over the years. Streams which once joined the Vyrnwy below the dam are now diverted into the reservoir by tunnels, and the aqueduct now consists of three parallel pipelines along which flow is speeded by pumps.

In post-war years, Liverpool has turned once more to Wales to quench its growing thirst. This time it was the headwaters of the River Dee which received attention. 8 kilometres north of Bala, the tributary Afon Tryweryn was dammed to create Llyn Celyn. This scheme differs from those of Rivington and Vyrnwy. The reservoir, together with sluices near the outlet of Lake Bala, is designed to regulate rather than impound the flow of the Dee. The level of the reservoir responds to variations in rainfall, but water is released into the river in amounts calculated to maintain a steady flow throughout the year. With volume ensured, Liverpool may safely take up to 290 million litres per day. Only a short aqueduct is needed for delivery to Prescot and Speke.

The developments described above were achieved by the Corporation of Liverpool. In 1974, water supply was

Fig. 72

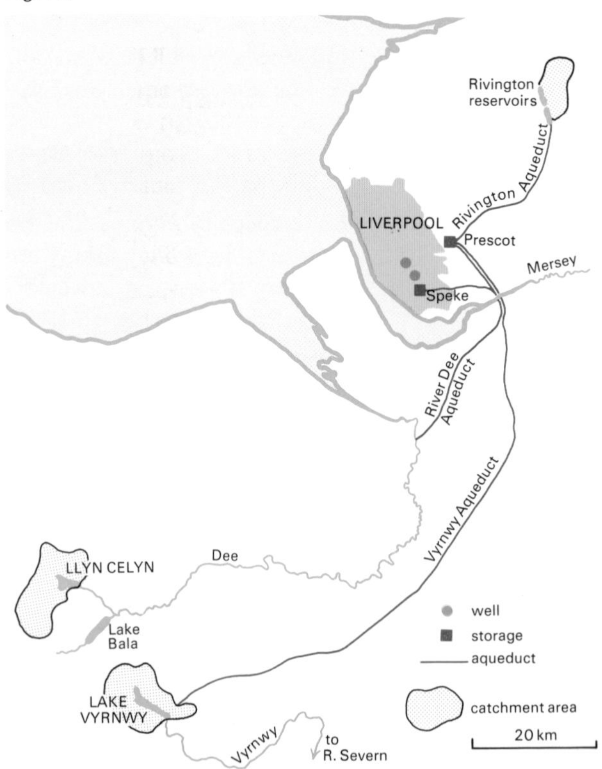

Fig. 73

reorganised on a national basis. Control passed from local government to the regional water authorities mapped in Fig. 74. Boundaries are based on natural drainage basins, and authorities have responsibilities not only for water supply but also for sewage disposal and all aspects of river management. It is the western division of the North-West Water Authority which supplies water to Merseyside. In 1976, it distributed 184522 million litres.

Over the country as a whole, demand for water has more than doubled in the last thirty years. It is now in excess of 43000 million litres per day. All types of consumer have contributed to this increased demand. More water flows into the average home as standards of living rise. Improved farming methods often require greater supplies – much is used in the modern milking parlour and the value of irrigation is increasingly appreciated in the drier parts of the English lowlands. Expansion of industry brings greatly increased demand. Nearly 200000 litres of water are used in the manufacture of one car tyre. 34 litres are needed to make a litre of beer. New power-stations need vast quantities of water for cooling purposes. It must be stressed, however, that much of the water used by industry for cooling is recycled, or returned to rivers to be used again by factories located downstream.

The demand for water continues to grow. It is estimated that supplies must be increased by more than 50 per cent before the end of the century. Expansion on this scale poses serious problems. Lowland towns will doubtless make increased demands on upland resources. Supplies in north-east England, for instance, will be augmented by the completion of the new reservoir at Kielder in Northumberland. This scheme, like Liverpool's Llyn Celyn, follows modern practice in making maximum use of rivers in the distribution of water to the consuming towns. The development of large, new reservoirs is expensive and often leads to conflict. Upland agriculture usually depends on the integrated use of valley-floor and bounding hillsides. Reservoirs which drown the former make the whole valley agriculturally unproductive. Opposition also comes from those who regard dams and reservoirs as destructive of the natural beauty of the landscape.

Fig. 74

1 Northumbrian
2 Yorkshire
3 North West
4 Severn-Trent
5 Anglian
6 Welsh National Water Development Authority
7 Thames
8 Southern
9 Wessex
10 South West

Problems of future supply are greatest in the south-east of England. In this area of restricted natural resources, population is increasing and industry expanding at a greater rate than in the rest of the country. Far from the wet uplands, more intensive use will doubtless be made of traditional sources. But even here, there are difficulties: underground water is not unlimited and a greater rate of extraction leads to a fall in the water-table. If more water is taken than precipitation can replace, exhaustion of resources will surely follow. There are also limits to the amounts that can be taken from surface sources. Rivers must continue to flow. Their waters are needed for other purposes, and form a rural amenity that overcrowded Britain can ill afford to lose.

Integrated use of rivers and rock can ensure increased supplies. The Thames ground-water scheme, now in its development stage, uses porous chalk as a natural reservoir. In times of abundance, water from the Thames is transferred to the rock for storage. In dry periods it will seep back into the river. Regulating the rate of flow in this way will make it possible for London to draw an additional 450 million litres of water per day.

Ways of satisfying demand in the more distant future are being actively considered by experts. London and the south-east could be served by the long-distance transfer of water from the highlands of Wales. With powerful pumps and a relatively short aqueduct, water from the River Severn could flow into the Thames. There is also the possibility of distilling salt water into fresh. Desalination, however, requires so much expensive power that it is unlikely to become an economic proposition in the foreseeable future. Of greater practical interest is the possibility of damming wide lowland bays and estuaries to create freshwater reservoirs. Solway Firth, Morecambe Bay and The Wash have all been considered, but the Dee Estuary is the most likely candidate. Such a scheme would be very costly but would have important secondary benefits. A road along the dam would shorten the journey from North Wales to Liverpool and the new lake would have an important amenity value.

4 Farm, Forest and Fish

Fig. 75

Farming

Fig. 75 portrays a landscape typical of much of lowland England. Mature trees rise above the sturdy hedge and fence which divide the land into a rural patchwork. Contented cattle graze permanent pastures. Distant crops of roots and cereals mature to harvest. The picture has a timeless quality which belies the nature of farming. The farmer's response to his environment is not inflexible. His use of the land is modified by changing circumstances. The present pattern of agriculture is the product of slow development over a period of many centuries. The process of change continues. In recent years change has been varied and pronounced.

The United Kingdom has a total area of approximately 20.5 million hectares and Fig. 76 indicates the share claimed by major types of land use. It also reveals important contrasts between the constituent countries. England, for instance, with her extensive lowlands of good soil and kindly climate, is the most favoured for agriculture. In Scotland, where highland relief and climate are dominant, rough pasture of low economic value is the principal land use.

Fig. 76

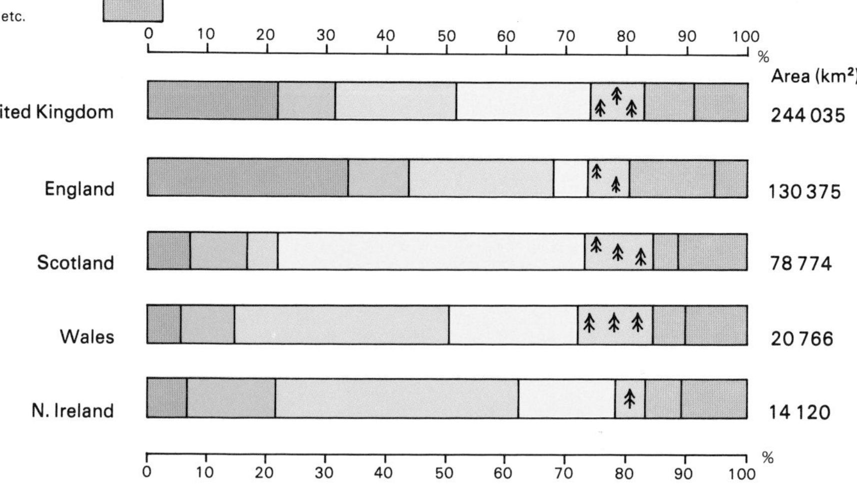

Fig. 77 *thousand hectares*

Agricultural land: U.K.	*1953*	*1965*	*1970*	*1976*
Arable	7333	7502	7204	6968
Permanent grassland	5246	4916	4948	5033
Rough grazing	6840	7221	6697	6511

In all four countries there is a decline in the proportion of land devoted to agriculture. Farms in marginal areas are being abandoned or planted with forests but more serious are the losses in lowland areas. As population increases and standards of living rise, new houses are built at lower densities and urban expansion gobbles up fruitful fields. Industry and motorway are also hungry for space.

Evidence of the reduction in agricultural land can be found in Fig. 77. Fig. 78 records changes in the popularity of selected crops. Temporary grassland shares the decline of pasture in general. Potatoes claim a shrinking share of the arable land, whereas other vegetables are gaining ground. Cereals show the greatest changes. Wheat has more than held its own, but oats are out of favour. Barley, aided by the introduction of new, high-yielding varieties, has risen to a position of dominance. Fig. 79 tables changes in livestock.

Land under selected crops: U.K. *thousand hectares*

	1960	1965	1970	1976
Wheat	851	1027	1010	1240
Barley	1366	2185	2246	2175
Oats	799	411	376	232
Potatoes	336	300	271	221
Sugar-beet	176	184	188	206
Fruit	115	99	83	71*
Vegetables (other than potatoes)	165	148	204	198*
Ley grass	2748	2640	2294	2159

*1975 figures

Fig. 78

Fig. 79
Livestock on agricultural holdings: U.K. *thousands*

	1960	1965	1970	1976
Cattle	11771	11943	12581	14013
Sheep	27871	29911	26080	28184
Pigs	5724	7979	8088	7932
Poultry	103005	118141	143431	122790

In recent years, in spite of the reduction in the amount of land available, agricultural production has risen impressively. Britain's farmers are making a growing contribution to the nation's food supply. Pre-war output represented a mere 30 per cent of total food consumption. Today, although there are nearly 10 million more mouths to feed, the figure is over 50 per cent. Crop yields per hectare may vary from year to year in response to weather conditions, but an overall upward trend is revealed in Fig. 80. Similar progress is recorded in animal husbandry: the average pasture yields more and better grass; the average cow is more prolific with milk; and the average hen is more generous with eggs.

Fig. 80
Crop yields per hectare: U.K. *tonnes per hectare*

	Average 1943/52	Average 1952/61	Average 1968/73
Wheat	2.54	3.14	4.08
Barley	2.37	2.91	3.63
Potatoes	17.82	19.58	26.86
Sugar-beet	24.60	30.37	36.78

Higher output is the rewarding result of changes in agriculture often described as a 'revolution'. British farming is becoming steadily more intensive as higher inputs prompt higher outputs. The farmer enlists the aid of the scientist: improved chemical fertilizers are applied to the fields in greater quantities; chemical sprays bring death to troublesome weeds and insect pests; new varieties of familiar crops are developed to give higher yields, and greater resistance to disease. Also scientific breeding programmes produce better farm animals. To a limited extent, the farmer may improve his environment. Investment in field drainage gives more manageable soils. In drier areas, irrigation facilities can increase the yield of many crops. These improved farming techniques are expensive, but the cost is repaid with interest at harvest time.

Government policy has speeded the process of change: farmers enjoy the security of a guaranteed minimum price for their produce; subsidies on cattle and sheep help farmers in marginal areas and grants are available for improvements to land and buildings. Entry into the Common Market has brought changes in the nature, but not in the principle, of financial support for the farming industry. Government has another vital role to play. Agencies of central government offer information and advice to the farming community.

Fig. 81

Fig. 82

Increased farm output is obtained with a dwindling labour force. Farm workers are leaving the land at a rate of about 20000 a year. Employment in agriculture has fallen by 50 per cent since 1960. The loss of labour is balanced by increased mechanisation. Tractors are commonplace. Combine harvesters sweep up cereal crops with speed and efficiency. Electric milking parlours have replaced the traditional bucket and stool. Today, there are few farm operations which must be done by hand. The potato harvest once involved long hours of tedious back-breaking toil. The modern method of gathering this staple crop is pictured in Fig. 81. Look to Fig. 82 for another example. As the 'peasmobiles' move smoothly over the field, they lift the vines, strip the pods and liberate the peas. The typical farm worker is now a skilled craftsman; the farmer a business man.

Increased mechanisation has brought changes in farm size. Modern machines are very expensive. If they are to repay their cost they must be used as much as possible. A farmer with just a few hectares would not be wise to invest in a combine harvester. Small farms, unable to support machinery, are incorporated in neighbouring units. Thus the average farm size increases, especially in arable districts. Mechanisation also makes an impact on the rural landscape. Sloping land, once safely turned by the horse-drawn plough, is seeded down to pasture. Heavy clayland is opened up for arable crops by powerful caterpillar tractors. Hedgerows are grubbed up and ditches filled to create larger fields. These activites release a considerable amount of land for profitable cultivation, and enable large machines to work at maximum efficiency.

Revolutionary changes have also taken place in the livestock branch of agriculture. In Fig. 83 we look inside a large, modern poultry house. Laying birds are closely confined in long, multi-tiered rows of wire cages. Their environment is entirely artificial. Light, temperature, humidity and the flow of air are closely controlled to maintain optimum conditions for egg production. Food in measured amounts is delivered automatically. Eggs roll forward for easy collection. Yield per hen is high. Production costs are low. This is an example of the efficient, large-scale methods of food production appropriately described as *factory* farming. Ninety per cent of the eggs we eat are laid in battery cages.

Similar methods are applied to other livestock. Battery pigs are seen in Fig. 84. They are the outcome of scientific breeding programmes; they fatten efficiently and have a high resistance to disease. Much of the pork, and

Fig. 83

Fig. 84

virtually all the chicken that appears on the table is the finished product of a factory farm. Even the dairy cow is not immune from the spread of intensive methods; an increasing proportion of the British herd spend all their time indoors and are fed on cultivated fodder crops.

Let Fig. 85 serve as a footnote to this story of continuing change. A field of corn has been harvested and the stubble burnt. The seeds for next year's crop are being drilled directly into the ground. With this new technique, the plough that has served man throughout the long history of cultivation is rendered obsolete.

Fig. 85

Farming landscapes

The farmer is a business man and increasingly so. He keeps an accountant's eye on his income and costs of production. He readily invests in new methods and techniques if confident of an adequate return. Sensitive to market demands, he endeavours to produce what the customer wants. The farmer's basic resource is his land, the fertility of which must be maintained or improved. He uses his land in the way that is likely to give maximum profit. To this, the fickle British climate adds the spice of uncertainty.

Choice of land use is influenced by the considerations indicated in Fig. 86. All are highly variable: even slight differences in altitude are reflected in rainfall and temperature; a single farm may contain soils of several types; a difference in slope of one degree may distinguish ploughland from pasture. In difficult but beautiful areas it is often government assistance and an income from tourists which keep the farmer in business. The British Isles have a more diverse physical environment than any other equivalent area. No two farms are identical. The typical farm is hard to find and the complex pattern of

Fig. 86

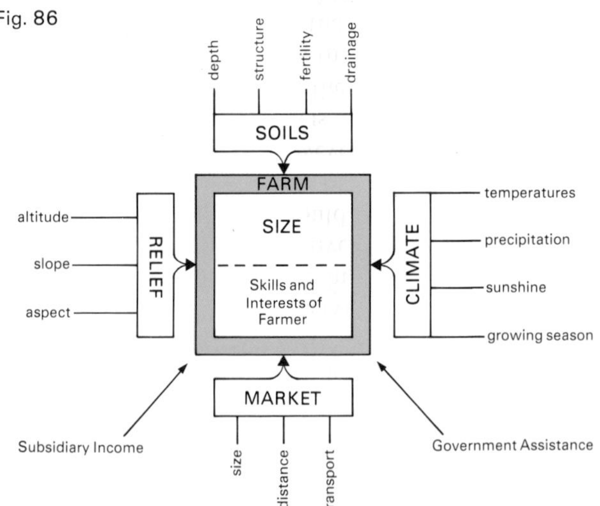

British farming is hard to plot on a small-scale map. Fig. 87 does no more than indicate the general distribution of important specialisations. Even so, it contains a strong suggestion of the important contrast between pastoral west and arable east.

Mixed farming

The area left unshaded in Fig. 87 is devoted to *mixed farming*. The integration of arable and pastoral activities brings many benefits. Most significant is its contribution to the maintenance of soil fertility. Natural manure is hoofed into the soil by grazing livestock. Winter accumulation from stall-fed animals is spread on the fields to enrich the soil. The diet of farm animals can be cheaply varied with waste materials from arable crops. Sugar-beet tops and the vines of the pea are familiar examples. The straw from cereal crops has several uses about the farm. It may, for instance, serve as bedding for cattle, or help to keep frost away from roots in storage. In mixed farming the need for fodder encourages varied rotations that are beneficial to land and crops. With the inclusion of clover, the soil gains nitrogen which is appreciated by next year's cereals. A mixed farm economy helps to spread labour requirements more evenly over the year. It also serves as insurance against the risk of inclement weather, insect pests, plant disease and variations in the market price. If one enterprise yields less than well, the others are there in support.

In view of these advantages, it is not surprising that the great majority of lowland farmers have interests in both crops and livestock. Relative importance varies greatly. At one extreme we have the Kent fruit farmer who keeps a few sheep to eat the grass that grows between his trees. At the other end of the scale is the Somerset grassland farm with a small orchard of cider apples which yield an annual harvest of cash. True mixed farming lies between these two extremes. Crops and livestock are more in balance, but the emphasis changes from region

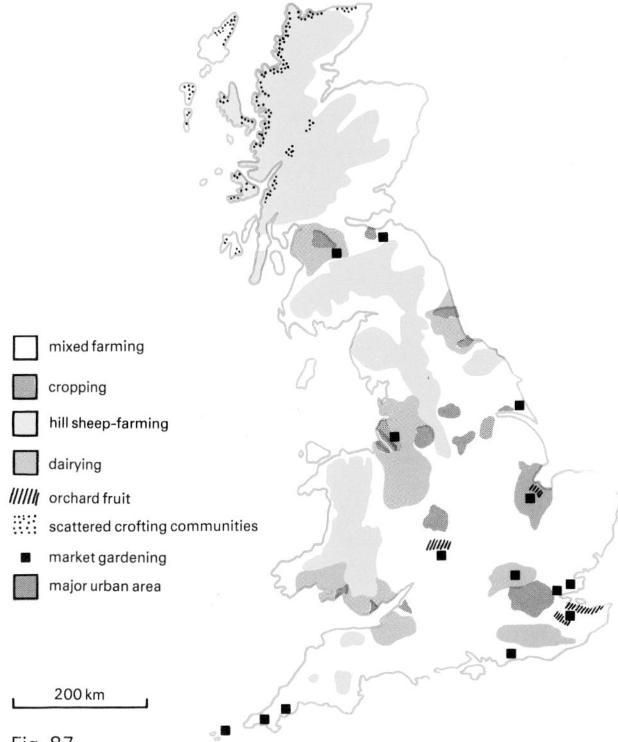

Fig. 87

to region. Farmers accept the advantages of mixed farming, but lean towards the aspect for which environment or market equips them best.

Take East Anglia for example. The gentle relief of these wide lowlands enable machines to be used with ease. Soils (Fig. 88) are mainly derived from glacial deposits. Some are naturally fertile. Others have been made rich by centuries of wise cultivation. The growing season is relatively dry. Annual rainfall averages less than 750 millimetres and long hours of sunshine are enjoyed. A selection of cash crops may be grown with profit. Wheat, barley, sugar-beet and field vegetables are all highly popular choices. Yet farmers plant considerable areas with grass to support a herd of dairy or beef cattle. With a mixed farm economy, the farmer can make use of any

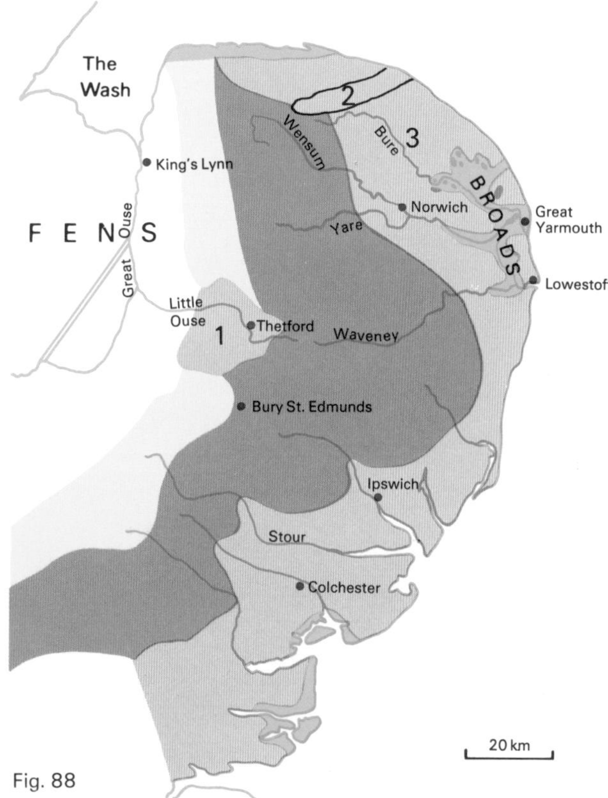

Fig. 88

rough grazing land or riverside pasture which may lie within his farm.

In Fig. 89 we fly over central Norfolk. Beneath us we see the land-use pattern typical of rural East Anglia. The close patchwork of differing tints and textures changes with the seasons. Rotations bring an annual shift, but do not change the essential balance between cash crops and fodder.

East Anglia may be contrasted with more westerly parts of England where rainfall is heavier and sunshine less certain. Grass grows green and rich. Here it is the dairy herd which takes pride of place and cash cropping is of secondary importance.

Hill sheep-farming

Fig. 90 was taken in the heart of the highland core of north Wales. We look along the Nantygwryd valley to the distant summit of Snowdon. The signs of glacial action are clearly seen. It is a landscape typical of much of highland Britain. Low, level land is extremely scarce. Only on the alluvial land of the valley floor is the farmer able to use the plough. Here the soil has reasonable depth and fertility, but drainage is often poor. Climate does little to encourage cultivation. Exposed to humid winds from over the sea, rainfall is heavy and the sun often obscured by cloud. In these conditions, the farmer's choice of crops is limited. Only grass truly appreciates the moist, cool growing season. The valley floor is devoted to permanent pasture.

The valley sides rise steeply to heights of 300 metres or more before easing into the more gentle slopes of the plateau surface. Outcrops of bare, polished rock penetrate a thin layer of infertile acid soil. Climate deteriorates with increasing altitude. The growing season shrinks as average temperatures fall. Precipitation is higher, and the bleak moorland summits may carry

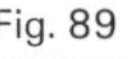

Fig. 89

Fig. 90

winter snows for several weeks. This harsh land supports a broken cover of poor vegetation which is dominated by tough, coarse grass.

Look again at Fig. 90. It illustrates Britain's most difficult farming environment. The extensive rearing of hardy sheep is the only productive way of using the land.

Upland grazings have carrying capacities which may be as low as one sheep per hectare. Farms must be large to support a flock of economic size. Their boundaries often enclose over 400 hectares. The bulk, of course, is rough pasture, but also included is a small patch of improved land – the farmer's share of the alluvial soils of the valley floor. Hill sheep-farming depends on the close integration of the two types of land.

For most of the year the rough uplands provide adequate support for the hardy and tolerant sheep. The permanent pasture on the valley floor gives a good yield of rich grass. Some is cut and dried as hay – no easy task in the moist summer. The rest is available to accommodate the animals when they are shepherded down from the hills. These visits are short and relatively rare. One example is in the depths of winter when hay is much appreciated. At lambing time, the ewes relish the new flush of spring grass. Stock may also be assembled for dipping, shearing and the selection of animals for sale.

With his limited area of good pasture, the hill farmer is unable to fatten his stock for market. His surplus lambs are sold to farmers in lowland districts. This is his main source of income. The wool clip is light in weight and poor in quality, and is of secondary importance.

Hill sheep-farming makes modest demands on labour. Expensive machines are not required. Farm buildings are small and simple. There is little need of fertilizer and seed. The farmer's costs are low, but so is his income. Profits are often too small to support an acceptable standard of living in lonely areas with few social amenities. Rural population declines as people move away in search of higher rewards for their labours. The number of farms decreases. Land is abandoned, converted to forestry or joined into larger units.

The farms that remain must often depend on government assistance or an income from the tourist trade. In many popular areas, farmers find caravans, catering or campsites more profitable than pasture.

Dairy farming

Milk is British agriculture's most important product. It accounts for roughly 25 per cent of the total value of farm sales. Output continues to satisfy a domestic market which expands with growing population, rising standards of living and the pressures of advertising. Surplus output is manufactured into significant quantities of cheese, butter, yoghurt and other dairy products.

Milk production is more widely distributed than any other form of farm activity. The dairy cow is a familiar sight in virtually all agricultural areas. The greater part

Fig. 91

of total milk output comes from dairy herds run as part of mixed-farming enterprises. There are, however, important areas where dairying is truly dominant. South Cheshire, Somerset, south-west Wales and the western half of Scotland's central lowlands are examples

Fig. 92

located on Fig. 87 (page 49).

South Cheshire has a firm environmental basis for the long-established interest in dairying which it shares with adjacent parts of neighbouring counties. The area experiences a climate which is happily free from extremes; mild winters bring little frost or snow and summers are relatively cool and cloudy. Cows appreciate these equable conditions. 10°C is the temperature considered ideal for milk production. An average annual rainfall of between 650 and 750 millimetres is well distributed throughout the year. Relief and soil have been developed on glacial deposits left behind by ice-sheets which intruded southwards over the lowlands between the Pennines and Wales. Uneven spreads of boulder clay are responsible for the rolling surface that is typical of south Cheshire. Soils derived from boulder clay are a mixed blessing. Fertility is often high, but, being stiff and heavy, they do little to encourage the plough. They readily retain moisture. Pastures remain fresh and green throughout the average summer, but may be damaged by grazing hooves in winter. Field drainage is often essential.

In this environment, grass has few serious rivals. Rich and abundant, it is the basis of cheap milk production. Once, south Cheshire profited from its proximity to large urban markets in the midlands and north-west. Today all milk is sold through the Milk Marketing Board which pays a standard price to producers in all parts of the country. This means that farm location is now of little economic significance. With a regular and reliable outlet for fresh milk, the farmhouse manufacture of milk products has declined. Only a handful of farms continue to make the famous cheese in the traditional way.

Fig. 91 shows the rural landscape on the southern edge of the Peckforton Hills. A typical farm is seen in Fig. 92. Land use in south Cheshire is dominated by grass. Two-thirds of the farmland is commonly devoted to leys and

Fig. 93

permanent pasture. The balance is shared by fodder crops which include oats, roots and kale. Stout thorn hedges parcel the land into small fields which are convenient for the close control of livestock. The black and white Friesian is the most popular breed. Not only does it give record milk yields, but surplus calves command a high market price, for they are much in demand for beef production in other parts of the country. Farms are generally of modest size – 40 hectares is typical. Farmhouses, alone or in small clusters, are sprinkled over the countryside. They are flanked by the elaborate outbuildings demanded by dairy farming. Examples include housing for cattle and storage of fodder.

Dairying is the most intensive form of pastoral agriculture. The small farm receives high inputs of labour and capital. The cow in milk has a seven-day week. Twice each day she demands attention. The farmer's day is long; his year unbroken by quiet times. Mechanisation, especially electric milking parlours, eases the farmer's burden, but only at high capital cost.

The current trend is towards even greater intensification. Increased use of fertilizers and more careful choice of seeds give improved pasture and heavier crops of fodder. In dry spells, spray irrigation is increasingly used to increase the yield of pastures (Fig. 93). Herd quality is improved by the service of pedigree bulls, now widely available through the artificial insemination scheme run by the Milk Marketing Board. By purchasing imported feeding stuffs, the farmer is able to increase the size of his herd and make more efficient use of his machines. In ways such as these, the farmer is able to squeeze increased output from his fixed area of land.

Cropping

Fig. 94 portrays a distinctive farming landscape. The characteristic features of the English countryside are hard to find. Flat land extends to the misty horizon. Rivers and roads do not twist and bend. The pattern is dominated by straight lines and sharp angles. Fields are bounded not by hedges but by water-filled ditches. Trees are few and farmhouses are dispersed over the farm land. The photograph, taken near Downham Market, is representative of the English Fenlands. It is essentially a human landscape, created by man from raw materials delivered by river and sea.

Fig. 94

The slow melting of the ice-sheets brought about a substantial rise in sea-level. Areas of clay lying between the Jurassic and Cretaceous cuestas were converted into a large, shallow bay. This was sealed by marine deposits to give the silt lands indicated in Figs. 95 and 96. Inland waters were colonised by marsh vegetation, the remains of which accumulated into thick beds of rich, black peat. Low islands of clay or gravel rose above the marsh-land and sluggish rivers, flowing on thick ribbons of alluvium, followed meandering courses to the sea.

Fig. 95

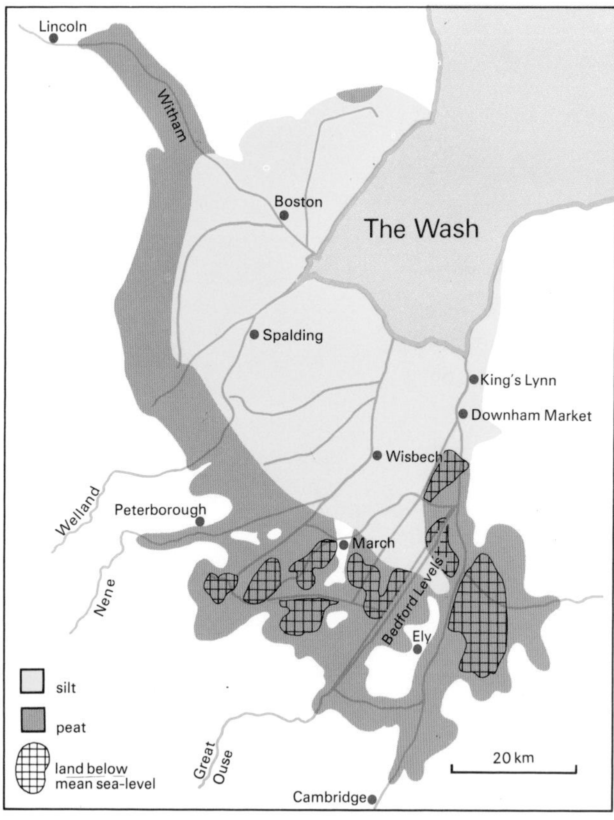

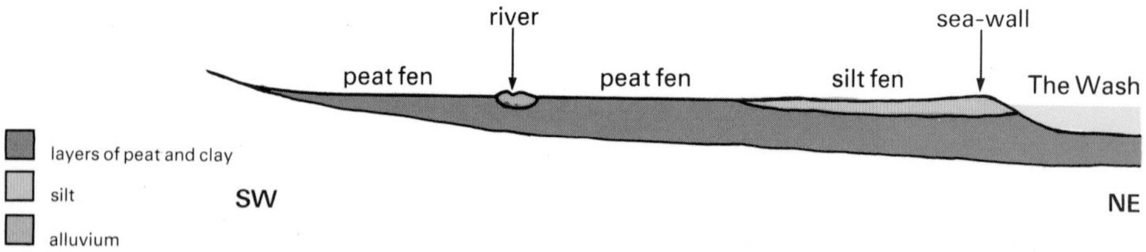

Man's efforts to create farmland out of this watery wilderness date back many centuries. The Romans nibbled at the edges. The Anglo-Saxons, from settlements on the silt lands, won new fields from inland fen and coastal marsh. In medieval times, it was mainly monastic establishments that shouldered the burden. Large-scale reclamation began in the seventeenth century, under the guidance of Dutch engineers. Rivers were straightened to improve the rate of flow. New channels were cut to further improve the drainage. A network of ditches was dug to deliver water to the major channels. This lowered the water-table and so made cultivation possible. Reclamation was virtually complete by the middle of the nineteenth century, but improvements in water control are still being made.

Reclamation has brought problems. Removal of water lowers the surface of the peat. Exposure to air causes further shrinkage. Under cultivation, the fine peat soils are subject to wind erosion. Today the peat lands are several metres below their original level (Fig. 96). In the

Fig. 96

river
sea-wall
peat fen
peat fen
silt fen
The Wash
layers of peat and clay
silt
alluvium
SW
NE

Fig. 97

south, wide areas lie slightly below mean sea-level. Look at Fig. 97. The river Little Ouse, safe on its bed of alluvium, flows above the surrounding farm land. It is embanked as a defence against flooding. Water from drainage ditches must be pumped up to the river. In some areas the shrinkage of the peat has been so severe that the plough now bites into the underlying clay.

Drainage works are expensive. The farmer must bear his share of the cost. His reward is in the quality of the soil. Both peat and silt are very fertile; yields per hectare are well above the national average. The fen-land farmer enjoys other advantages. The smooth relief encourages the use of labour-saving machinery. Climate is highly favourable. Average rainfall of less than 600 millimetres is generally adequate, for a slight summer maximum coincides with the greatest need of moisture. The warm growing season meets the requirements of wheat, sugar-beet and other valuable crops. Long hours of sunshine help the crops to ripen. Winter frosts help to break down the soil and impose a check on insect pests.

Livestock are of little significance in fen-land farming. Cattle may graze areas still liable to flooding, or be fed on arable waste, but the land is generally too valuable to be put down to pasture. Intensive cash cropping is the dominant type of farm economy. Farms of modest size carry a high investment in terms of machinery, labour and chemical fertilizer. The last item is particularly important in view of the shortage of animal manure. Potatoes, wheat, barley and sugar-beet are the dominant crops of the peat fen. These crops also feature in the more diversified cropping pattern of the silt lands. Here vegetables are a major interest. Grown in variety and abundance they are trucked to markets in London, the midlands or even further afield. An increasing proportion of the harvest is delivered under contract to processing factories or large retail outlets. Some districts boast local specialisations. In the Wisbech area, for instance, much land is devoted to soft fruit and apple orchards. Fig. 98 provides a colourful example of specialisation. It shows a spring scene near Spalding, the centre of Britain's bulb production.

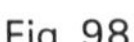
Fig. 98

Fruit

Orchards are commercially important in several relatively small districts. Wisbech has already been mentioned. Apples grown near Hereford support the local manufacture of cider. The Vale of Evesham is noted for the production of plums. Orchards make their mark on the rich farming landscape of south Essex. These areas are overshadowed by Kent, which maintains its long-established leadership in this branch of agriculture.

The concentration of orchards in south-east England reflects the significance of climate in the cultivation of fruit. Dry, sunny conditions encourage ripening and reduce the incidence of plant diseases and insect pests. An average annual rainfall of between 500 and 750 millimetres is generally adequate, but farmers are discovering that irrigation brings a substantial increase in yield. Climate does, however, hold hazards. A sharp frost when the blossom is on the bough can put a whole year's crop at risk. Strong winds when the fruit is on the tree may bring serious losses. These dangers can be reduced by the careful siting of orchards. Planting on a slope gives free air drainage and allows frosty air to flow down and away. A naturally sheltered site may give some protection from the wind, or windbreaks may be planted to achieve the same ends. Soils must be deep and well drained to allow the development of healthy root systems.

Kent offers the fruit farmer a favourable climate and considerable areas of suitable relief and soil. One of these areas is found on the dip-slope of the North Downs, within easy reach of the large London market.

Orchard fruit is seldom the farmer's only interest. In fact, the cropping pattern is highly diverse. Apples, pears and cherries are grown, often in several varieties. The farmer has a long list of soft fruits from which he may choose, and strawberries, gooseberries and black-currants are popular. Kent is responsible for roughly half of Britain's hop production, and orchard districts claim a major share. Vegetables are often important. Large farms may include fields of cereals and roots.

There are advantages in this variety. It smooths out the demand for labour, and enables efficient use to be made of permanent staff. Even so, casual workers must be employed at busy times. The fruit harvest, so dependent on the weather, is highly fickle. Yields may differ by more than 100 per cent from one year to the next, and a variety of fruit serves as insurance.

A well-tended orchard may last for fifty years. In spite of this, fruit farming is not immune from the mood of change that is characteristic of British agriculture. Old orchards are grubbed up and replaced by new varieties which give high yields but mature at modest heights and so make harvesting easier and cheaper. Public taste is also subject to change and as a result, dessert apples enjoy increased popularity, but fewer cherries are grown. The quality of the fruit improves as new chemical sprays destroy pests and prevent diseases. The farmer pays greater attention to grading and packing, now often a large-scale co-operative enterprise. Many farmers, or groups of farmers, have invested in special storage facilities which extend the marketing season by several months.

With entry into the European Economic Community, fruit farming faces the prospect of severe competition from Continental producers. Growers in the south of France and the north of Italy, for instance, have warmer, sunnier climates with little risk of frost. Output per hectare is often twice the figure achieved in Kent. Perhaps the superb flavour of traditional English varieties plus lower transport costs will be an adequate safeguard to the livelihood of farmers in the county sometimes described as the 'Garden of England'.

Market gardening

The main elements in the landscape of market gardening may readily be identified in Fig. 99. The photograph was taken near Shoreham in Sussex. Open land on the edge of the built-up area is in close cultivation. Individual plots are striped with the varied hues and textures of a wide range of crops. The road is flanked by batches of glasshouses.

Some market-gardening enterprises occupy a hundred hectares or more, but these are rare exceptions. The typical holding is less, often considerably less, than 10 hectares. Only by the use of highly intensive methods of cultivation may such small units be made to prosper. The level of investment is high. Crops receive lavish, almost personal, attention. The reward is a very high output per hectare.

The market gardener chooses his crops with care. He concentrates on those which command a high market price. Cauliflowers and Brussels sprouts are typical vegetables. Valuable salad crops include lettuce, spring onions, tomatoes and cucumbers. The production of flowers and bedding plants is commonly important. Crops such as these demand much skill and care in cultivation. Long hours of costly manual labour are involved. Mechanisation has made little progress on the

Fig. 99

typical market garden; the holding is too small, the crops are too varied and the necessary operations are often too delicate to be done by machines. A plough or rotary-cultivator may prepare the soil, but hand tools are much in evidence.

The heated greenhouse is evidence of the high level of investment. Expensive to construct, it is costly to run. Moisture and temperature can be closely controlled to create artificial climates which are useful in several ways. They permit the cultivation of crops such as the tomato which is more at home in warmer regions. Lettuces, for example, may be grown out of season when prices are high. Plants started in the glasshouse may be planted out to mature early, again when prices are high. By this method, a plot of land may yield two or more crops in the course of a year.

Market gardening has developed on a variety of soils. High fertility is not a prime consideration for, in view of the small areas involved, they may readily be enriched by natural and artificial fertilizers. Light, well-drained open soils are generally favoured, for they are easily worked by manual methods. In addition, their high air content causes them to warm up rapidly in spring, and so encourage early growth.

A popular location for market gardening is where areas of suitable soil enjoy ready access to large centres of population. The Vale of Evesham, for example, is well placed to serve the towns of midland England. London draws in supplies from the Lea Valley, and parts of Bedford, Essex and Kent. Proximity to market offers important advantages. Produce may be delivered in prime condition and transport costs are low. A location too close to an urban area may also pose problems. As towns expand, the enriched soils of market gardens are often buried under the tide of bricks and mortar. Air pollution, by impeding the sun's radiation, may reduce the efficiency of glasshouses. London's Lea Valley, which once supplied most of the capital's needs, has suffered in both respects. In compensation, the Worthing district, which enjoys the clean air and sunny skies of the Channel coast, has expanded its area under glass.

Market gardening is also important in the Isles of Scilly and on patches of light soils in sheltered Cornish valleys. These are exceptional locations, for they lie far from the main centres of population. The climate of the extreme south-west of England gives the market gardener a considerable advantage over his rivals in other parts of the country. Southerly latitudes and constant exposure to maritime air brings winters of exceptional mildness. Temperatures high enough to encourage plant growth are commonly experienced as early as February, and the harvest is similarly advanced. Daffodils, cauliflower, broccoli and early potatoes are important crops. With efficient packaging and transport they can be sold in distant urban markets when prices are high.

Crofting

The Atlantic fringe of highland Scotland is the setting for a type of agriculture which is a relic of earlier, more simple times. Crofting is basically a subsistence form of economy. Once common and widely distributed, it has suffered a long and persistent decline. Today there are fewer than 15000 working croft units. They lie scattered within the area indicated in Fig. 87 (page 49).

Fig. 100

A typical crofting landscape is viewed from the air in Fig. 100. Here, on the Isle of Skye, opportunities for agriculture are severely restricted. The distant peaks rise steep and bleak and the rock-pierced foreground supports the poorest of pasture. The small area of cultivatable land stands out as strips of brighter green between the scarps and along the coast. It is only here that the land will support the plough.

The environment poses farming problems not seen in the photograph. Heavy rainfall and a cloudy growing season effectively limit the range of possible crops. Soils are leached and acid, and their successful cultivation demands heavy applications of lime and fertilizer. Remote and isolated crofting communities are poorly served by means of transport. They generally lack a market for their produce, for towns in this part of Scotland are small and few.

In Fig. 101 we take a closer look at a crofting community or *township*. This is a view of Balallan on the Isle of Lewis. Houses are sprinkled over the cultivated land. Each stands within its patch of arable land. Stacks of peat, dug on the uplands, are drying close at hand. Crofts are small; seldom do they exceed 25 hectares and most are less than 4 hectares. Potatoes are the main food crop and common vegetables such as carrots and cabbages are also grown for the kitchen. The rest of the land yields oats and grass. Simple methods of cultivation often involve the use of spade, fork and scythe. For heavy tasks the crofter may borrow a tractor and appropriate attachments owned jointly by the township.

Livestock plays a significant role in the crofting economy but numbers are usually small. The typical croft can only raise winter fodder sufficient for two or three cows. Served by the township bull, they more than meet domestic milk requirements, and surplus is made into butter and soft cheese. Sheep are more numerous. They receive a little hay in winter, but for most of the year they depend on the scanty hillside pastures. Grazing rights are held in common by the township. The share of

Fig. 101

the individual crofter is measured in terms of the number of sheep he can graze. Livestock provides the crofter with his only saleable produce. Wool clip and surplus animals will stand the cost of transport to distant markets.

Landholdings are generally too small to give full-time employment to the crofter. Output is seldom sufficient to afford an adequate standard of living for his family. Crofting has traditionally been combined with other employment such as fishing or weaving. Even with an outside source of income, crofting is a hard life with few amenities and little financial reward. For many decades, people have been leaving the land and migrating to urban areas or overseas countries. The signs of rural depopulation may be recognised in the many abandoned and decayed crofts that dot the countryside.

In recent years, conditions have improved in the crofting counties. The steep downward trend of population has been checked, and in some areas is beginning to show a slight increase. Today there are more varied opportunities for employment. Forestry and tourism may be quoted as examples. Many crofts have a steady summer income from the accommodation of visitors to this remote but beautiful part of Scotland. The influx of tourists creates a slightly larger market for farm produce, especially milk and vegetables. Crofters now receive considerable financial assistance from the government; grants are paid for such things as buildings and fertilizers, and subsidies are paid on livestock. Reseeding of naturally poor pastures improves their carrying capacity. The Highlands and Islands Development Board encourages new development with advice and finance.

But agriculture is slow to improve. The difficulties of land, climate and isolation are ever-present. Crofts are too small to adopt modern farming techniques. Amalgamation into units of economic size is made difficult by the large number of crofts that would be involved, and the strong attachment of the individual crofter to his own particular patch of land. It is likely that crofting will remain a part-time occupation.

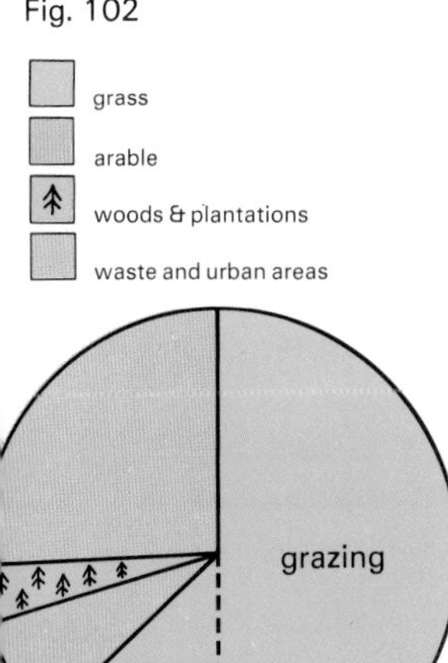

Fig. 102

Agriculture in the Republic of Ireland

Agriculture plays a far more significant role in the economic life of the Republic than it does in the United Kingdom. The land gives direct employment to over 25 per cent of the working population. Farm produce accounts for nearly half of the total exports. Most of this trade is directed to Britain, and the presence of this large market, virtually on Ireland's doorstep, has a great influence on Irish agriculture. The United Kingdom takes more than half of the Republic's exports, which are particularly strong in livestock and dairy produce.

Fig. 102 indicates the use made of the land and reveals the great importance of grass. For this, climate bears the main responsibility. The price of Ireland's exposed position on the edge of the wide Atlantic is a climate dominated by maritime influence. Mild, moist winters are followed by cool summers which are only slightly less damp. Cloud rolls in on the persistent westerly winds, and severely restricts the hours of bright sunshine. The rarity of winter frosts and snow is some small compensation. Grass is the crop best suited to these conditions. On all but the poorest soils it grows long and lush. The winter check to growth is of short duration, and the risk of summer drought is slight. Throughout Ireland, grass, and the animals it nourishes, are of prime importance in the farming economy.

The climate, so favourable to grass, has little to offer the arable farmer. Wheat, for instance, is slow to ripen and is susceptible to disease. Nevertheless, most parts of the Republic have an interest in tillage. Often this is merely the occasional small field of potatoes or oats. The bulk of the arable land is concentrated in the drier east and south. Only in the area shaded yellow in Fig. 103 does the tilled area exceed 20 per cent of the land in agricultural use.

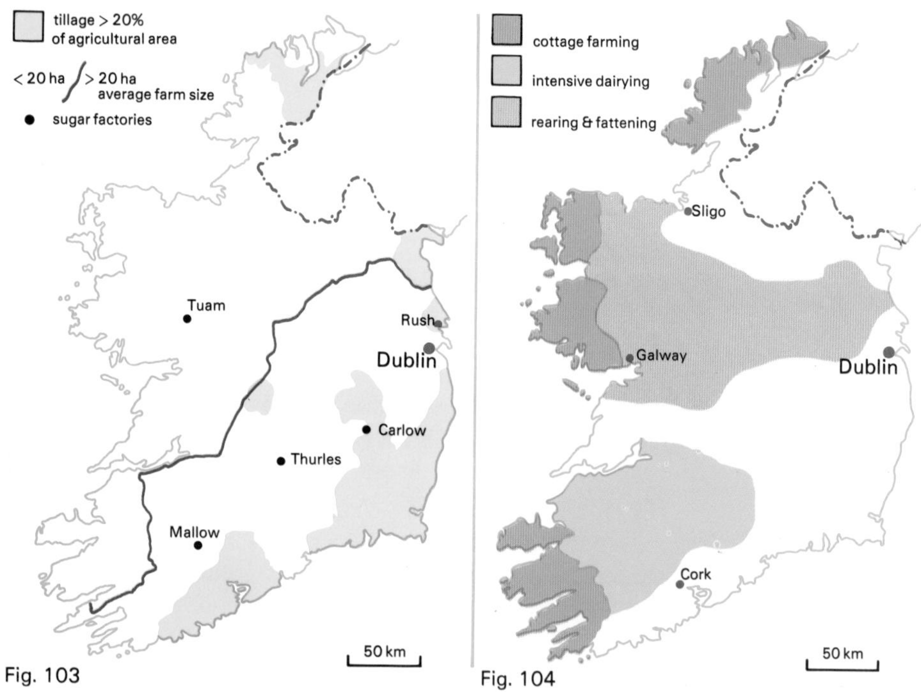

Fig. 103

Fig. 104

Barley is the most important cereal. As in the United Kingdom, its popularity as a fodder crop has increased with the introduction of new high-yielding varieties. Malting qualities are grown in quantity to supply the breweries, especially that of the Dublin-based firm of Guinness. The cultivation of wheat for milling is stimulated by government subsidies. Sugar-beet is produced on a significant scale in areas of suitable soil within range of the factories located on Fig. 103. Potatoes are grown virtually everywhere, mainly for domestic requirements. The area under this traditional food crop has declined in recent years. This is a response to improvements in national diet, and increased yields per hectare. Market gardening is concentrated near the coastal village of Rush, 20 kilometres north of Dublin. This district is favoured by proximity to the capital; by light, easily-worked soils, and by the mildness of the winter climate.

Today, the Republic is a land of small owner-occupied farms. This is in marked contrast to the situation in the nineteenth century, when the great majority of farmers were tenants of large landholders. This transformation has been brought about largely by the activities of the Land Commission. Established in 1881, it has been responsible for the purchase of more than a million hectares of land, and its resale on favourable terms to former tenants. Only in the counties south and east of the line indicated in Fig. 103 does average farm size exceed 20 hectares. In the far west it is only half as much. Small landholdings encourage pastoral farming, for few farms are large enough to support mechanised production of arable crops. The present work of the Land Commission is to encourage a general increase in farm size, and, especially in the west, to consolidate fragmented holdings into more economic units.

Regional variations

The Republic of Ireland, though small in area, shows significant variations in farming activity. Climate, relief and soils are the major factors of influence. The peat-bogs of central districts, for instance, offer little opportunity for productive agriculture. The Wicklow Mountains, rising above the level of cultivation, are largely devoted to sheep rearing. The market gardening district of Rush is a further illustration. These are local examples. On a broader scale, variations in farming are more subtle. Often it is only a slightly different emphasis in the dominant pastoral interests that leads to change. Distinctive farming characteristics are, however, displayed by three regions indicated in Fig. 104.

Cottage farming

It is in the west that conditions for agriculture are most difficult. Relief is rugged and well over half the land is unproductive. Soils are thin, acid and infertile. Cloudy skies weep rain on more than 250 days in the average year. Communications are poor and the major markets for farm produce are far away. Landholdings are small even by Irish standards. Less than 12 hectares is the average size. In these conditions, profitable agriculture is hard to achieve.

Fig. 105, a photograph taken near Derrynane in County Kerry, shows a typical farming landscape. Single-storied farm cottages sit amidst a patchwork of small, stone-walled paddocks, most of which are put to pasture. As on the crofting coast of Scotland, there is a strong element of subsistence in the farm economy. Tiny plots are spaded over and planted with potatoes and vegetables for the family table. Livestock add milk and eggs to the diet. The poor land is reluctant to yield a surplus; the occasional sale of calves or young stock brings in a little cash, but it is seldom sufficient to meet essential needs. The family must look beyond the land for support. The government creates new jobs in industry and tourism. Additional family income comes from relations overseas, or seasonal labour at home or even abroad.

Fig. 105

Dairying

In counties Tipperary and Limerick and adjacent parts of Kerry and Cork, dairying is the dominant type of farm economy. This activity is greatly encouraged by conditions of climate and soil which favour the growth of grass. This, the cheapest fodder, grows abundantly throughout the long growing season. The landscape features fields of permanent pasture framed by stout thorn hedges. Only a tiny fraction of the land is under the plough. Cattle can be out in the pastures as early as March. There they can stay until November, when the heavy land is wet and soft, and open to damage from trampling hooves. The mild climate makes costly winter housing unnecessary. Open paddocks or the simplest of shelters are all that is needed. Silage is the popular winter feed, for hay is often difficult and tedious to make in the damp summer months.

In the absence of large urban markets, milk is delivered to the co-operative creameries that are scattered over the region. It is processed into butter and other dairy produce, most of which is exported to England via the port of Cork.

Rearing and fattening

In a belt which widens westwards from Dublin to Galway and Sligo, land use is again dominated by permanent pasture. Here, in contrast to the south-west, milk is of little importance. In the western half of the belt, rearing is the main activity. Calves are bred on the small farms and additional supplies are brought in from the cottage and dairy-farming regions. They are nourished until about two years old and then sold as stores. In areas of poor land and pasture, sheep are of greater importance.

In the east of the region, farms are larger and grassland is better. Rearing is still important, but fattening for the butcher is also of significance. Dublin is a factor in this. As a city it provides a market for fresh meat and as a port it offers an export link to the United Kingdom for live cattle.

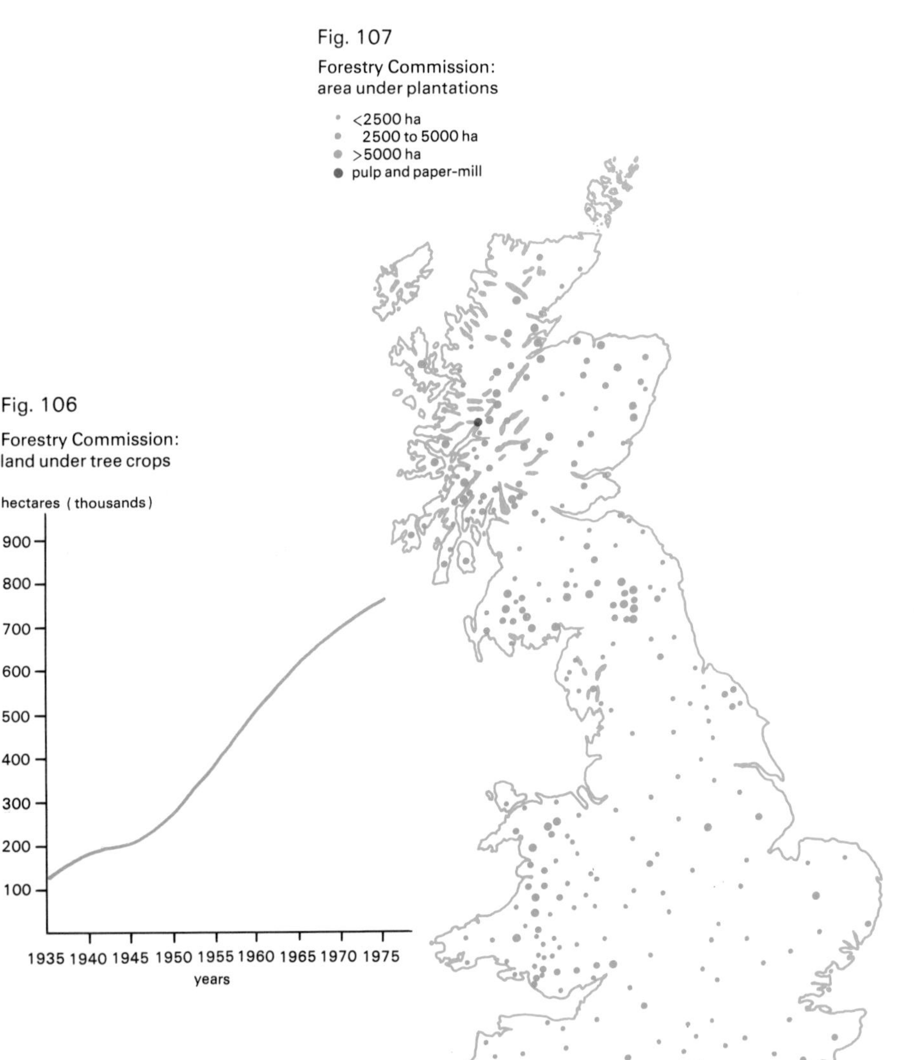

Fig. 107
Forestry Commission: area under plantations

Fig. 106
Forestry Commission: land under tree crops

Forestry

Over the greater part of the British Isles, forest is nature's natural response to the environment. Only at the highest elevations, and on coasts exposed to salt-laden winds, are conditions too harsh for trees to flourish. In former times, the British Isles were clothed with dense forests, mainly of broad-leaved deciduous species, among which the oak was dominant. Local conditions brought variety to the forest scene. The thin, dry soils of chalk cuestas carried wide stands of beech, but ash was typical in limestone areas. Over the lower slopes of the Scottish highlands, the Scots pine, Britain's only native conifer, formed a distinctive forest type.

Today, this natural vegetation has all but disappeared. Only in remote and isolated areas do tiny remnants remain. Throughout history, forests have been devastated to meet the needs of man: the creation of agricultural land demanded the clearance of trees; timber was vital in the construction of buildings and boats; and much was consumed as domestic and industrial fuel.

The woodlands which so often add to the charm of present-day landscapes are there by the grace of man. In lowland areas, landowners established small plantations to serve local needs, or simply to decorate their estates. Deciduous trees were popular, and they included alien species, such as the sycamore. Where soils were poor, especially in upland areas, coniferous trees were established. Plantations were typically small and scattered, and their yield was meagre. They could meet only a tiny fraction of Britain's growing appetite for wood and wood products. Britain's dependence on imports was underlined during the First World War.

The Forestry Commission, established in 1919, has the task of stimulating home production. By 1935 it had 136 000 hectares under tree crops and later progress is graphed in Fig. 106. Today, nearly half the forest land in Britain is administered by the Commission.

Fig. 107 locates the Forestry Commission plantations. A widespread distribution reflects a climate that is generally favourable to tree growth. The quality of soil is the chief factor influencing the choice of site, for the Forestry Commission restricts its purchase of land to areas that are unable to support profitable agriculture. Such areas are occasionally found in lowland districts. Indeed, Britain's largest forest, 18 987 hectares, is near Thetford, on the infertile, sandy soils of the Breckland district of East Anglia.

Fig. 108

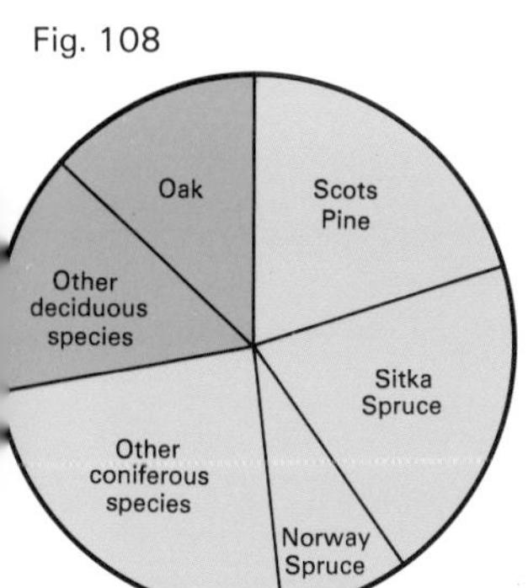

The greatest opportunities are found in highland Britain. Extensive plantations make more productive use of land which formerly supported only poor sheep pasture.

Fig. 108 indicates the character of Britain's forests. Conifers are dominant, but deciduous species claim over 25 per cent of the total area. This is a situation that will slowly change. Fig. 109 illustrates current planting by the Forestry Commission. Many private land-owners, encouraged by grants and guidance from the Commission, are following similar programmes. Current plantings are the basis of future forests; deciduous species will become progressively rarer, as mature forests are cleared and replaced by conifers. There are sound economic reasons for this concentration on coniferous trees. They are softwoods, which represent 90 per cent of Britain's current timber consumption. Quick-growing conifers commonly yield three times as much marketable timber as deciduous species. They are, moreover, better suited to the poor land that is available for forestry.

Fig. 109

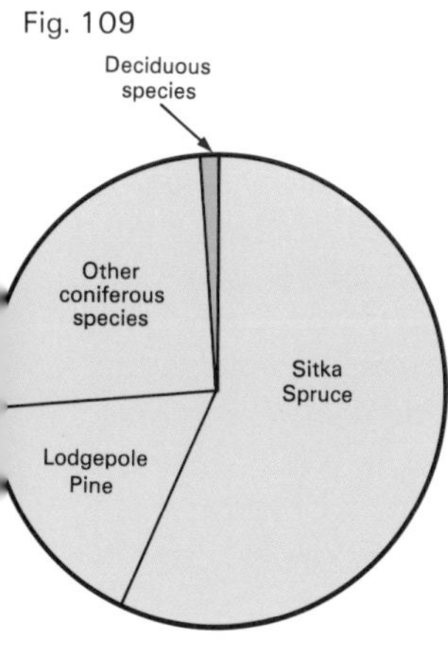

Coniferous species are planted in great variety. More than a dozen have a share of Forestry Commission plantations. Care is taken to select the type best suited to local environments. Sitka spruce holds pride of place. It is tolerant of poor soil and bleak exposures, yet gives a good harvest. Its nearest rival is the lodgepole pine which also yields well under harsh conditions.

Fig. 110

The growing dominance of coniferous trees, although supported by economic arguments, does not meet with universal approval. It is felt by many that the advance of close-packed regiments of alien spruce and pine detracts from the natural beauty of many wild and majestic upland landscapes. Your own assessment may follow study of Fig. 110, which shows part of the Beddgelert Forest in Snowdonia.

The forester's skill must be matched by patience, for forestry is a long-term undertaking. At least 15 years must elapse before new plantations can be thinned to give a first harvest of saleable timber. Subsequent thinnings ensure that surviving trees have space to grow to a maturity that may take 60 years to achieve. Only then is the land clear-felled and reafforested.

The annual harvest from all Britain's forests exceeds 1.5 million cubic metres, but this represents a mere $7\frac{1}{2}$ per cent of current timber consumption. Production of softwood from Forestry Commission plantations is graphed in Fig. 111. Extended by forecasts of future output, the curve rises with increasing steepness. This reflects the

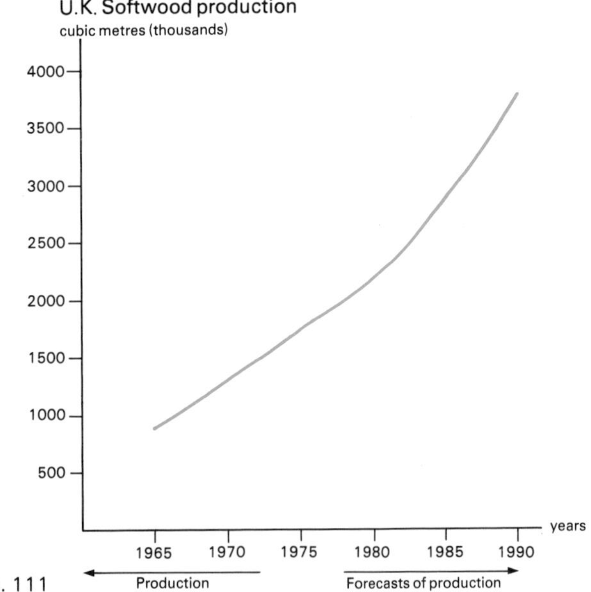

Fig. 111

Fig. 113

growing maturity of established plantations.

Home-grown softwood finds a ready and varied market. Telegraph-poles and pit-props are an obvious outlet. Saw-mills rip logs into building timber. Trees are raw material for fibreboard and chipboard. Increasing output stimulates the establishment of new processing factories, and the largest example is located on Fig. 112 and viewed from the air in Fig. 113. This is the pulp and paper-mill of Wiggins Teape Ltd. at Corpach, near Fort William in the highlands of Scotland. Opened in 1966, it now employs a work-force of nearly 1000. Annat Point on the north shore of Loch Eil affords a level site within range of many scattered areas of productive forest land. Abundant supplies of pure water are locally available and the site is served by both road and rail communications. Artificial islands created in the deep waters of the loch give berthing facilities for vessels of up to 14000 tonnes d.w.t. Each day, lorries, trains and coastal vessels together deliver 1000 tonnes of Scottish coniferous timber. This is joined by hardwood chippings brought in by sea from Canada. The mills are powered by electricity generated on site. The fuels used are oil, and the waste organic material extracted from timber during processing. Annual pulp production is over 80000 tonnes

Fig. 112

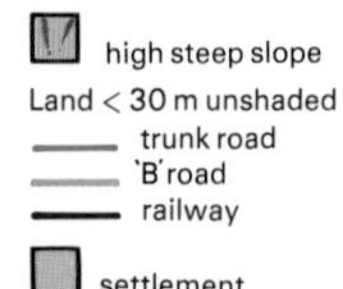

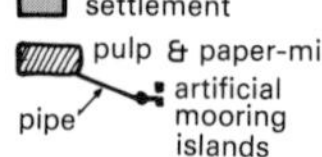

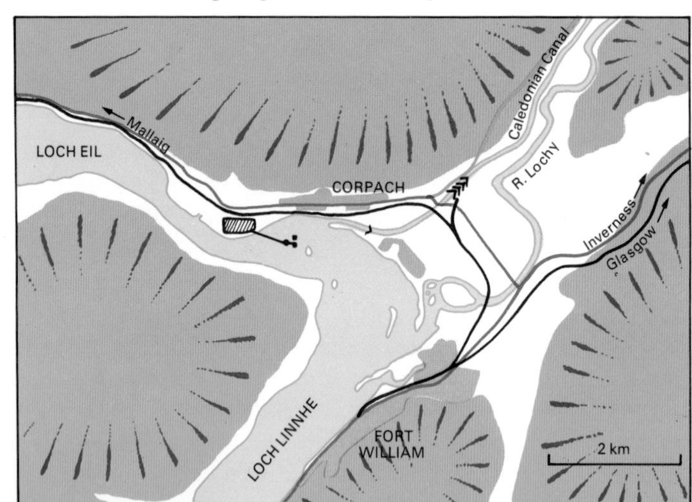

and more than half of this is converted into high-grade paper. Pulp and paper are despatched by rail and road to markets in the United Kingdom.

There is more to the work of the Forestry Commission than the growing of trees. It has a part to play in the creation of employment opportunities in remote highland areas that have been declining in population for many decades. In addition, forest land is developed to provide leisure amenities such as campsites and forest walks. These aspects of the work of the Forestry Commission are considered in Chapter 9.

Fishing

Fig. 114 emphasises that the British Isles rise from the platform of an extensive continental shelf. Shallow surrounding seas are easily penetrated by the rays of the sun and this prompts the growth of plankton, the basic nourishment of marine life. An abundance of plankton supports rich resources of fish which are exploited by vessels based on many of the sheltered havens afforded by a long and indented coastline. Britain's population, clustered in urban centres, provides a large and appreciative market. Efficient transport systems speed the catch to the consumer. Fishing is not restricted to sea areas within easy reach of the coast and modern trawlers make regular voyages to the Barents Sea, Greenland, and other distant fishing-grounds.

Fig. 114

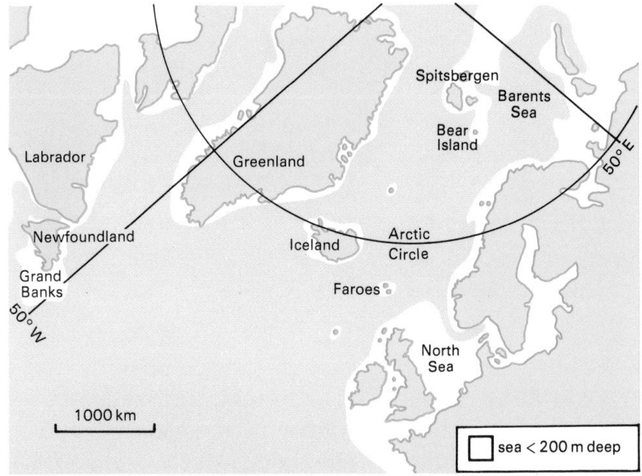

The waters fished from Britain are home to a variety of palatable species which afford a source of high-protein food. Three broad groupings are recognised. *Demersal* species are those which mainly dwell on or near the seafloor. They form the backbone of the industry; haddock, hake and sole are common examples, but the cod takes pride of place. Present in all areas, cod dominates the catch taken in distant waters. *Pelagic* species spend most of their time near the surface, often in shoals of enormous size. The herring is the most important example; others include mackerel and sprat. Pelagic fish tend to be of lower value than demersal. Smaller in average size, they are less to the public taste and are generally processed before they reach the market. Most herrings, for instance, are eaten as kippers. *Shellfish* in rich variety are taken close to the coast. They are normally regarded as a delicacy, and though the catch is light in weight, its value is relatively high. Cockles and mussels are humble examples. Lobster and crab are held in higher esteem. The Norwegian lobster, sold as scampi, has suffered an increase in popular consumer demand, and landings have risen impressively in recent years.

Fishing is a primitive economy; it is hunting in a watery environment. The fisherman can do nothing to increase the resource on which he depends. Indeed, the greater his success, the more bleak his future, because the more fish he catches, the fewer remain to produce future supplies. *Overfishing* quickly brings serious reduction in fish stocks. With the development of new techniques, fishing becomes more efficient. As population rises, the demand for food increases. So, too, does fishing activity by maritime nations, whose vessels compete for the available fish. Overfishing has become a serious problem in recent decades; traditional fishing-grounds, once alive

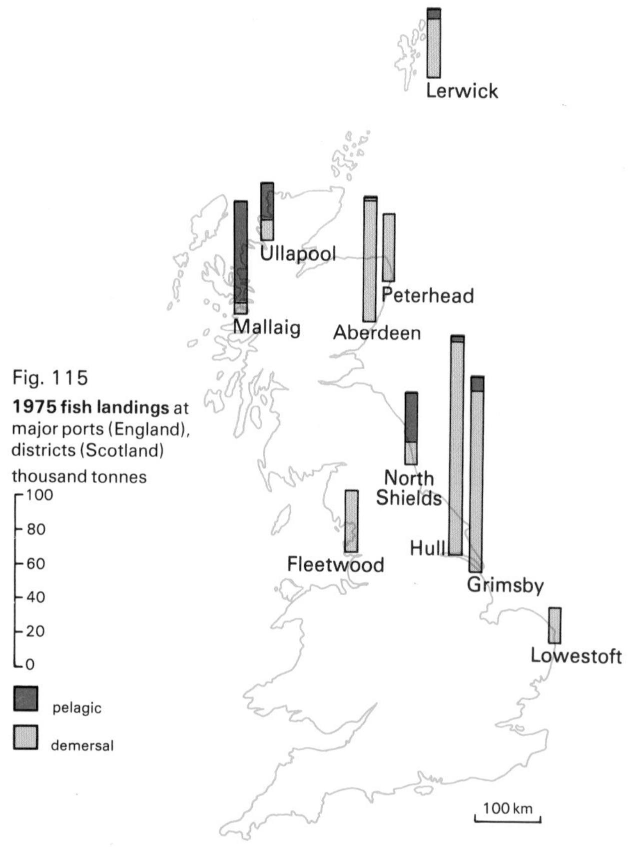

Fig. 115
1975 fish landings at major ports (England), districts (Scotland)

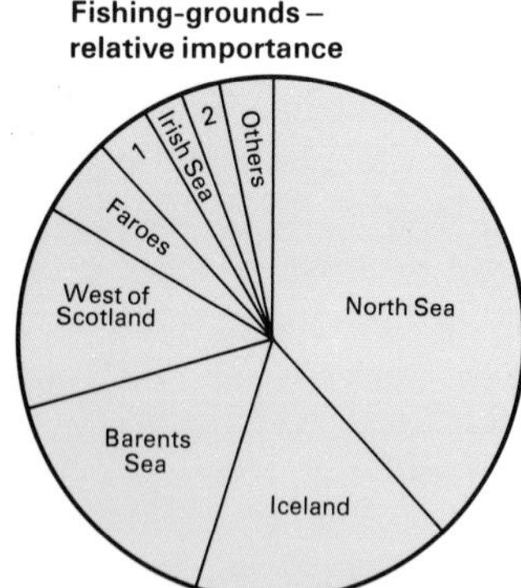

Fig. 116
Fishing-grounds – relative importance

with fish, now give meagre returns and the need to restrict the international harvest of the sea has never been more urgent.

Commercial fishing is widely but unevenly distributed around our coasts. Fig. 115 locates the important centres. Fig. 116 indicates the relative importance of fishing-grounds in terms of the value of British landings in 1975.

Mallaig lies on the southern shore of the Sound of Sleat which separates the Isle of Skye from the Scottish mainland. Beyond the sheltered waters of the Minches lie the Outer Hebrides which break the force of Atlantic storms. In Fig. 117, we look across the simple harbour, cluttered with fishing craft. The vessels are small and their equipment simple. A handful of men will serve as crew. Seldom do they stay long at sea. Throughout the year, but mainly from October to March, they seek the herring.

The herring is widely found over the continental shelf. At spawning time it congregates in coastal waters. Shoals appear in different areas at different times of the year, and once located, offer a rich harvest. The herring catch has steadily declined over the years; landings are now less than half what they were before the war and markets at home and abroad have dwindled. The industry has suffered severely from overfishing, especially in the southern North Sea, which was the most productive area. Great Yarmouth, once a major centre, now has no interest in the herring fishery.

Today, the herring is mainly taken in Scottish waters, especially those off the west coast. In the last decade or so, shoals in the Minches have been larger and more numerous. This has been appreciated by fishermen based on Mallaig and Ullapool, where landings have increased. In 1975, Mallaig's total was 52 444 tonnes. Some was exported to markets in northern Europe. More was kippered to meet home demands and the balance was converted into meal and oil.

The herring is of little significance at Britain's major fishing ports. Vessels sailing out of Hull, Grimsby, Aberdeen, Peterhead and Fleetwood seek demersal species. The North Sea is still important and is actively worked, especially by vessels based on Grimsby and Aberdeen, but yields show the steady decline which results from overfishing.

The development of Hull as a major fishing port dates back to the middle of the nineteenth century. In 1850, a fishing smack sailing out of Scarborough was blown off course in a gale. Before it gained sanctuary in the Humber, it had discovered the prolific 'Silver Pits'

Fig. 117

fishing-grounds, just 110 kilometres east of Spurn Head. Many of the vessels which flocked to exploit these and other North Sea grounds favoured Hull as a base. It offered the advantages of sheltered waters and port facilities. Men trained to the sea in a declining whaling industry were available to crew the fishing craft. Developing rail services could quickly take the catch to the large markets of London and the expanding towns of the industrial north of England. Progress was rapid. Larger vessels were launched. Timber gave way to steel. Sail gave way to steam and then to diesel engines. Voyages in search of fish became progressively longer. Today, the Hull trawler fleet is exclusively concerned with the distant water fishing-grounds.

As vessels increased in number and size, so, too, did the facilities essential for their accommodation and service. The port of Hull, outlined in Fig. 118, developed rapidly in the nineteenth century in response to general trading needs. Fishing interests became concentrated at the western end of the port complex. Fish markets rose from the dockside Factories meeting such varied and essential needs as paints, nets, pumps and protective clothing were established nearby. So, too, were factories using fish as a raw material in the production of fish-meal, fertilizer and cod-liver oil. St. Andrew's Dock was closed in 1975, and it is now the Albert and William Wright Docks which welcome the home-coming trawler. New facilities for the discharge and processing of fish have been developed, and the port now boasts the most modern and efficient fish docks in Britain. The many rail tracks which once served the fish docks are now obsolete, for distribution is now entirely by road.

In Fig. 119, a ship sets out for Arctic waters. This vessel is typical of the modern *freezer* trawlers which harvest distant seas. She has the strength and stability to withstand the winter perils of fierce gales, tumultuous waves and severe icing which are common at her destination. The most up-to-date equipment is carried; in addition to

Fig. 118

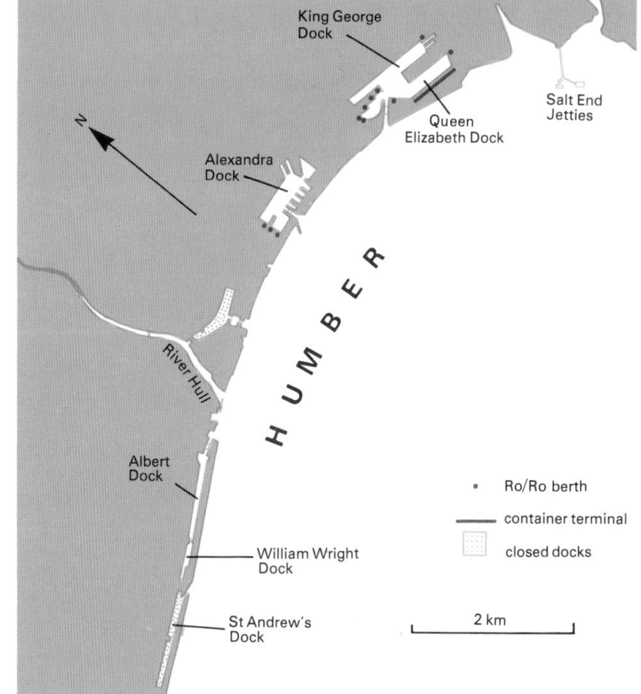

Fig. 119

radio and radar, she has electronic fish-finding gear. The trawl is hauled in over a ramp at the stern and its contents are sorted and gutted on a fully enclosed processing deck. The fish are then frozen in blocks and stored in refrigerated holds. The *factory* trawlers now coming into service go one stage further. The catch is filleted before freezing and waste is converted into fishmeal for animal feeding. The modern vessel is a highly efficient means of catching fish. Range is not limited by the perishability of its catch; it commonly stays at sea for three weeks or more, and for most of this time it is busy fishing.

In 1976, Iceland extended her territorial waters to 320 kilometres from her coastline and her example was followed by other maritime nations. Now Icelandic cod is mainly reserved for Icelandic nets. The British fishing industry faces an uncertain future. Hull and Fleetwood, once largely dependent on Icelandic waters, are hardest hit. Expensive trawlers are laid up, and fishermen are out of work. Service industries are also affected. The search for alternative grounds and other species is active, but there is little prospect of success.

Increased efforts are made to conserve fish stocks within the extended territorial waters of the U.K. and her E.E.C. partners, but even so, it is likely that the decline of the British fishing industry, tabled in Fig. 120, will continue.

Fig. 120

Fishing Industry: Great Britain

	Landings (thousand tonnes)				*Fishermen*	
	Cod	*Other Demersal*	*Herring*	*Other Pelagic*	*Full-time*	*Part-time*
1948	343	99	270	15	38826	8821
1960	315	72	110	11	22007	6247
1971	306	63	146	59	17898	4115
1975	242	94	112	109	17061	5073

5 Fuels and Power

Fig. 122

Coal output and markets

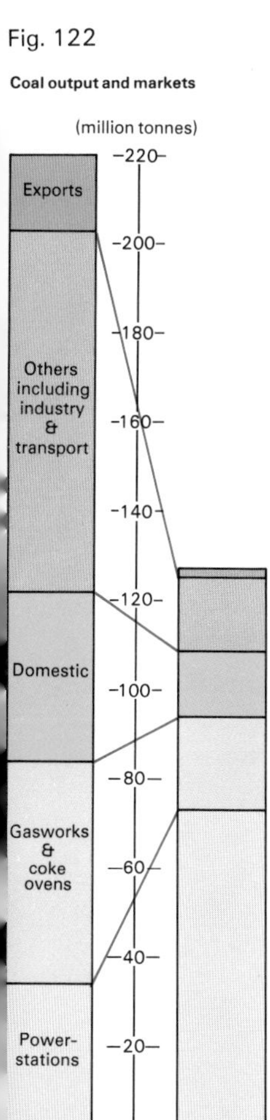

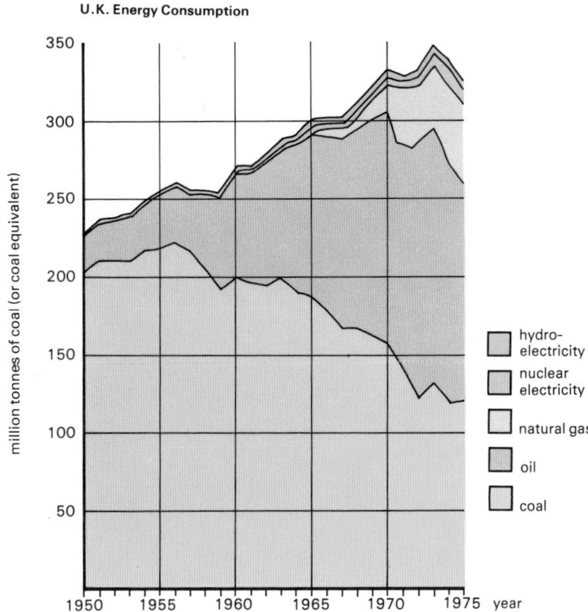

Fig. 121

Coal

Exploitation of Britain's rich and varied coal resources, discussed in Chapter 2 and mapped in Fig. 125, page 70, reached a peak in 1913, when production exceeded 293 million tonnes. The industry has since experienced fluctuating fortunes but the general trend has been one of decline. From the early 1960s, coal experienced a decade of severe economic difficulties which increased the rate of decline and accelerated the important changes that were taking place on the coalfields.

The National Coal Board's major problem has been severe competition from cheaper and more convenient fossil fuels. Imported oil has flooded in to capture markets traditionally served by coal. The recent arrival of natural gas has further reduced demand. Fig. 121 illustrates coal's declining share of the U.K. energy market. Look also at Fig. 122. In gasworks, industry, transport and the home, the use of solid fuel has fallen dramatically. The increased consumption of coal in the production of electricity does not compensate for these losses. Electricity generation is now coal's most important outlet.

In response to the stiff challenge of competition, the coal industry has contracted to the extent indicated in columns 1, 2 and 3 of Fig. 123. At the same time it has become more efficient. Many unprofitable mines have been closed. Others have been rescued by large-scale modernisation. Several large new mines have been established in favourable areas. Conversion to mechanised mining is now virtually complete. Fig. 123 shows the results of these efforts in terms of output per man-year.

Fig. 123

Coal industry: U.K.

	1 *Output (deep-mined) (million tonnes)*	2 *Active collieries*	3 *Manpower (thousands)*	4 *Mechanised output (%)*	5 *Output per man-year (tonnes)*
1950	206	901	691	3.8	298
1955	211	850	699	11.1	302
1960	187	698	602	37.5	309
1965	186	534	491	75.0	379
1970	142	299	305	92.3	464
1975	117	246	246	93.5	475

In the general contraction of post-war years, some coalfields have suffered more than others. This has produced the changes in relative importance indicated in Fig. 124. Several mining areas, notably Scotland, South Wales

Fig. 124

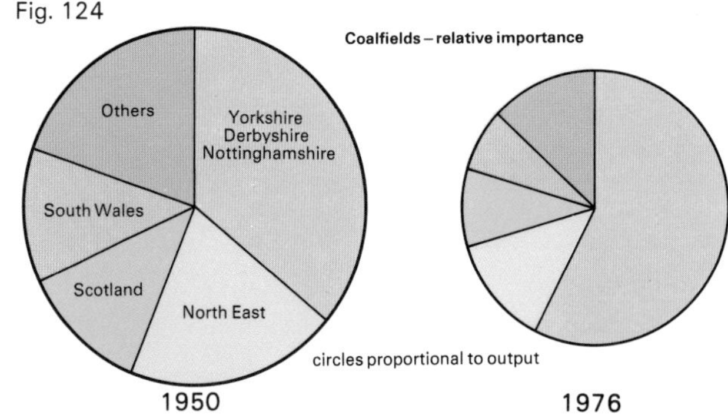

and the scattered fields of the north-west, have experienced serious decline. As we saw in the case of Lancashire (page 17), these fields are paying the price of many decades of intense exploitation. In these declining coalfields, the downward trend will doubtless continue. Many mines remain active only because they meet local needs, or produce coal of a special quality, such as anthracite.

It is worth noting that even where deep mining has ceased, exposed coalfields may still make a contribution to total output. Isolated pockets of coal are worked by small-scale private undertakings. Few in number, their combined annual output is less than a million tonnes.

Fig. 125

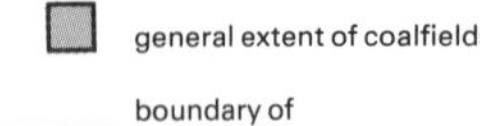

Fig. 126

More significantly, seams which lie near the surface may be cheaply mined by opencast methods (Fig. 126). In 1975, 9 million tonnes were obtained in this way.

The coalfields that have grown in relative importance include the South Midlands fields and the great Yorkshire, Derbyshire and Nottinghamshire coalfield discussed in Chapter 2. These fields enjoy a central location and are well placed to serve markets in many parts of the country. They have benefited from the growth of electricity generation, for large supplies of cheap coal have attracted many large, new power-stations.

The Yorkshire, Derbyshire and Nottinghamshire now holds pride of place amongst British coalfields. This may be appreciated from Fig. 125 which gives the distribution of active collieries. Its dominance in terms of output is emphasised in Fig. 124.

Kellingley Colliery, located in Fig. 127, makes a worthy contribution to the output of Britain's greatest coalfield. Its tall, modern winding-gear is pictured in Fig. 129. In the late 1950s, test borings proved the geological

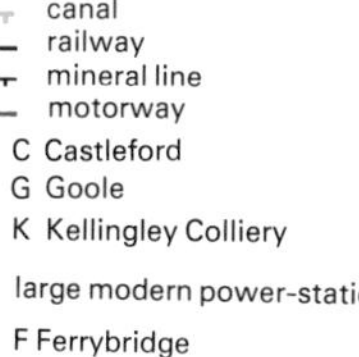

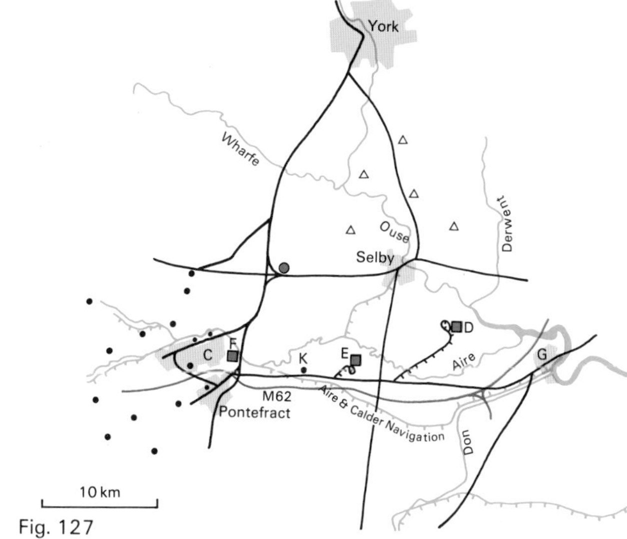

Fig. 127

sequence simplified in Fig. 128. The Coal Measures, concealed beneath 153 metres of younger strata, hold eight seams of varying thicknesses. The three of greatest significance, each between 2 and 3 metres thick, are named on the section. To tap these rich reserves, estimated at nearly 200 million tonnes, twin shafts 8 metres in diameter were sunk to a depth of 700 metres. The

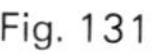

Fig. 128

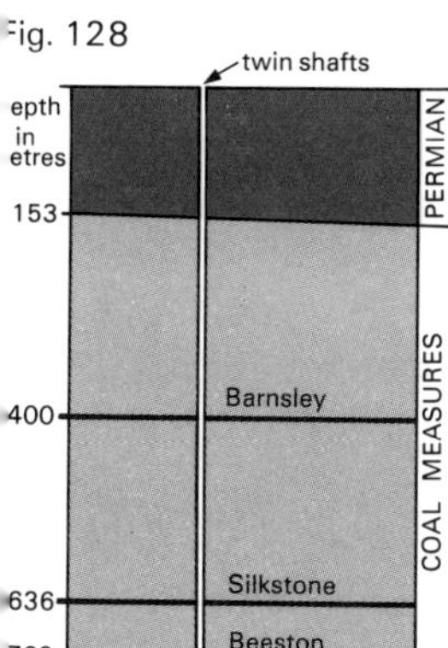

Fig. 129

Fig. 130

Permian strata are water-bearing, and the rock had to be frozen to permit excavation. It took two and a half years to reach the level of the thick and valuable Beeston seam.

Coal was first produced in 1965. Today, four faces, all on the Beeston seam, yield over a million tonnes a year. Annual output is expected to double by the early 1980s. All faces are fully mechanised (Fig. 130); coal is transported to the foot of the shaft by a high-capacity conveyor system (Fig. 131) and lifted to the surface in 18-tonne loads. Kellingley has a work-force of nearly

Fig. 131

1500 men. Thick seams and mechanisation make for efficient mining; output per man is twice the national average.

Surface installations wash and grade the coal. Waste material is not piled up into unsightly slag-heaps but is taken by road to fill abandoned limestone quarries, or help in the reclamation of nearby marshland.

Kellingley coal finds a ready market in the power-stations plotted on Fig. 127. Delivery is efficient and cheap; fuel for Ferrybridge is barged along the Aire and Calder Navigation, and Eggborough and Drax are served by a highly-automated 'merry-go-round' rail system. The trains never stop; at Kellingley, they are loaded in motion, and at the power-station, while moving at 1 km/h precisely, the wagon bottoms open automatically and the coal is discharged into underground hoppers.

In the early 1970s, coal enjoyed an upturn in its economic fortunes. The oil-exporting countries raised the price of crude oil by 500 per cent and suddenly coal became cheaper than its major rival. The need to make full use of Britain's own fuel resources became more urgent. The future of coal looked brighter.

In 1974, the National Coal Board drew up a plan for the development of the industry. It anticipates a future of steadily rising output. By 1985, it is expected to reach 150 million tonnes. To achieve this increase, the plan allows for a greater output from many existing mines, and a larger contribution from opencast workings. More important, however, will be the extension of deep mining into areas as yet untouched.

The most exciting of these new developments is to take place between Selby and York (Fig. 127), where drillings revealed an extension of the Yorkshire coalfield. Five workable seams are present. The best, the Barnsley seam, ranges in thickness from 2 metres to 3.25 metres and offers a reserve of over 600 million tonnes of good quality coal. Mining conditions are excellent. In the south, the Barnsley seam lies 250 metres beneath the surface but dips north-eastwards to greater depths.

This major new addition to Britain's fuel resources is to be exploited by the most modern techniques. A long, gently-inclined drift mine is to be driven along the dip from a point 10 kilometres west of Selby. This will be the route to the surface for coal mined over an area of 250 square kilometres. A high-capacity conveyor system will raise the coal and deliver it to wagons waiting on an adjacent railway line. Five pairs of shafts are to be sunk at wide intervals over the countryside. They will take men, materials and fresh air to a developing network of underground workings. It is anticipated that by 1986, this one mine will yield 10 million tonnes of coal a year, a rate of production that can be maintained well into the twenty-first century.

Exploration continues. In 1976, large reserves of high-quality coal were proved to lie beneath the attractive landscape of the Vale of Belvoir in east Nottinghamshire. The same year brought news of a new field near Musselburgh on the southern shore of the Firth of Forth, with estimated reserves in excess of 50 million tonnes. These new discoveries are a welcome addition to Britain's resources and will do much to encourage the resurgence of the coal-mining industry.

Gas

In the years since the war, the fuel and power industries have all responded to changing circumstances. In the case of gas, however, change amounts to a transformation. Major developments since 1966/7 are graphed in Fig. 132. Consumption has increased dramatically and shading records changes in the source of gas consumed.

In 1950, gas was obtained exclusively from coal. It was manufactured in almost 1000 works which served small local areas. The gasholder was a familiar urban landmark. By 1955, oil refineries were making a contribution to gas manufacture and this had increased to 25 per cent

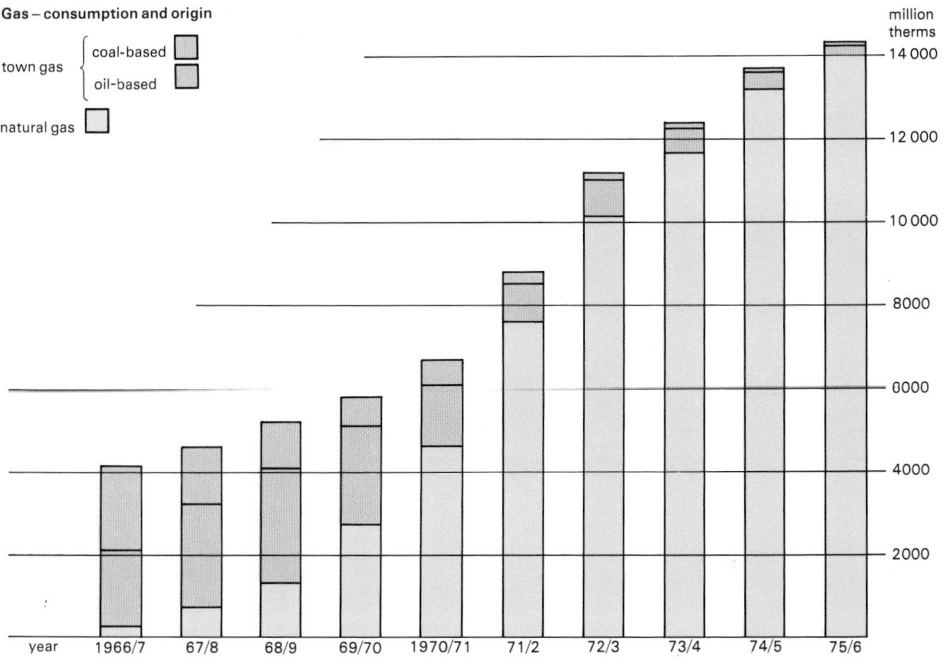

Fig. 132

by 1965. Today, virtually all gas is natural gas. Its introduction was prompted by its several advantages. It has twice the heating value of coal gas and can be obtained without manufacture. It is not poisonous and its burning does not pollute the atmosphere.

Britain's first significant supplies of natural gas came, not from the North Sea, but from the Sahara Desert. In Fig. 133 a tanker is seen at its moorings in the Thames Estuary. It has just completed a voyage from Arzew on the coast of Algeria. There its refrigerated holds were filled with natural gas that had been liquefied by cooling to −160°C. Now its cargo is being discharged into the terminal installation on Canvey Island.

The North Sea made its first contribution in 1967. Supplies rapidly increased as fields were developed and brought into production. Delivery to nearly 14 million individual customers is a complicated undertaking. Fig. 134 maps the progress that has been made in the development of a national transmission system. The gas is treated at terminal installations and pressured into a growing network of large-diameter pipelines. These are frequently tapped by smaller pipes to meet local needs. Winter gas consumption is two and a half times that of summer, and storage is therefore essential. Storage facilities were incorporated in the initial Canvey Island project and can be identified in Fig. 133. They take two forms; insulated tanks that rise above the flat coastland and cavities in frozen ground capped by large flat discs. Tanks and cavities are filled with liquid natural gas. In its liquid state it occupies only 1/600th of its normal volume. Fig. 134 shows that storage facilities have been constructed in areas of high demand. Ambergate in Derbyshire is supplied by road tanker from Canvey Island, otherwise gas drawn from the pipelines is liquefied on site. At Hornsea, a project is under development for the storage of gas in cavities leached out of underlying beds of salt.

The gas industry shows every sign of future expansion. The supply of this convenient fuel increases as new North Sea fields are brought into production. New

Fig. 133

pipelines ensure its efficient distribution. Its market increases as coal and oil become relatively more expensive. It is estimated that by the end of the century, natural gas will provide 20 per cent of Britain's total energy requirements.

Fig. 134

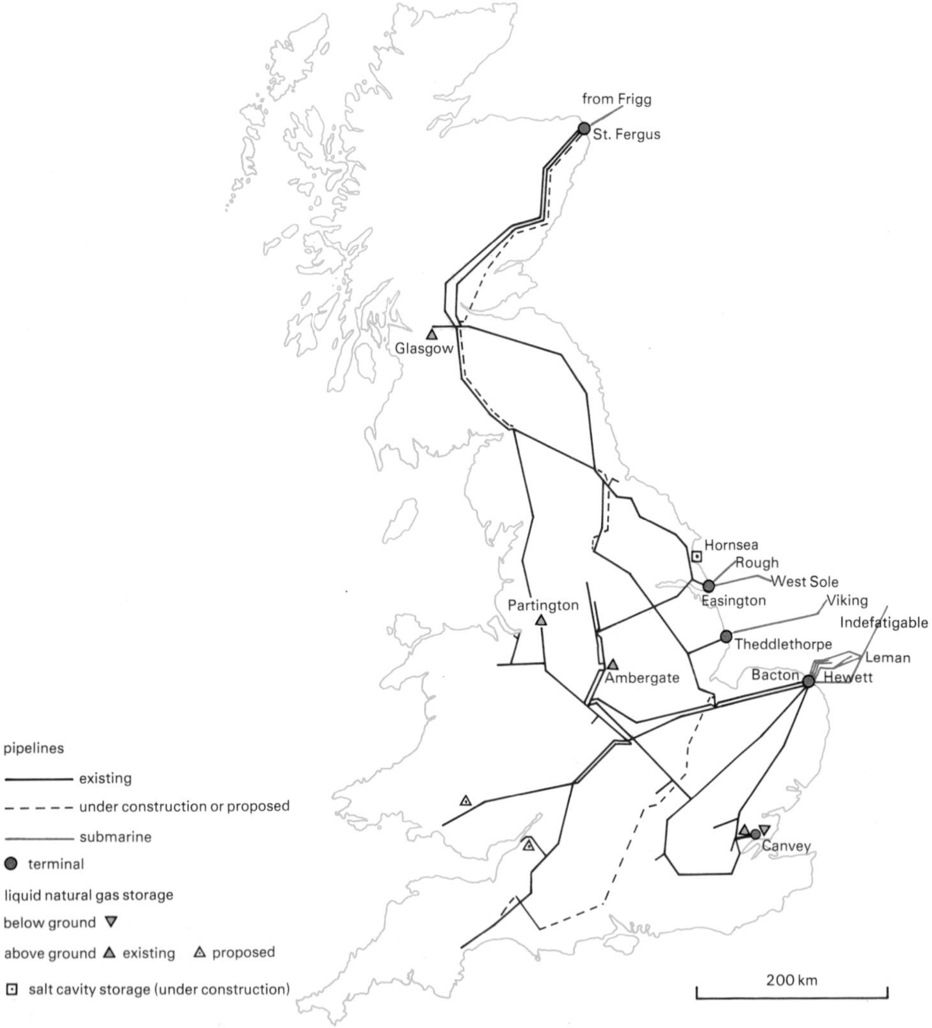

from Frigg
St. Fergus
Glasgow
Hornsea
Rough
West Sole
Easington
Viking
Indefatigable
Partington
Theddlethorpe
Leman
Ambergate
Bacton
Hewett
Canvey
200 km

pipelines
existing
under construction or proposed
submarine
terminal
liquid natural gas storage
below ground
above ground existing proposed
salt cavity storage (under construction)

Fig. 135

Oil

Fig. 135 portrays an impressive human contribution to the landscape of the northern shore of the Thames Estuary. Many slim steel towers are linked to a multitude of storage tanks by an angular web of pipework. This is the Shell refinery at Shell Haven, Essex. It covers an area of 400 hectares and has the capacity to process 10 million tonnes of crude oil a year.

Fig. 136

Crude oil is a mixture of hundreds of different hydrocarbons. These substances consist mainly of the elements hydrogen and carbon in varied and often complex combinations. Oil is seldom of use in its natural state, but when the hydrocarbons of similar molecular structure are sorted into groups or *fractions*, oil yields a wide range of valuable products. This is the task of the oil refinery.

One small corner of Shell Haven is pictured in Fig. 136. This is the Crude Distillation Unit, which is the start of the refinery process. Its operation is shown diagrammatically in Fig. 137. Crude oil, heated to a temperature of 340°C, is pumped into the fractionating column. Heavy hydrocarbons remain liquid and sink to the bottom, but the lighter ones turn to gas and slowly rise to progressively cooler parts of the column. In sequence, fractions return to the liquid state and are trapped on special trays. The lightest, simplest hydrocarbons remain as a gas which collects at the top of the column. Fig. 137 names the main fractions and indicates their principal uses. The importance of oil products in modern transport may be emphasised.

The fractions produced by primary distillation are pumped to other parts of the refinery for further processing. Impurities are removed and quality improved. Some fractions are converted into others for which demand is greater. In addition, subtle techniques lead to the extraction of a wide range of *petrochemicals*. These are supplied as *feedstocks* to chemical plants where they are built up into a range of familiar products which include plastics, detergents and synthetic rubber.

Fig. 137

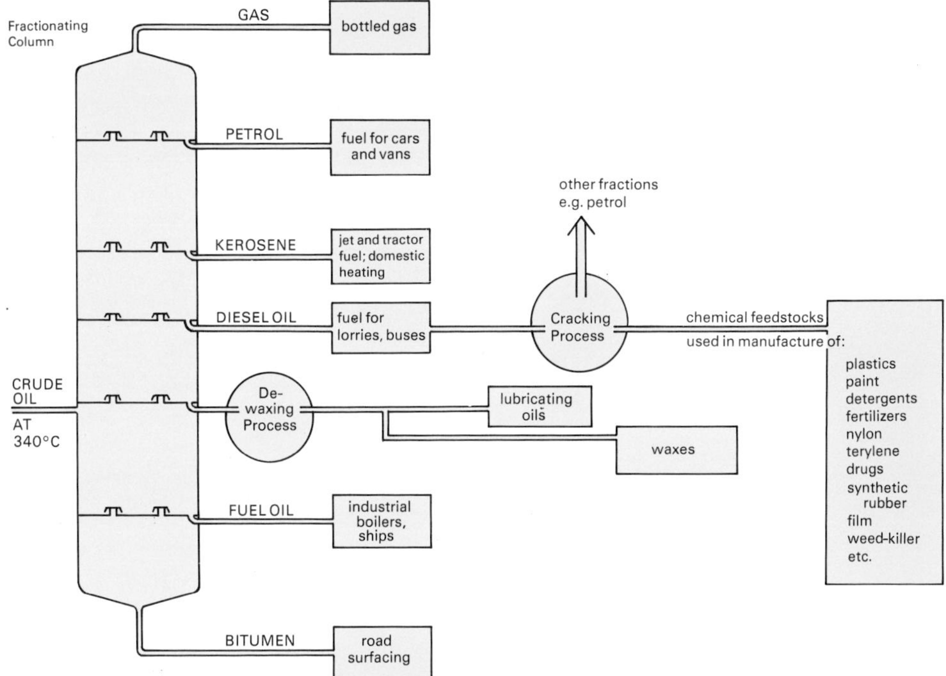

The Shell Haven refinery represents an investment of many millions of pounds, and its site was chosen with great care. A large area of level land was available at reasonable cost. Jetties built into deep water allow large tankers to discharge their cargo directly into the refinery. Shell Haven is well placed to serve the large markets of south-east and midland England. Similar factors have influenced the siting of other refineries in the British Isles. The coastal distribution plotted in Fig. 138 is hardly surprising in view of the overseas, or North Sea, origin of crude oil supplies.

The larger the tanker, the lower the transport costs per tonne of oil. The refining industry has taken steps to avail itself of the economies afforded by the use of larger vessels and in recent years there has been a great increase in the size of tankers coming into service. Channels, such as the one giving access to Fawley, are dredged to give the greater depth of water needed by larger tankers. The Grangemouth refinery is fed by a 93-kilometre pipeline from a deep-water terminal at Finnart on Loch Long. The Shell refinery at Stanlow has been forced to make a series of adaptations. It was originally served by tankers small enough to enter the Manchester Ship Canal. Later, a special dock, able to accommodate tankers of 30 000 tonnes d.w.t., was constructed at the canal entrance. Later still, Stanlow received its crude oil from a terminal at Tranmere, near the mouth of the Mersey, where water is deep enough for vessels of 60 000 tonnes d.w.t. Today 250 000-tonne tankers moor at a huge buoy off Amlwch on the Anglesey coast and oil is pumped to Stanlow through a 125-kilometre pipeline.

Fig. 138

Adequate depth of water is of prime importance in the siting of new refineries. Milford Haven (Figs. 139 and 140) is deep and wide enough to accommodate tankers of over 200 000 tonnes d.w.t. It supports four large refineries, all established since 1960, and also forwards oil by pipeline to Llandarcy. The significance of tanker size is well illustrated by the development of a major terminal at Bantry Bay, Republic of Ireland, where water is deep enough for tankers of 326 000 tonnes d.w.t. The Gulf Oil Company operates a fleet of six of these mammoth vessels which shuttle in with crude oil from the Persian Gulf. Storage facilities can hold a million tonnes, and the oil is redistributed in smaller tankers to the Gulf refinery at Milford Haven, and to others on the mainland of Europe.

The market for oil products is varied and widespread. It ranges from the vast quantities burnt in power-stations to the humble can of paraffin carried home for a domestic heater, and petrol is required by motorists everywhere. To service such a market demands a highly complex and efficient distribution system. To achieve this, several forms of transport are closely integrated. Refineries serve as distribution centres for their local areas, and deliveries are made by road. Elsewhere, strategically sited storage depots are supplied by rail, by small coastal tankers, or, to a limited extent, by barges on inland waterways. Cost is the deciding factor. The link from depot to factory, farm, school, office and service station is forged by road vehicles. Increasingly, oil-product pipelines are joining the distribution system, and Fig. 138 includes some important examples. Pipelines are commonly used to take fuel oil to power-stations, and feedstocks to chemical plants.

In the years following the end of the Second World War, the refinery industry experienced the tremendous expansion that is recorded statistically in Fig. 141. Oil profited greatly from the rise of road and air transport. In industrial and domestic markets it gained at the expense of coal, over which it enjoyed considerable advantages: oil

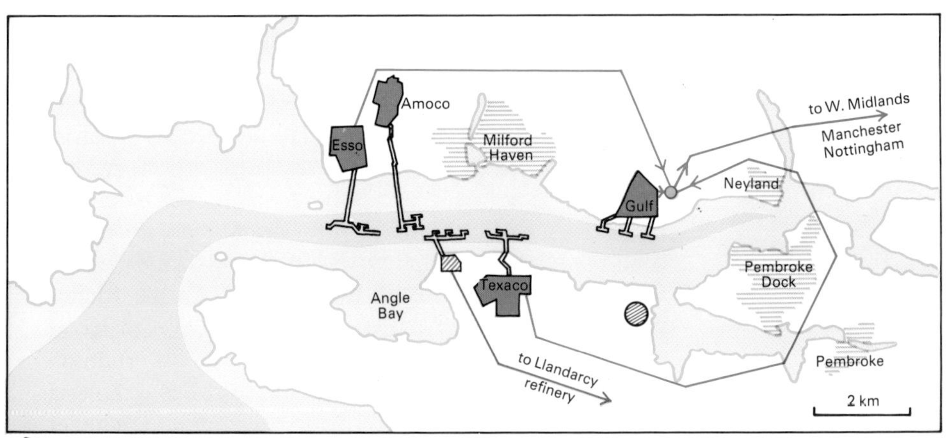

oil refineries
other shore installations
products pipeline
crude pipeline
pipeline station
oil-burning power-station
deep-water channel

Fig. 139

was considerably cheaper than alternative fuels, easily handled and cheaply transported; its heating value is 1.7 times that of an equivalent weight of coal, and the heat it provides can be more accurately controlled.

The rapid rise in the use of oil was checked in 1972. In that year, the Organisation of Petroleum Exporting

Fig. 140

thousand tonnes

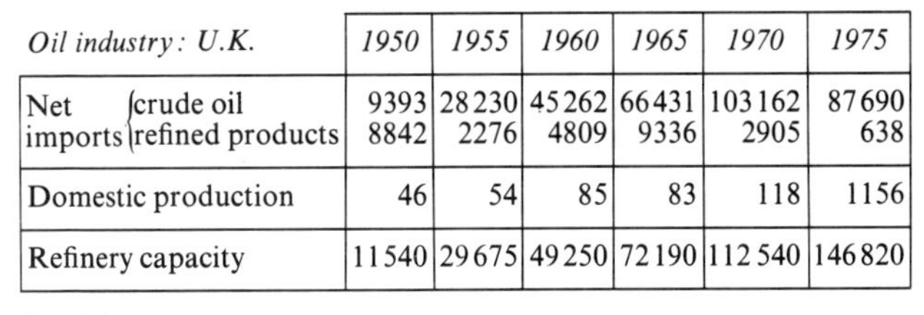

Oil industry: U.K.		*1950*	*1955*	*1960*	*1965*	*1970*	*1975*
Net imports	crude oil	9393	28 230	45 262	66 431	103 162	87 690
	refined products	8842	2276	4809	9336	2905	638
Domestic production		46	54	85	83	118	1156
Refinery capacity		11 540	29 675	49 250	72 190	112 540	146 820

Fig. 141

Countries (OPEC) greatly increased the price of crude oil. At a stroke, oil was no longer cheap. Economies were made but Britain had to pay vastly increased amounts of foreign currency for her supplies of essential oil, and great economic difficulties ensued. The first North Sea oil trickled ashore in 1975. It is anticipated that by the early 1980s Britain will be self-sufficient in oil, and may have a surplus for export. For reasons suggested in Chapter 2, North Sea oil is not cheap. No great reduction in the cost of oil products can be expected. But domestic production, by eliminating the need for imports, will greatly strengthen Britain's position as a major trading nation.

Electricity

In 1831, Michael Faraday demonstrated that mechanical energy could be converted into electrical energy. Forty years were to elapse before the generation of this new power became a commercial possibility, and the first power-stations for public supply were not established until the 1880s. Following this slow and hesitant start, electricity has made tremendous progress. Fig. 142 graphs the production in England and Wales since 1920. The steeply rising curve reflects the industrial expansion and higher living standards of recent decades. Electricity is now indispensable in home, factory, school, farm; indeed, in all aspects of life. Readily available at the touch of a switch, its tremendous value is often only fully appreciated when, for some reason, we are deprived of its services.

Electricity—production in England and Wales

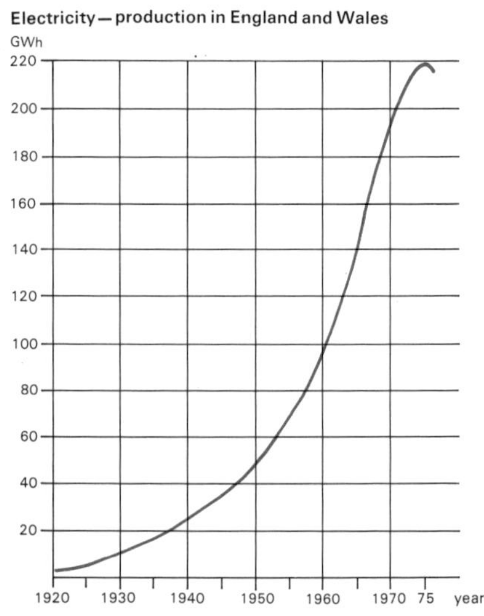

Fig. 142

Fig. 143 Electricity—generation in Great Britain

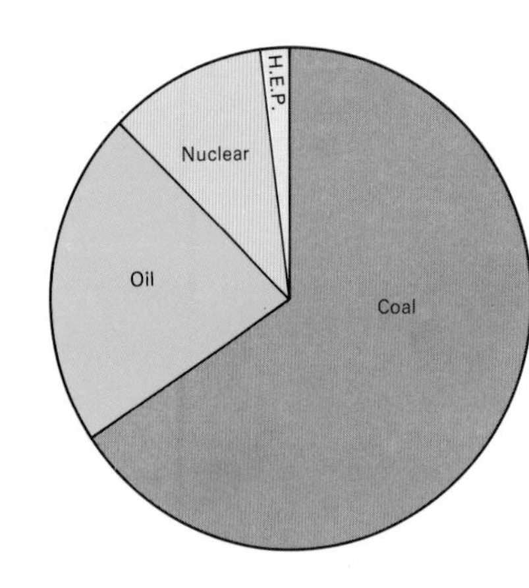

Faraday's discovery is embodied in the modern turbo-generator. As the shaft of the turbine rotates, a powerful electromagnet turns within heavy coils of copper and the current flows. Rotation is all important and may be achieved in a variety of ways, but most commonly the motive force is steam at high pressure. In the *thermal* power-station, fossil fuels are burnt to provide the heat needed to convert water to steam. In the *nuclear* power-station, the heat liberated by nuclear fission is utilised to raise steam. Falling water accurately directed at the blades of the turbine is the basis of *hydro-electricity*.

Fig. 144

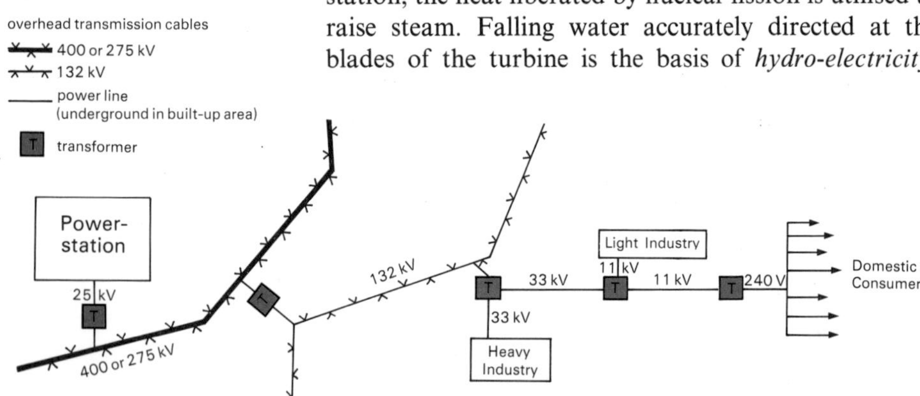

Great Britain makes use of these methods in the proportions indicated in Fig. 143.

In England and Wales the electricity supply industry has nearly 19 million customers. To make electricity so widely available, an extensive and intricate distribution network is essential. Power-station output is transformed to 400 kV or 275 kV and fed into the *national grid*. This is an interconnected system of high-tension cables slung from the tall transmission towers which are so often a prominent feature of the landscape. Current is progressively stepped down by transformers to the voltages required by individual consumers. Fig. 144 provides simple illustration.

The grid system is useful in other ways. Formerly, because of losses of energy in transmission, power-stations had to be built near the consuming centres. Now, with efficient high voltage lines, they can be sited where production costs are low. The grid evens out regional contrasts in capacity and demand; power produced in Yorkshire, for instance, may light lamps in London and Lancashire. Equipment failures in individual power-stations need not lead to an interruption of local supplies, for demand can be met from other areas. The grid also makes possible the most efficient use of generating equipment. Electricity cannot be effectively stored; production must be finely tuned to a demand which varies from minute to minute. Thanks to the grid, efficient modern power-stations, wherever located, can be run continuously to meet the basic needs of the nation. Less efficient stations need only be used during periods of peak demand. Submarine cables laid under the English Channel link the grid systems of Britain and France to the benefit of both countries.

Thermal power-stations

The north bank of the Mersey between Widnes and Warrington is dominated by Fiddler's Ferry power-station, mapped in Fig. 145 and pictured in Fig. 146.

Fig. 145

Fig. 146

Occupying a site area of over 400 hectares, it cost £100 million, and took six years to build. The eight massive cooling towers are each 114.3 metres high and have a base diameter of 87 metres. The turbine hall which houses four 500 000 kW turbine generators is nearly 300 metres long. Fiddler's Ferry is typical of the new generation of thermal power-stations. The decision to build such large-scale undertakings is not taken lightly. Several basic requirements must be met if electricity is to be produced at economic cost.

The thermal power-station has a healthy appetite for fuel and must be located within range of cheap and abundant supplies. Vast quantities of water are essential for cooling purposes. This may be taken from sea, river or canal, and a through-flow of as much as 60 cubic metres per second may be necessary. In addition, water of a high degree of purity is needed for steam raising. In view of this thirst, it is understandable that water is recycled through expensive cooling towers. Site requirements impose other limitations. A large area of cheap land is needed free from the risk of flooding and offering firm foundations for the great weights of construction. In the case of coal-fired stations, there must be facilities for the disposal of fuel ash.

Fiddler's Ferry is coal-fired. Annual consumption exceeds 4.5 million tonnes. Suitable coal in such large quantities is not available from the nearby but declining Lancashire coalfield, and supplies are brought in from Yorkshire and the East Midlands. Transport costs are kept to a minimum by the 'merry-go-round' rail system (page 72). Powerful conveyor systems move the coal from hopper to stockpile, or directly into the power-station where it is ground to a powder before being blown into the boilers. The coal burns, heat is liberated, but ash remains. Each day demands the disposal of 5000 tonnes of ash. Some is sold, but the greater part is being used to reclaim neighbouring marshland for eventual agricultural use. The pure water needed for steam is supplied by the regional water authority. The tidal

River Mersey is the source of cooling water. Each day 182 million litres are pumped up to large storage lagoons which ensure that water is available whatever the state of the tide.

The generating capacity of Fiddler's Ferry – 2000 MW – is enough to meet the needs of six towns the size of Liverpool. That this great capacity may be achieved around the clock with a workforce of 500 is an indication of the highly automated techniques employed in the modern power-station.

Fig. 147

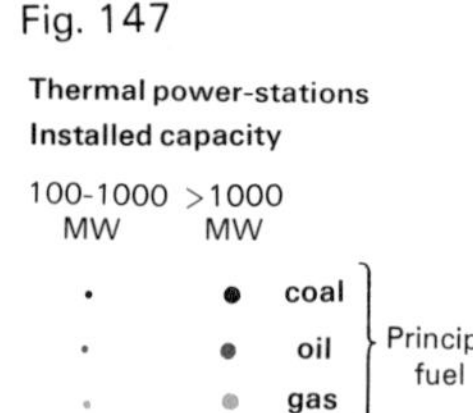

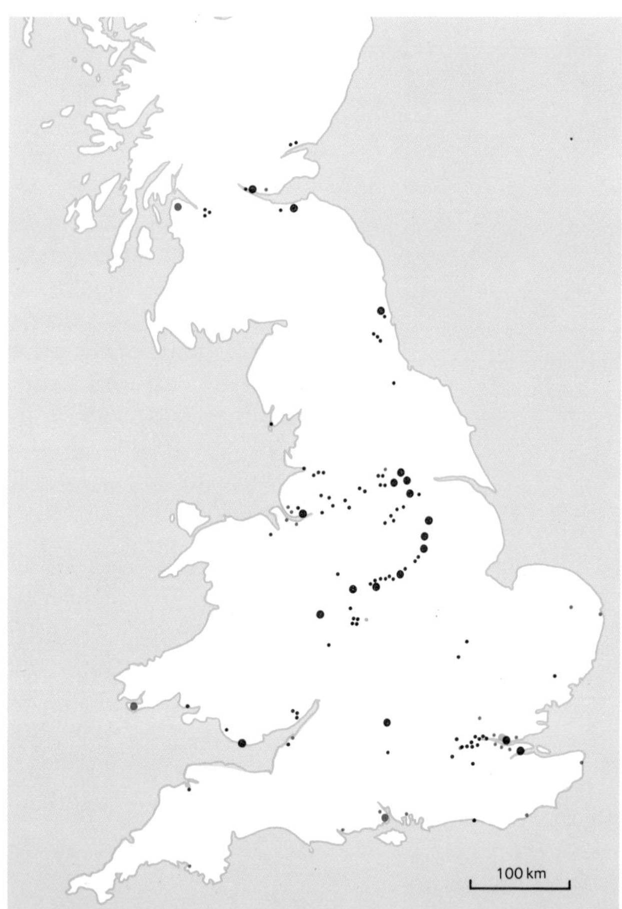

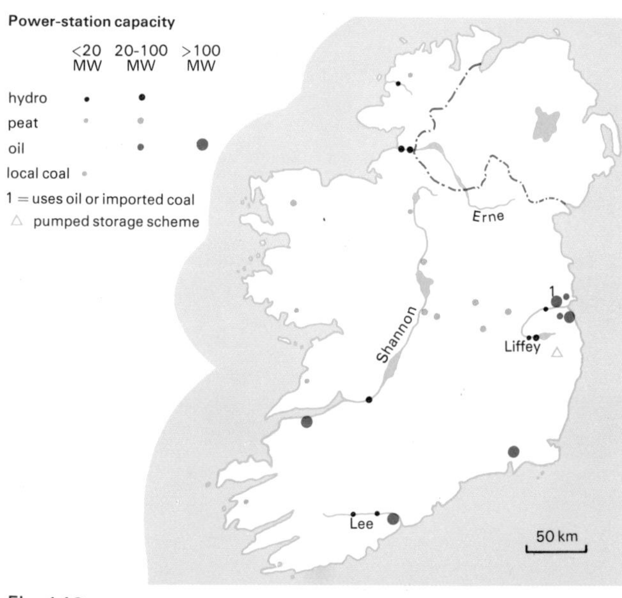

Fig. 148

Fiddler's Ferry is but one of over 100 thermal power-stations which together supply the greater part of Britain's electricity. Fig. 147 locates those with a capacity of more than 100 MW, and indicates the fuel burnt. The uneven distribution reveals the influence of major locational factors. Coalfields have an obvious attraction; there is a great demand for electricity and fuel is normally available. There are concentrations of stations on the flanks of the Pennines, in the midland counties and in the central lowlands of Scotland. The valley of the lower Trent is particularly noteworthy. Dry, level sites on the banks of the river support a series of large stations which are cheaply fuelled by modern collieries on nearby coalfields. The flow of the Trent contributes vital cooling water, much conserved by cooling towers. Away from the coalfields, many coal-fired stations enjoy a coastal location. Seas and estuaries provide cooling water and the chosen fuel is cheaply delivered by ship. Coastal sites are also favoured by oil-burning stations. Oil is a handy fuel; it is easily moved

Fig. 149

by pipeline and presents no problem of ash disposal. Until 1972, it could be imported at a highly competitive price, and its use increased rapidly. Several large power-stations have been established close to major oil-refining centres. Fawley and Milford Haven may be quoted as examples. Oil shares with coal the fuel burden of the clutch of power-stations which line the lower Thames. The advent of North Sea gas has provided the electricity supply industry with an alternative fuel. First used in 1967, the gas consumed in electricity generation is the equivalent of over 2.5 million tonnes of coal.

Fig. 148 gives the overall picture of power production in the Republic of Ireland. Imported oil is of vital importance, but one-third of electricity output is derived from peat. This is an inferior fuel; calorific value is less than half that of an equivalent weight of coal, but it can be cheaply prepared by machine. Peat-burning stations are of small capacity. The example viewed in Fig. 149 is at Bellacorick, County Mayo. It rises from the dreary boglands that are its source of fuel.

Nuclear power

Calder Hall, on the coast of Cumbria, claims the distinction of being the world's first nuclear power-station to operate on a commercial scale. It made its initial contribution to the national grid in 1956. Two years later a similar undertaking was commissioned at Chapelcross in Scotland. Success led to the adoption of Britain's first nuclear power programme. This was completed by 1970 and consisted of nine stations. The fuel is natural uranium canned in tubes of magnesium alloy *('Magnox')*. One tonne of uranium can be used to produce as much electricity as 10 000 tonnes of coal. The five stations of the second nuclear power programme (1972–9) incorporate the advanced gas-cooled reactor *(AGR)* fuelled by enriched uranium oxide canned in stainless steel. Prototypes of new and more efficient types of nuclear power-stations are operational at Winfrith and Dounreay.

The brief history of nuclear power has been marked by rapid technical progress. The AGR stations have a generating capacity of nearly five times that of Berkeley, the first of the magnox variety, and produce electricity at much lower costs. With the recent steep rise in the cost of fossil fuels, the modern nuclear power-station is a highly competitive producer of large amounts of electricity.

Nuclear power-stations use fuel in such small quantities that it is not a factor influencing location. They do, however, share with their thermal counterparts the need for cheap, level sites which offer firm foundations and access to vast quantities of water for cooling purposes. Coastal sites have an added advantage in that the sea will safely receive low-active liquid waste. Early public concern about the safety of nuclear power encouraged location in remote areas. Today, with confidence supported by an impressive safety record, they may be built near large centres of population. Heysham and Hartlepool are examples.

Fig. 150

Fig. 151

Fig. 150 maps the distribution of nuclear power-stations. It will be noted that all but one are close to the coast. Fig. 151 shows the exception, Trawsfynydd, sitting on the shore of an enlarged reservoir which was originally developed to serve a small hydro-electric scheme.

Hydro-electric power

The Shannon, the largest river in the British Isles, flows sluggishly south over the low, level plains of central Ireland. Its slow flow is regulated by passage through the large loughs of Allen, Ree and Derg. Below Killaloe, however, gradients are steeper and the Shannon rushes to meet the sea near Limerick. On the last lap of its journey, the bulk of the flow is diverted from its natural course and led by canal to the hydro-electric power-station at Ardnacrusha. Here, a fall of nearly 30 metres has been harnessed to create a generating capacity of 85 MW. Electricity thus produced is relatively cheap. Water flows freely. The station must be manned, and its equipment maintained, but it does not bear the heavy burden of fuel costs.

In its use of a large lowland river, the Shannon scheme is exceptional. It is the elevated parts of the British Isles which offer the greatest potential for the generation of hydro-electric power. Heavy rainfall and impermeable rocks give abundant surface flow, and high, steep heads of water are easier to find in areas of pronounced relief. Many lakes provide natural water storage, and deep glaciated valleys offer additional storage potential. Good dam sites are rare, however. Lengthy dams are often needed to close the wide valleys, and construction may be complicated by the fact that the solid rock is often thickly plastered with glacial drift. A more serious disadvantage is that upland drainage basins are of limited extent, and rivers are small in volume.

Fig. 152 shows the distribution of hydro-electric power-stations, and emphasises the significance of highland areas. The importance of Scotland will be readily appreciated. Since its establishment in 1943, the North of

Fig. 152

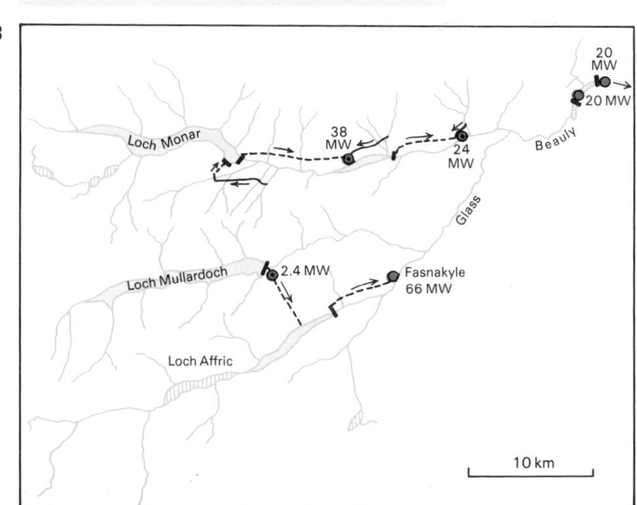

Fig. 153

Scotland Hydro-Electric Board has made great progress in power development. Over 90 per cent of the potential within the Board's area has been harnessed. Electricity is supplied to over 98 per cent of potential customers in the thinly peopled highlands, and total installed capacity of the hydro stations exceeds 1500 MW. It must be borne in mind, however, that this is appreciably less than the capacity of one thermal station of the stature of Fiddler's Ferry.

The River Beauly flows into the Moray Firth to the west of Inverness. Fig. 153 illustrates how its headwaters are harnessed. Six power-stations have a combined capacity of 170.4 MW. The largest, that at Fasnakyle, is pictured in Fig. 154. Aqueducts and tunnels capture minor streams and so increase the volume of water passing through the turbines.

Hydro-electricity is the basis of new pumped-storage

Fig. 154

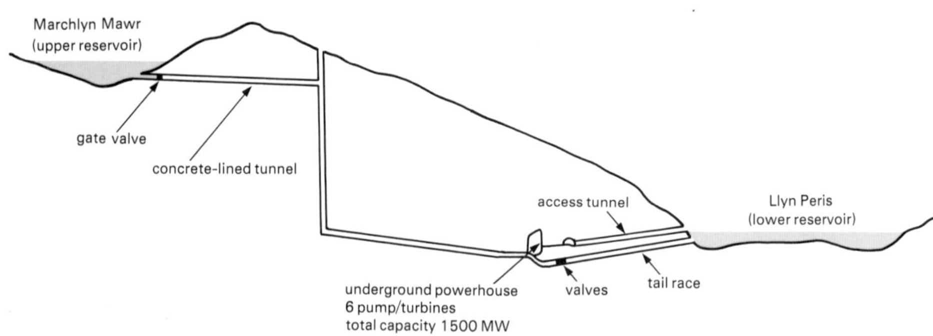

Fig. 155

schemes. These schemes require two reservoirs at different levels. During times of peak demand, falling water activates turbines in the normal way, and power is fed into the grid. At night, low-cost electricity is taken from the grid to pump water up to the higher reservoir. Thus potential energy is stored for future use.

Fig. 155 illustrates the Dinorwic pumped-storage scheme which is scheduled for completion in 1979. Marchlyn Mawr lies more than 500 metres above Llyn Peris, and both lakes have been enlarged by dams. They are connected by concrete-lined tunnels 10 metres in diameter. Water rushing down these tunnels will activate six pump/turbines with a combined capacity of 1500 MW. At night the same machinery, working in reverse, will return 6.5 million litres of water to Marchlyn Mawr. Note from Fig. 155 that the installations are housed deep under the hillside in a huge man-made cavern.

Freight traffic: Great Britain — *thousand million tonne-kilometres*

	1962	*1965*	*1970*	*1974*
Road	54.9	68.8	85.0	90.0
Rail	26.3	25.2	26.8	24.2
Coastal shipping	23.4	25.0	23.2	20.7
Inland waterways	0.3	0.2	0.1	0.1
Pipelines	0.6	1.3	2.9	3.4

Fig. 156

Passenger transport: Great Britain
thousand million passenger-kilometres

		1955	*1960*	*1965*	*1970*	*1974*
Air		0.3	0.8	1.6	1.9	2.3
Rail		38	40	35	36	36
Road:	Public services	80	71	63	56	54
	Private transport	87	144	233	306	350

Fig. 157

Factories must have their raw materials. Finished products have long and complex journeys before they reach the customer. Electricity is delivered at the touch of a switch. Farmers need access to market. Milk flows from cow to tanker to float to doorstep. Letters and parcels are posted daily. Words speed along wires or through the air. People, too, are constantly on the move; they journey to factory, office, school or about the world on business. Holidays are spent away from home.

Advanced nations depend on rapid and abundant movement. This vital need is met in a variety of ways: ships plough their way across seas and oceans; other vessels keep to coastal or inland waters; aircraft hum through the air above landscapes which are patterned by road, rail and cable; and many kilometres of wires and pipes are hidden from view beneath our feet.

The British Isles are the meeting-point of many important international trade routes; sea lanes focus on the shallow seas around our shores and Heathrow (London) is one of the world's busiest international airports. Domestic needs are met by transport systems of great complexity. Not all parts of the British Isles are equally well served. Communications develop in response to the demand for the services they offer; areas with many people and busy industry – lowland England, for instance – are greatly favoured. Remote and poorly developed regions are ill-equipped in terms of transport; central Wales and northern Scotland are notable in this respect.

The present pattern of communications is the result of centuries of development; a modern road may follow the line paced by Roman soldiers and the country lanes which wander from village to village may first have been trod by Saxon farmers. The story of transport tells of the many changes prompted by inventions which offer the customer a cheaper, quicker or more convenient service. Different modes of transport are in constant competition; the old decline and the new expand. Thus the canal gave way to the railway which has since been effectively challenged by modern road transport. For cross-channel services, the aircraft is now more popular than the ferry, but both face competition from the hybrid hovercraft.

Some recent changes are indicated in Fig. 156. The volume of freight traffic expands steadily in response to industrial growth. The railways are in decline, and so, too, is coastal shipping. The contribution now made by

Fig. 158

Fig. 159

inland waterways is insignificant. Pipelines are more popular. The dominant feature of Fig. 156 is the development of road transport. This is also seen in Fig. 157 which is concerned with the movement of people. The private motor car is responsible for the present high level of personal mobility. Buses and trains compete for a diminishing share of the traffic. Aircraft, although of great importance for overseas journeys, have made little impact on travel within Britain.

Fig. 160

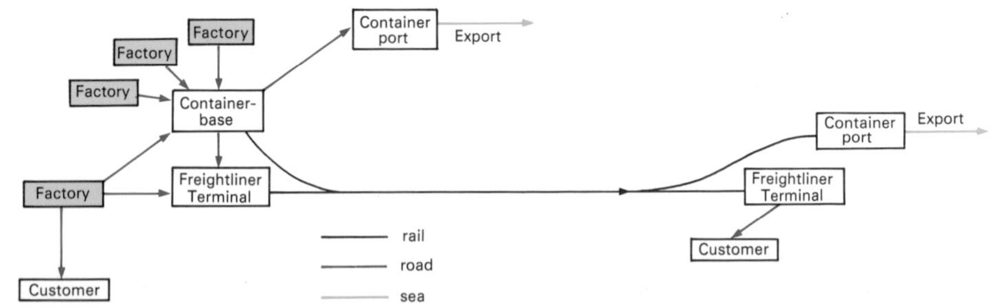

Other major changes have taken place in recent decades. Goods are moved in larger units: the oil tanker (page 77) is one example and the juggernaut lorry another. Average speeds are generally higher. This is true, for instance, of movement between cities by both road and rail.

One important development is seen in Fig. 158. A *container* made of tough but lightweight aluminium alloy rests on a trailer. Its doors are open and it is being loaded with manufactured goods. With doors shut and sealed, the contents are safe and secure. The great advantage of containers is that, being of standard sizes, they can be neatly carried by all modes of transport and speedily transferred from one to another. In Fig. 159, a container is lifted from road to rail; the operation takes sixty-five seconds. Speed of handling makes for great savings in cost. Containers permit greater integration of the means of transport, each of which may be used to its best advantage; the speed of long-distance rail transport can be married to the flexibility of road vehicles for collection and delivery. Containers may be stacked like bricks in the holds and on the decks of special ships.

Fig. 160 illustrates in a simplified way the workings of the container system. Containers packed at the factory may, of course, be trucked directly to the customer, but for journeys of over 150 kilometres, it is usually cheaper and quicker to make use of rail services. Containers are received at special terminals which offer the necessary facilities. There they are quickly lifted on to flat waggons, permanently coupled into trains, for rapid transport to a distant terminal where road transport waits to complete delivery. Goods for export go straight to a port with appropriate facilities. *Containerbases* assemble small consignments from different factories into full loads for onward despatch by various means. They are subject to customs control and do much of the work traditionally associated with the dockside.

Within the limits imposed by standard dimensions, containers are made to meet the special requirements of

Fig. 161

goods such as liquids, gases or perishable items. Fig. 161 provides illustration. The *Remuera* sets sail from Liverpool's Gladstone Dock. Part of its cargo, kept safe in refrigerated containers, is a consignment of frozen fish fingers on its way to Australia.

Railways

For over a century, the railway dominated transport within the British Isles. After Liverpool and Manchester had been profitably linked in 1830, an intricate network was rapidly created. Soon, few settlements of any importance were out of range of their nearest station. Rail transport, quicker and more widely available than canals, nourished the great industrial expansion of the nineteenth century, and gave people increased mobility for business and pleasure. The expansion of the rail system was achieved in a haphazard fashion; lines were created by a multitude of small private companies eager for profit and routes between urban centres were often duplicated in the competitive scramble for traffic. For journeys between Liverpool and Manchester, for instance, passengers came to have the choice of no less than five different routes.

Since 1930, when route length amounted to nearly 33000 kilometres, the railway system has suffered a steady decline. Road transport has been the chief culprit, but there have been other contributory factors; aircraft compete for long-distance passenger traffic, and with the growing use of electricity there is much less coal to carry about the country. The movement of iron-ore is also much reduced.

Railways are fighting back. Great changes have been brought about, especially since the early 1960s. Unprofitable lines have been closed in great numbers and others are retained only with the help of financial aid from the government. The network has shrunk dramatically (Fig. 162). Large amounts of capital have been invested in schemes of modernisation. The busiest routes are electrified. Elsewhere, motive power is the diesel locomotive. Track is rebuilt, rolling-stock redesigned and new signalling methods are installed.

The new streamlined system which is developing concentrates on the tasks for which the railway is best suited. In the case of passenger transport, these are the linking of major city centres and commuter traffic.

The Inter-City services of British Rail offer comfortable journeys at high speed. The train now leaving London's Euston Station (Fig. 163) will arrive in Glasgow in 5

Fig. 162

British Railways	*1964*	*1970*	*1974*
Route open for traffic *(km)*	25735	18988	18168
Stations	5129	2868	2790
Locomotives	15063	9537	8665
Passenger journeys *(millions)*	923	824	733

Fig. 163

Fig. 164

hours 10 minutes' time. Its average speed will be 125 km/h. Fig. 164 gives us a glimpse of the shape of things to come. It shows the prototype Advanced Passenger Train (APT). This train of revolutionary design will run on existing track at speeds as high as 240 km/h. Its introduction on the London–Glasgow run in late 1977 brings the journey time down to less than 4 hours.

Commuter traffic is of particular importance in south-east England. Roads are congested and journeys are slow. Rail is often preferred for the daily journey to work. Fast electric services radiate from the capital. During the morning rush hour, frequent trains are packed with London-bound commuters. Early evening sees the flow reversed. Each day between 07.00 h and 10.00 h over a million people enter central London. Fig. 165 records the contribution made by the railways.

Fig. 165

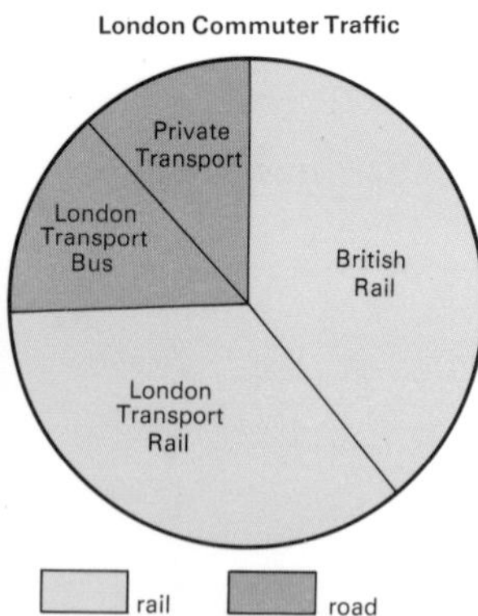

Fig. 166 shows the present rail network, and emphasises the Inter-City routes. Note the pronounced focus on London. Direct cross-country routes are rare. Note, too, the variations in the density of the network. In Lancashire, Yorkshire, the midlands and the south-east, it is still relatively dense but other areas are now poorly served by railways.

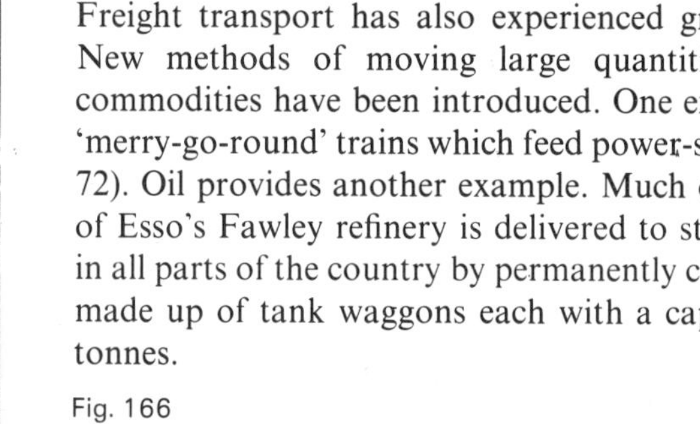

Freight transport has also experienced great changes. New methods of moving large quantities of bulky commodities have been introduced. One example is the 'merry-go-round' trains which feed power-stations (page 72). Oil provides another example. Much of the output of Esso's Fawley refinery is delivered to storage depots in all parts of the country by permanently coupled trains made up of tank waggons each with a capacity of 100 tonnes.

Fig. 166

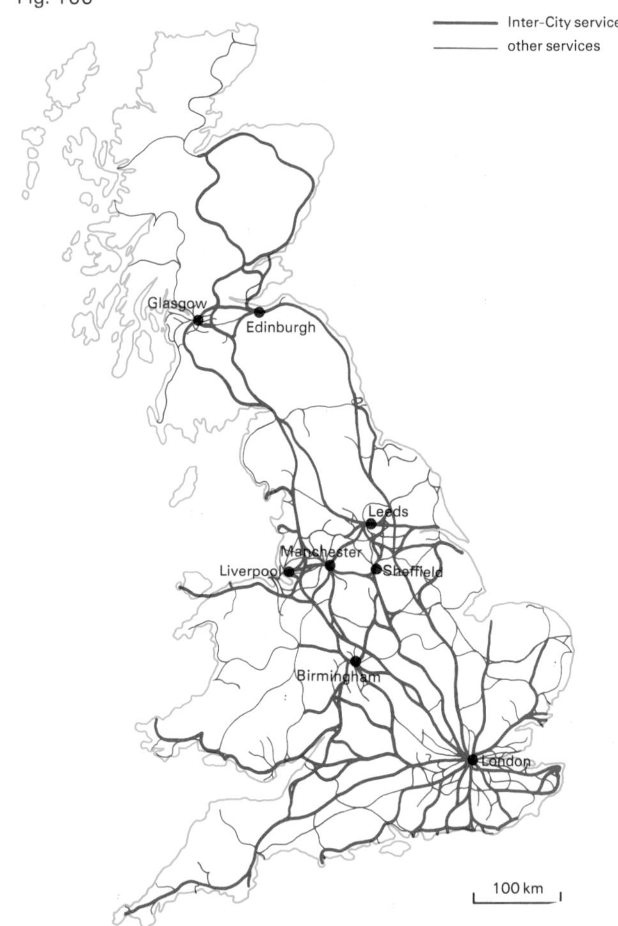

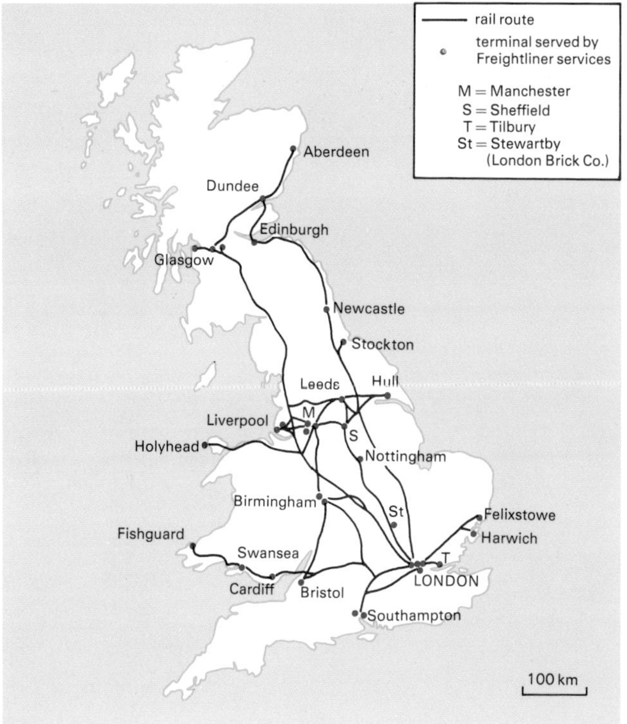

Fig. 167

For the movement of more general merchandise, British Rail have shared in the container revolution with their aptly named Freightliner services. Fig. 167 plots the terminals designed solely to handle containers. Between them, trains run to a regular timetable at average speeds as high as 120 km/h. The Freightliner service started in 1965 and since then much goods traffic has been snatched from the backs of lorries. British Rail now operate about 200 daily Freightliner services and handle 750 000 containers annually. Speed and reliability are great attractions to manufacturers. It makes it possible, for instance, for cakes baked one afternoon in Leith (Scotland) to be on sale in London early the following morning.

Roads

A car gives its driver the choice of time and route. The lorry offers a door-to-door service. The bus can stop at any convenient point on the kerbside. Flexibility and convenience are the great advantages of modern road vehicles, which have multiplied to the extent indicated in Fig. 168.

Britain's road network, developed in the leisurely age of the horse, was ill equipped to meet the onslaught of the internal combustion engine. Major routes focused on London as they did in the time of the Romans. In the intervening centuries they had gained little in width, and had lost much of their former directness. In rural districts, roads wandered from village to village. It was with poetic justification that G. K. Chesterton wrote, 'the rolling English drunkard made the rolling English road'. As with other forms of transport, the network reflected man's need of movement. It achieved a high density in prosperous lowlands but was thin and patchy in remote upland areas. Nevertheless, every settlement could be reached by road.

Adaptation of the network to the requirements of the modern vehicle has been hesitant and piecemeal; a new road here, a bypass there and a new bridge somewhere else. Dangerous bends have been smoothed and carriageways widened. Small local developments have added up to considerable overall improvement. In recent years, increased capital investment has accelerated the rate of progress.

Fig. 168

Licensed road vehicles *thousands*

	1950	*1955*	*1960*	*1965*	*1970*	*1974*
Private cars and vans	2307	3609	5650	9131	11 802	13 948
Public transport vehicles	140	105	95	98	105	109
Goods vehicles	916	1134	1433	1642	1659	1801

—— motorway
.... under construction

BE — Belfast
G — Glasgow
E — Edinburgh
N — Newcastle
C — Carlisle
LE — Leeds
H — Hull
M — Manchester
LV — Liverpool
SH — Sheffield
ST — Stoke-on-Trent
NO — Nottingham
LI — Leicester
B — Birmingham
CO — Coventry
SW — Swansea
CF — Cardiff
BR — Bristol
EX — Exeter
S — Southampton
LO — London

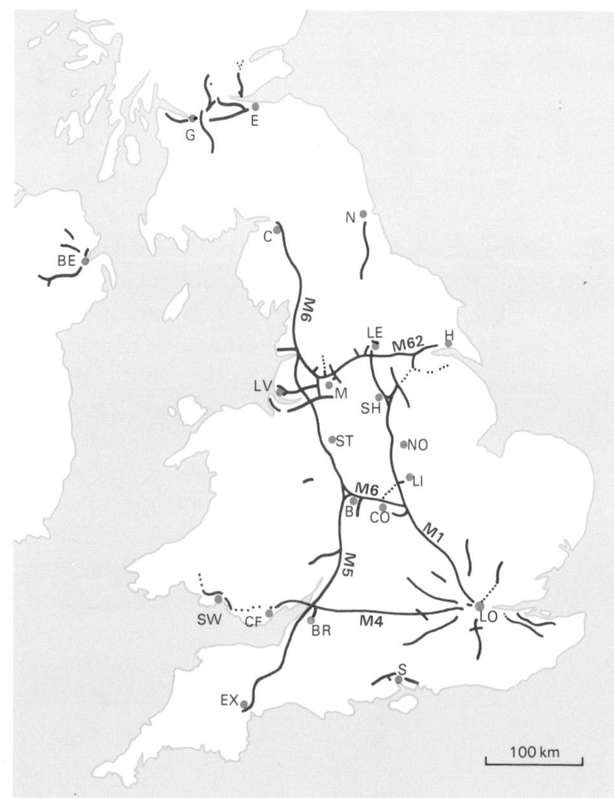

Fig. 169

the motorway. Two or three lanes in each direction permit uninterrupted high-speed progress. Service stations at appropriate intervals provide the traveller with food, fuel and other conveniences. Safety measures are given high priority. Carriageways are separated by tough steel barriers. Signs are clear and plentiful. Hard shoulders accommodate breakdowns which would otherwise cause dangerous obstructions. No stranded driver is further than 800 metres from an emergency telephone. Accidents, often serious, do occur, especially in fog, but the motorway has proved itself the safest type of road.

The motorway does not always shorten the distance between any two points, but it greatly reduces the time needed for the journey. This is appreciated by the private motorist, and to the commercial user it represents a great saving in cost. Proximity to the motorway

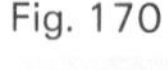

Fig. 170

Britain had to wait until 1958 for the first small stretch of roadway specifically created for the motor vehicle. The short Preston bypass, now incorporated in the M6, was the beginning of the motorway system mapped in Fig. 169. Now totalling more than 2000 kilometres, it is designed to link the major centres of industry and population which generate the heaviest traffic.

The motorway has many distinctive features. Access points are few in number, and minor forms of transport are excluded (Fig. 170). Cuttings, embankments and viaducts eliminate all but the most gentle gradients. Changes of direction are achieved by wide sweeping curves. Local traffic of all types is bridged over or under

Fig. 171

network is now a factor which often influences the location of industrial enterprises, and may also stimulate suburban development.

The benefits of the motorway have not been cheaply bought. Even in rural areas the cost is often £2 million per kilometre. The maze of interweaving carriageways seen in Fig. 171 is the Gravelly Hill interchange where M6 meets A38(M). It represents a capital investment of many hundreds of millions of pounds. There are further costs to be borne in mind. Motorways eat up large areas of land, often of high agricultural value, and have detrimental effects on the environment. The constant roar of vehicles speeding along a motorway is not appreciated by people living within earshot. The M62 cuts through an area of woodland once valued as a tranquil local beauty spot. The same motorway does nothing to improve the rural serenity of the lonely Pennine farmhouse pictured in Fig. 172.

Fig. 172

The speeds achieved on motorways are in great contrast to conditions within the towns they serve; it is here that the pressure of motor vehicles on available roads is greatest. Serious congestion is a feature of town centres, for movement is irritatingly slow as cars, lorries and buses compete for space on narrow streets. Exhaust fumes of idling engines pollute the atmosphere and room to park the car is hard to find.

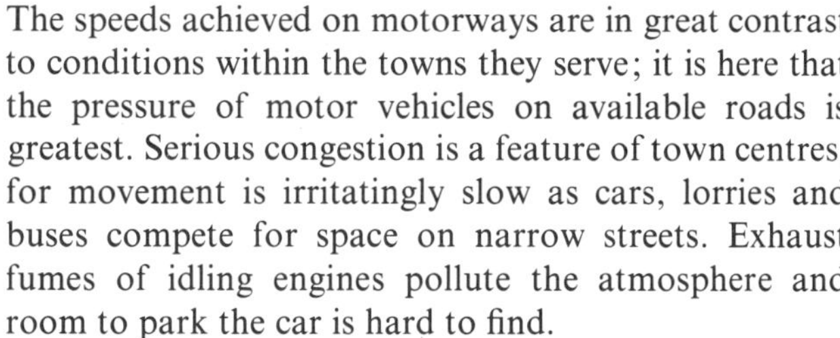

Many steps are taken to improve the flow of urban traffic. Elaborate systems of one-way streets have been evolved and special lanes may be reserved for public transport. Parking restrictions are doubly underlined in yellow and parking-meters have their watchful traffic wardens. Wide new roads carry traffic to and from the centre, which may be bypassed by 'roads in the sky', such as the one in Fig. 173. These new roads are appreciated by the motorist, but are costly to build, occupy much valuable land, and do nothing to improve the urban landscape.

The problem has been eased but not solved. Further improvements are sought. The local paper will inform you of traffic experiments being tried in your nearest large town. Perhaps the motor vehicle has no place in the middle of the modern city! Hope for the future possibly lies in a city centre ringed by parking space, but served exclusively by public transport. The pedestrian precincts, flanked by multi-storey car-parks, which have been established in many towns, point in this direction. Improvements in public transport, possible on uncluttered streets, would soften the blow for the motorist.

Fig. 173

Air

The aircraft wings its way at speeds that cannot be matched by surface transport. This is its great advantage and one for which passengers are prepared to pay a higher fare. For movement within Britain, however, there are limitations which restrict the full development of air transport. Britain is small in area, and urban centres are clustered close together. Glasgow, for instance, is only 550 kilometres from London, as the crow flies. Airports must of necessity, be located on the outskirts of towns, and the often lengthy time

Fig. 174

taken to reach the city centre, the destination of the majority of passengers, detracts considerably from the benefits of high-speed flight. In Britain, moreover, the aircraft must compete with efficient and well-organised surface transport. In particular, the fast Inter-City services of British Rail (page 87) are proving highly competitive.

For the movement of freight, the limitations of air transport are even more severe. Only those goods which are valuable in relation to weight can withstand the higher costs of air transport. Freight generally does not need to be moved with the same urgency as passengers, but exceptions include highly perishable commodities, and desperately needed spare parts.

In spite of its handicaps, air transport within the United Kingdom is of increasing importance. Growth is impressive, but it must be borne in mind that air transport only accounts for a tiny fraction of total passenger and freight movement.

The distribution of airports served by scheduled services is indicated in Fig. 174. The country is criss-crossed by domestic air routes. As in the pattern of road and rail communications, they show a pronounced focus on the national capital. The importance of a particular route reflects distance and the size of the urban areas served. The greater the distance, the more valuable is the speed of flight. The larger the urban area, the more traffic it is likely to generate. Thus, it is not surprising that London–Glasgow is Britain's busiest service. Between London and Belfast, air traffic is encouraged by the fact that for part of the journey, it competes with slow and often uncomfortable sea transport. For the same reason, aircraft forge convenient links between the mainland and detached areas such as the Isle of Man and the Channel Islands, especially in the busy summer holiday season. Remote island groups off the western and northern shores of Scotland are similarly served.

Fig. 175

Airports—relative importance

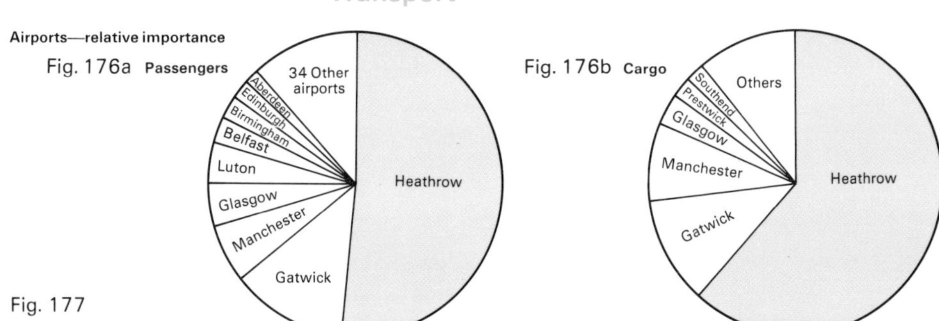

Fig. 176a **Passengers**

Fig. 176b **Cargo**

Fig. 177

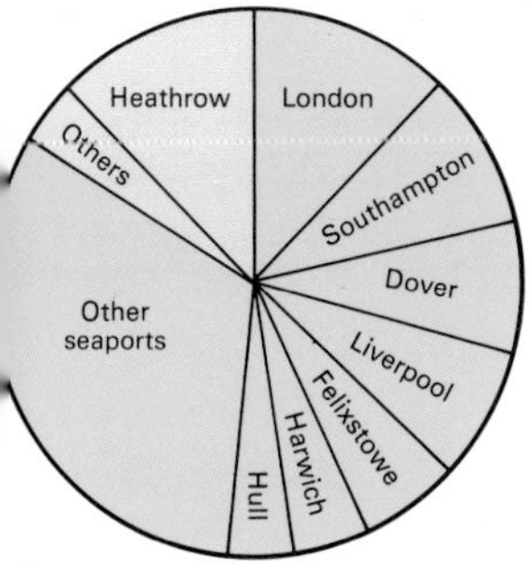

Heathrow
London
Others
Southampton
Dover
Other seaports
Liverpool
Felixstowe
Harwich
Hull

Ports: share of foreign trade by value

airports seaports

Operating from simple landing grounds – the one on Barra is pictured in Fig. 175 – aircraft bring scattered populations much nearer in time to vital mainland services such as hospitals.

It is over the much longer distances of international routes that the aircraft's speed advantage is most apparent. Australia is only a flying-day away from London, whereas a fast ship needs three weeks for the same journey. Air transport now dominates passenger movement to and from the United Kingdom; well over half the passenger journeys between Britain and her European neighbours are accomplished by air and for more distant continents, the figure is almost 100 per cent.

South-east England is the magnet for international as well as domestic air services. The dominant role of Heathrow will be readily appreciated from Fig. 176. Heathrow is used by all the world's major international airlines. On average, an aircraft takes off or lands every 2 minutes. In 1975, the airport handled 21.6 million passengers. Air freight amounted to over 400 000 tonnes, which may not appear an impressive total until it is remembered that it is made up of valuable items such as precious metals, intricate machinery, jewellery and pharmaceuticals. London airport now challenges London seaport for leadership in terms of the value of exports and imports (Fig. 177).

Air operations on this scale demand extensive ground facilities. Fig. 178 gives a plan of Heathrow. The total site area is over 1100 hectares. To accommodate the huge aircraft now in service, the main runways are

Fig. 178a

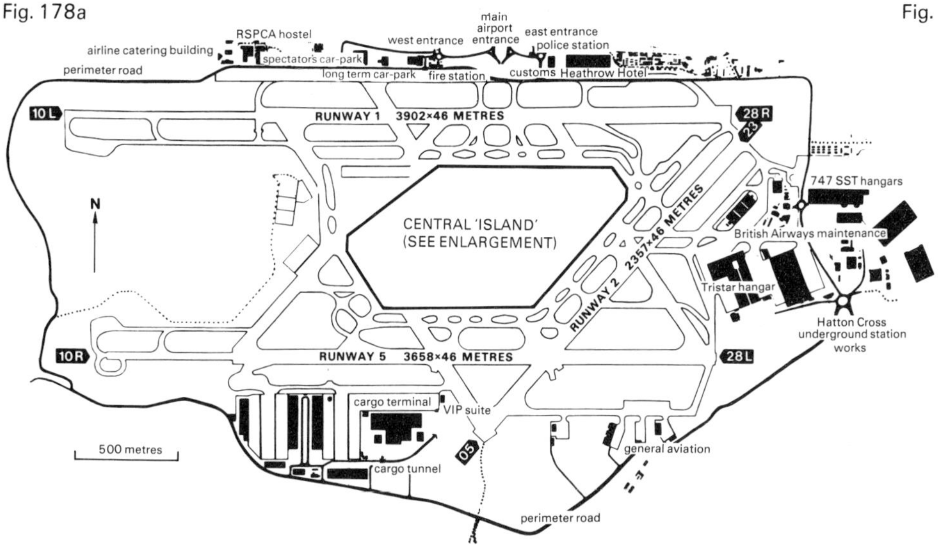

Fig. 178b **Central 'Island'**

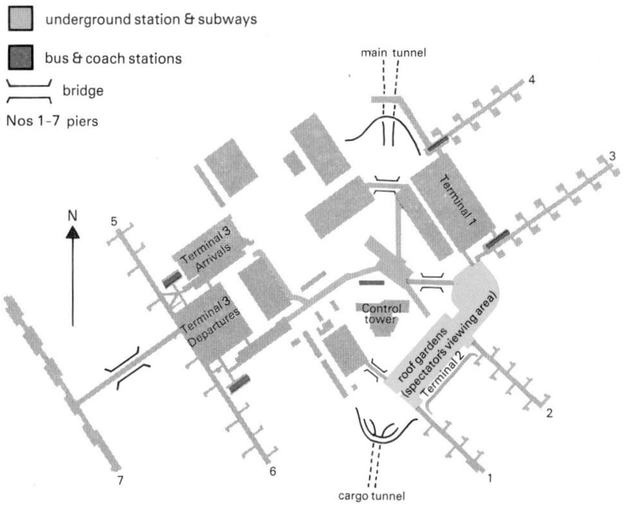

underground station & subways

bus & coach stations

bridge

Nos 1-7 piers

Fig. 179

over 3.5 kilometres long. Their alignment reflects the prevalence of westerly winds, for it is into the wind that aircraft prefer to take off and land. The large central 'island' (Fig. 179) houses passenger-handling facilities and air-traffic control. Maintenance, refuelling and cargo operations make great demands on space. The airport gives employment to 52 000 people.

Heathrow illustrates the factors which influence the location of major airports. Lying 25 kilometres west of central London, it has ready access to the great urban area which provides the bulk of its traffic. The large level site is firm, adequately drained, and well able to support the thick layers of concrete that form the runways. The lowland relief of the surrounding area gives aircraft a safe and gentle approach from all points of the compass. Heathrow does not suffer unduly from thick fog which is air transport's major weather hazard. London's smoke and fumes, which may impair visibility, are swept away from the airport by the prevailing westerly winds.

Inland waterways

When road transport was slow, cumbersome and horse-powered, rivers offered a tempting alternative for the movement of bulky goods. In Britain, however, opportunities were limited. Rivers were generally short, shallow, and followed tortuous courses. Limited improvements were possible. Artificial cuts through the necks of large meanders could effectively shorten a river, and the construction of locks could increase its depth. Even so, few parts of Britain could make commercial use of their rivers.

In the late eighteenth and early nineteenth centuries, the benefits of water transport were widely extended by the construction of canals. By 1790, the estuaries of Mersey, Humber, Severn and Thames were linked by water. By 1830, the year the railway proved itself, a network of nearly 6500 kilometres was in existence. Britain's canals were ill equipped to meet the growing challenge of the railway. In conquering a varied relief they had gained winding courses along a convenient contour, and elaborate sets of locks, such as the flight seen in Fig. 180; both made canal transport slow and tedious. Moreover, many canals were narrow, and their barges could only carry small cargoes. Traffic on river and canal was rapidly lost to the railway, which offered a quicker and more efficient service.

Many canals now lie abandoned. The waters of others are disturbed only by the propeller of a passing pleasure cruiser, or the plop of a fisherman's hook. Fig. 181 shows the canals that still have some commercial significance. There is no question of a network – merely a few short stretches which represent extensions of England's major estuaries.

Fig. 180

Fig. 181

Fig. 182

One area where inland waterways are still of some importance is mapped in Fig. 182. This region of busy industry is served by rivers and canals of above-average dimensions which open into the deep, broad waters of the Humber. Trains of barges move coal from colliery to power-station or to Goole for export. The Aire and Calder Navigation supports a regular service of tanker barges each loaded with 500 tonnes of petroleum products. Other commodities handled in bulk by the depot at Leeds include newsprint, steel, plywood, and copper tubing.

New developments in cargo handling point to greater future use of these and other inland waterways. The ship pictured in Fig. 183 rides peacefully at anchor in the Humber. Of novel design, it is the first of its kind in the world. It is of catamaran construction, for aft of the bridge it slims into twin hulls. A submersible elevator quickly lifts barges with a cargo capacity of 140 tonnes to the deck where ten such barges can be stowed. With three larger barges loaded between the hulls, total cargo capacity is 2700 tonnes. This ship is called *Bacat 1*. The name is significant. It stands for 'Barges Aboard

Fig. 183

Catamaran'. Look now at the foreground of the photograph. A Bacat barge, off-loaded from its mother ship, is being pushed upstream to Leeds by a gaily-painted tug.

The Humber is linked to the Rhine by regular Bacat services inaugurated in 1974. Barges are shipped to Rotterdam for onward despatch by continental waterways. Thus cargoes packed in Leeds or Doncaster can proceed undisturbed to Cologne and Dortmund. In the reverse direction, imports can be delivered direct to inland centres.

The Bacat system provides a convenient, direct and economic transport link between areas of increasing mutual trade. It will doubtless stimulate interest in Britain's neglected waterways. After many years of decline, much improvement is possible. The Sheffield and South Yorkshire Navigation provides an example. Planned improvements would enable vessels loaded with 700 tonnes of cargo to reach Rotherham. The estimated cost of this development which would bring cheap water transport into the heart of South Yorkshire is less than the cost of 2 kilometres of new motorway.

An exceptional inland waterway is mapped in Fig. 184. The Manchester Ship Canal enables vessels of 12 500 tonnes d.w.t. to berth in the heart of Greater Manchester. Cargoes can be loaded and discharged at many points along the canal, and these facilities are appreciated by the many industries established along its banks. In effect, the Manchester Ship Canal is a single harbour more than 50 kilometres long.

Fig. 184

Pipelines

Day and night, large quantities of vital commodities are moving silently and unseen beneath our feet. They are being pushed by pumps through pipelines. This relatively new form of transport is totally inflexible, expensive to construct and can be used only for liquids and gases. Nevertheless, the total length grows annually. Pipelines now play a vital role in the distribution of crude oil, refined products, chemical feedstocks and natural gas. For the movement of large quantities between fixed points, pipelines are unrivalled. They offer safe, reliable

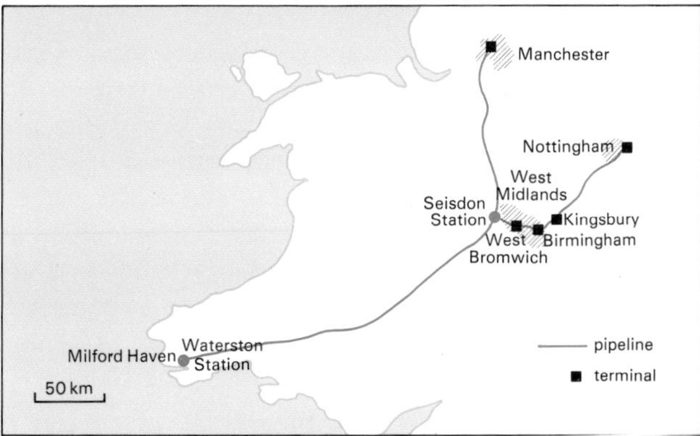

Fig. 185

transport at low cost. Buried a metre or more beneath the surface, the pipeline has no harmful effects on the environment, is free from weather hazards, and, if properly protected, will last virtually for ever.

With the growth of oil refining on the shores of Milford

Fig. 186

Haven, a distribution link to the large markets in the West Midlands and north of England became essential. The pipeline named *Mainline*, which is mapped in Fig. 185, was the chosen solution. The laying of 460 kilometres of welded steel pipe was necessary. In rural areas, with the aid of bucket-wheel trenchers like the one seen in Fig. 186, progress was rapid, but, for 32 kilometres, built-up areas could not be avoided. In addition, the line had to cross 22 rivers, 17 canals, 93 major roads and 23 railways. After 8 months of effort, and the investment of £15 million, Mainline was opened in the summer of 1973.

A pipeline may transport more than one product. Mainline carries kerosenes, aviation fuels, petrol and diesel oils in 'parcels' belonging to different owners. This is possible because, moving under pressure, there is very little mixing. Products from the Esso, Texaco and Gulf refineries are received at Waterston pipeline station (Fig. 139, page 77) and forwarded to Seisdon control centre where they can be shunted along either branch to company terminals at Manchester, Birmingham and Nottingham. Mainline has the capacity to deliver up to 16 million litres a day.

Seaports

The British Isles have long and tortuous coastlines. Wide bays are protected by prominent headlands. Broad estuaries extend deep, sheltered waters far into prosperous lowland areas. Land and sea routes make frequent contact and ports are numerous. Indeed, port facilities are maintained at nearly 300 points around our coast. They range from harbours of world renown to lonely quays used by fishing smacks and the occasional coaster. Only the more important are recorded on Fig. 187.

Britain's ports have a role to play in domestic transport. Many small vessels are busy about our coasts, concentrating on the cheap movement of bulky commodities. Coastal power-stations are fed with fuel by colliers

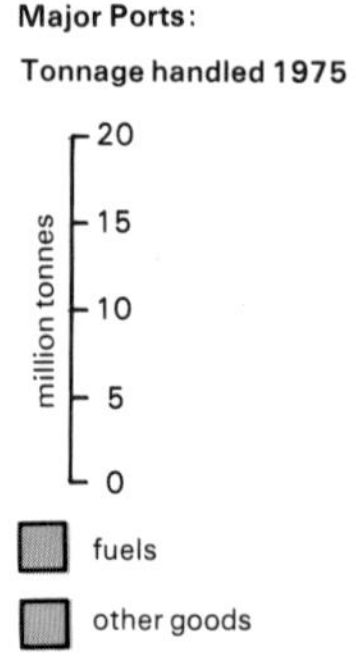

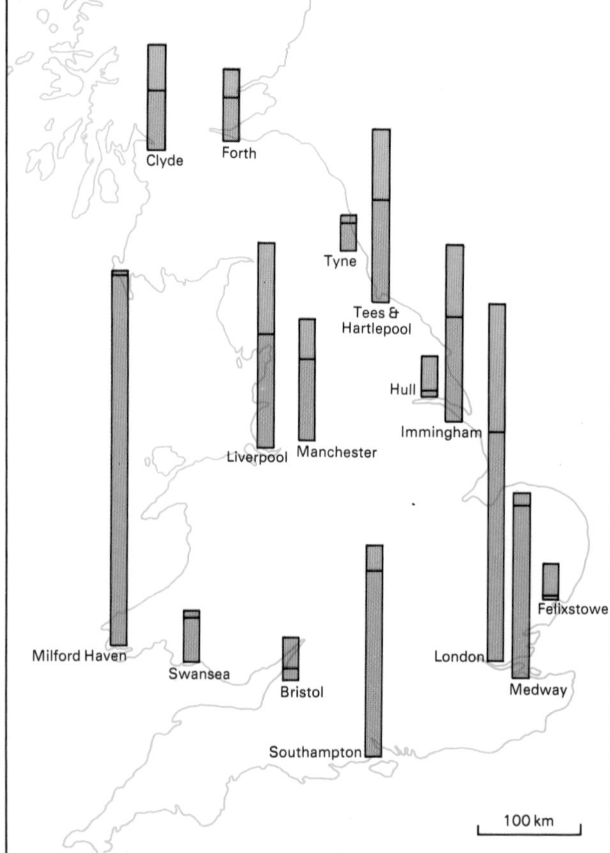

Fig. 187

loaded on the Humber and Tyne. Refineries pump petroleum products into small tankers for delivery to coastal depots. Building materials and fertilizers are other common cargoes. Coastwise traffic amounts for over 30 per cent of the tonnage handled by British ports.

Ports are the gateways of international trade. In Britain their significance increased enormously with the industrial expansion of the nineteenth century. Mills and factories demanded imported raw materials in ever-increasing quantities, and outlets were needed for their manufactured products. Ports expanded in step with the growth in trade. Major estuaries, such as Thames, Mersey, Humber and Clyde, held favoured sites. Natural shorelines were lost beneath the elaborate dock systems which solved the problem of tidal variation. Tall cranes sprouted from the dockside to rise above large transit sheds and warehouses. Rail tracks knitted together the port facilities and linked them to their hinterlands. Factories and close-packed housing were built close at hand to complete the picture of traditional dockland that may, in some measure, be appreciated from Fig. 194, page 102.

With their great advantages of fine estuaries and productive hinterlands, London (page 100) and Liverpool (page 136) came to achieve dominance in Britain's overseas trade. They remain Britain's premier ports for general cargo, but have declined in relative importance. Together, in 1960, they handled 60 per cent by value of U.K. trade. Today the figure is only 20 per cent. Recent decades have seen a great expansion in the total volume of trade, but much cargo is handled at new sites and by new methods. Crude oil claims the greatest share of increased imports. Estuaries servicing large refineries, Medway and Southampton Water, for instance, have gained prestige (Fig. 187). Milford Haven (page 76) has enjoyed a spectacular rise. Bantry Bay (page 76) is now the Republic of Ireland's leading port in terms of tonnage handled. The search for deep water close to existing oil refineries has led to the development of more port facilities. Page 76 records how the Stanlow refinery is supplied with crude oil from a monobuoy anchored off the coast of Anglesey. Another example is afloat at Tetney Haven off the mouth of the Humber.

Other commodities have benefited from improved bulk-handling facilities. New iron-ore terminals have been established at Port Talbot (page 109) and at the mouth of the Tees. At South Killingholme, near Immingham, a high-capacity conveyor system takes coal from a rail-fed stockpile to a deep-water jetty in the Humber, where it slides directly into the holds of waiting ships. Old

Fig. 188

established ports adapt to new and specialised methods of bulk-handling. At Liverpool, for instance, Canada Dock has special facilities for liquid cargoes, and the Royal Seaforth Dock has computer-controlled facilities for grain and timber.

The handling of more general cargo has also been revolutionised in recent years. One example is the now widespread use of containers. From Fig. 188 we may appreciate some of their advantages as applied to sea transport. A container ship is berthed at Liverpool. Its holds are of a special cellular construction and can accommodate upwards of 2000 containers. More can be carried as deck cargo. The ship can be loaded and unloaded simultaneously and special cranes make both operations quick and efficient. Ships can be in and out of a port in hours rather than the days demanded by traditional methods. A swift 'turn round' means that a ship spends less time in port and more time earning its keep on the open seas. Fewer vessels are therefore needed to service a particular shipping route, and costs are again reduced. Today, all major ports are equipped to handle containers.

Fig. 189, a photograph taken at Felixstowe, shows another new method of handling cargo. A loaded trailer is backed aboard a specially designed vessel. Parked with others, it forms part of the cargo. At Rotterdam the trailer will be shunted ashore, hitched to a tractor unit and sped to its destination. The same ship accepts loaded lorries which are driven directly on board. In this case the cargo handles itself. Transit is quick, and costs are low. These roll-on/roll-off *(Ro/Ro)* services are particularly well suited to the short sea crossings between Britain and neighbouring countries. These happen to be areas where mutual trade is increasing rapidly.

Fig. 189

Fig. 190

Felixstowe (Fig. 190), at the mouth of the Orwell, is one port which has benefited greatly both from proximity to mainland Europe, and from improved methods of cargo handling. The small dock, opened in 1876, could squeeze little trade from a mainly agricultural hinterland. But Felixstowe was a leader in the cargo-handling revolution. Heavy capital investment brought the early introduction of container and Ro/Ro berths. Helped by wise management and good labour relations, the port earned a reputation as the most efficient in Europe. Quick reliable service attracts exports from far afield, and the port has become a favoured point of entry for imports from Europe. Scheduled freightliner services from Birmingham, Coatbridge, London, Liverpool and Manchester converge on Felixstowe, which is linked by regular sailings to ports in Europe, North America, and the Middle and Far East. Fig. 191 illustrates the growth of trade through the port.

In spite of growing competition from air travel, passenger transport remains an important function of numerous ports, particularly those that can offer a short voyage costing appreciably less than the price of the equivalent air fare. Fig. 192 maps the major routes. Dover is pre-eminent. It earns its status by proximity to large centres of population on both sides of the English Channel, and its command of the shortest crossing. Dover is largely an artificial creation. Long breakwaters swing out from the town to enclose twin harbours. In 1976, 6783000 passengers passed through the port. This figure represents nearly 50 per cent of sea-borne passenger movements.

The greatest of all Britain's ports provides further illustration of the changing nature of port activity. Since the distant days of its Roman foundation, London has been well served by the Thames. For many centuries, the Pool of London, hard by the bridge that never did fall down, was the effective head of navigation for sea-going vessels. Riding at anchor, or beached on mudflats, ships were unloaded with the aid of lighters of shallow draught.

Fig. 191 **Cargo handled at Felixstowe**

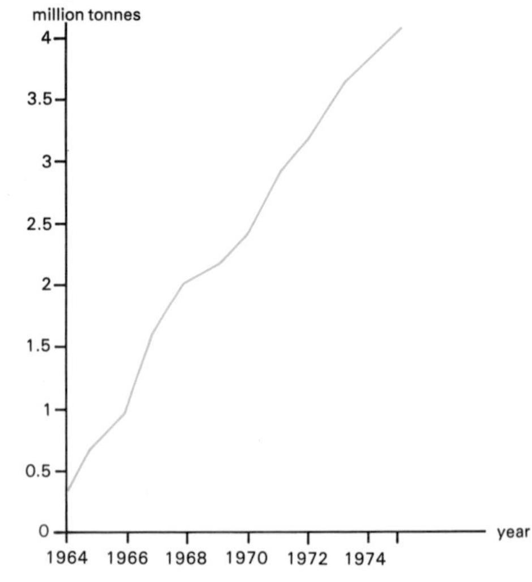

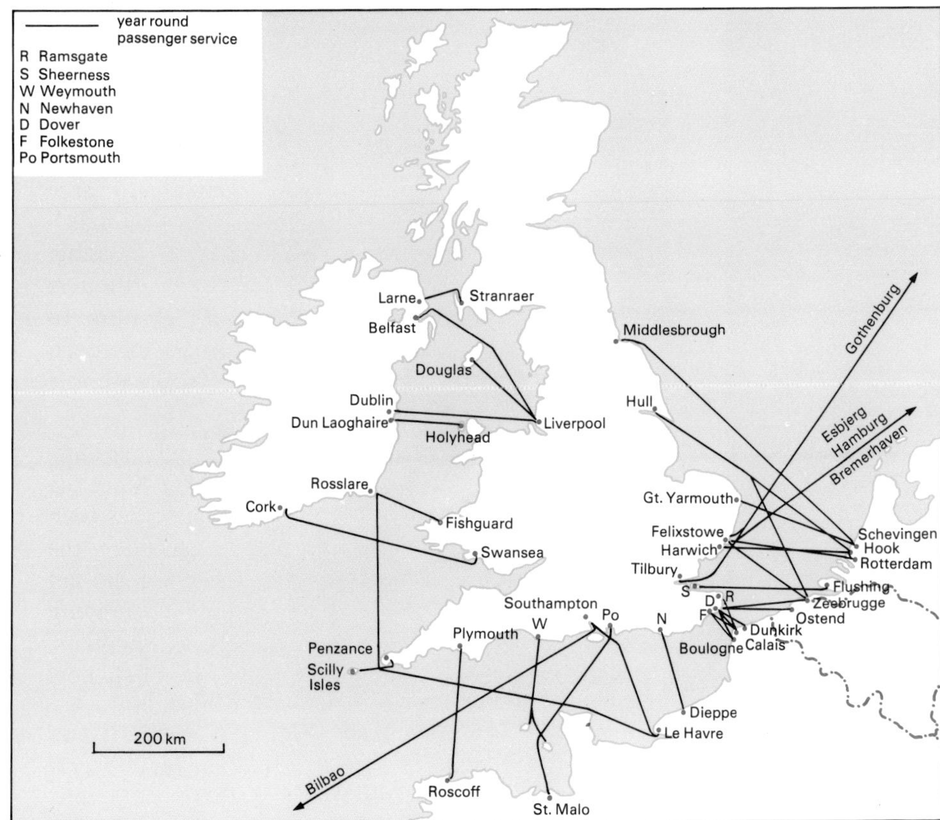

Fig. 192

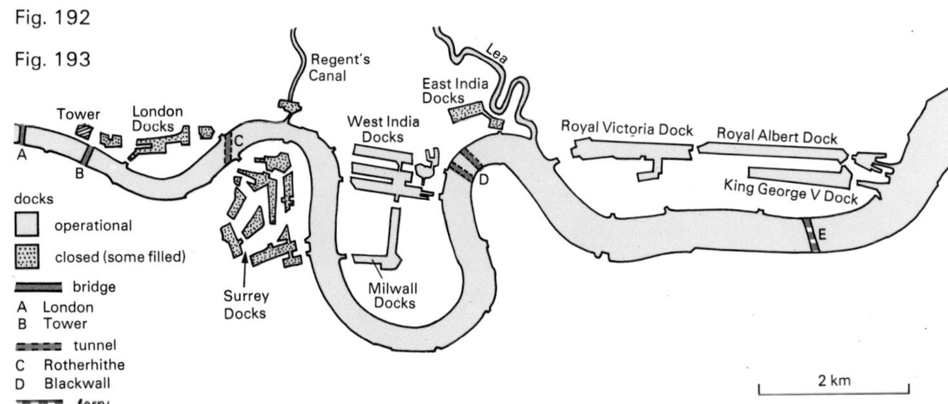

Fig. 193

London claimed its full share of the steady growth of trade in the nineteenth century. As Britain's largest urban centre, and the capital of a vast empire, it attracted imports from all over the world, and provided many return cargoes. Road and rail routes which fanned out in all directions extended its hinterland over most of southern and central England. Port improvements kept pace with increases in the size and number of visiting ships.

The earliest docks were opened in the first decade of the nineteenth century. By 1921, the inner estuary had achieved the dock complex outlined in Fig. 193. Construction was favoured by local conditions: the river was bordered by wide expanses of marshland, uncluttered by settlement; the soft alluvium and underlying clay were easily excavated; and dock systems could be neatly fitted within the embracing arms of wide meanders.

The winding Thames is glimpsed to the left of Fig. 194 which looks westward over the Royal group of docks, the largest in the inner estuary. It illustrates the traditional dockland landscape. Over 30 ocean-going vessels are moored at the docksides, which are paralleled by lines of cranes, transit sheds, railroads and roadways. Clusters of lighters shuttle between the docks and riverside factories and warehouses.

Many older upstream docks, hampered by small size and congested locations, have been closed in recent years, and large dockland areas are in the process of conversion to other uses. The site of St. Katharine Dock, for instance, has been redeveloped and now includes a large modern hotel, and a marina for pleasure craft. The Royal group still echoes to the sounds of port activity, but not as loudly as in the past. Modern developments are taking place in the deeper waters of the outer estuary (Fig. 195) where large ships can be handled with ease. The Port of London is moving east.

Fig. 194

Fig. 195

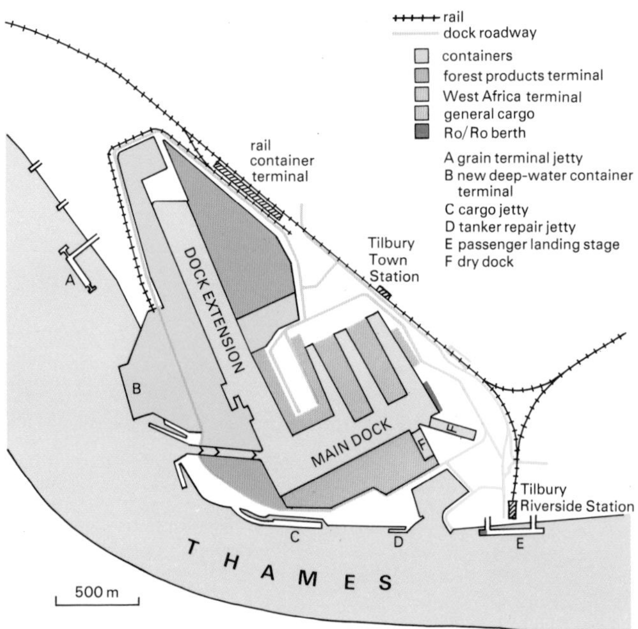

Fig. 196

Tilbury, 40 kilometres below London Bridge, has benefited greatly. The main dock (Figs. 196 and 197) was opened in 1898 and enlarged in 1912. The large extension – nearly $1\frac{1}{2}$ kilometres long – dates from the mid-1960s and was built to accommodate the container revolution. Berths have deep water and are backed by ample space for the marshalling and storage of containers. The entrance lock can take vessels of 30 000 tonnes d.w.t. When the riverside extension is completed in 1979, a deep-water quay over 300 metres long will accommodate the largest container ships in service. This new development will strengthen Tilbury's position as Britain's premier container port.

Below Tilbury, the jetties serving the Shell and Mobil oil refineries lie within the Port of London. They make a major contribution to the total of tonnage handled. Maplin Sands will be the ultimate eastward shift of the Port of London. Plans exist, but have yet to be

Fig. 197

approved, for the creation of a major port complex located close to natural deep-water channels. It will be able to receive the largest ships afloat – even the mammoth 500 000-tonne d.w.t. tankers.

7 Industry

One indication of the importance of industry in Great Britain is revealed in Fig. 198. Manufacturing provides employment to over one-third of the working population. This is enhanced by the fact that employment in service occupations such as power, transport, banking and insurance depends in large measure on manufacturing. Although imports are considerable, U.K. factories satisfy by far the greater part of domestic demand for manufactured goods. In addition, these items dominate exports to the extent indicated in Fig. 199. They pay for essential imports of food, fuel and raw materials. The economic well-being of Britain depends primarily on the health of her factories.

Industry does not play such an important role in the economy of the Republic of Ireland. Figs. 200 and 201 enable comparisons to be made.

In the U.K., industrial development has a long and eventful history. In medieval times, manufacturing was an urban activity. Towns were few in number and small in size, but each had its tiny workshops where craftsmen laboured to produce the range of simple products in common use. There was little specialisation. Poor transport facilities limited distribution.

In the eighteenth century, the old towns lost their dominance. Industry sought the valleys of swift-flowing streams where water-power could ease the burden on human muscle. The development of machinery reinforced the advantages of a riverside location. It was the waterwheel which powered the first factories born of the Industrial Revolution.

The nineteenth century brought dramatic change. The development of the steam-engine made power more abundant, more reliable and more widely available. Coal was the chosen fuel. Coalfields attracted industry, and small villages grew into great towns. Railways facilitated distribution, and encouraged local specialisations which have persisted to this day.

In the present century, industry has been slowly freed from its dependence on coal. Power in the form of electricity has become available virtually everywhere. Road vehicles have given transport a greater flexibility. For many types of industry it is the market – the major urban areas – that is their main magnet.

Since the end of the Second World War, the speed of change has accelerated. Advances in science and technology have brought new materials and new methods. Manufactured goods are available in vastly increased volume and variety; plastics, transistors, and aerosols, for instance, are the basis of many new products which are now part of everyday life. Greater affluence has created or enlarged the demand for goods which, although by no means essential, are useful, entertaining, decorative, convenient or labour-saving. Felt-tipped pens, television sets, ceramic wall tiles, paper towels, and frozen chipped potatoes may be quoted in illustration.

Factories are becoming increasingly interdependent; one firm's finished product is another firm's raw material. Components made in factories scattered throughout the country are assembled to make a T.V. set. A breakdown in the supply of just one item can halt production.

The average size of factories increases. Large-scale mechanised production reduces the unit cost of manufactured goods which are therefore in greater demand. Output is marketed in new and more efficient ways. A shorter working week provides more time for the enjoyment of a higher standard of living.

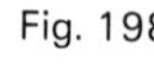

Fig. 198

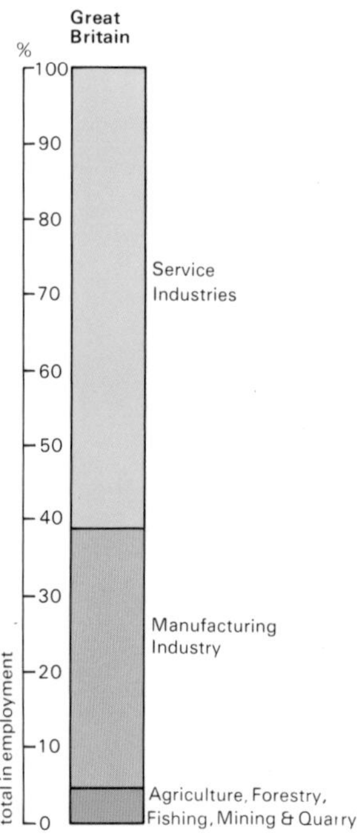

Fig. 199

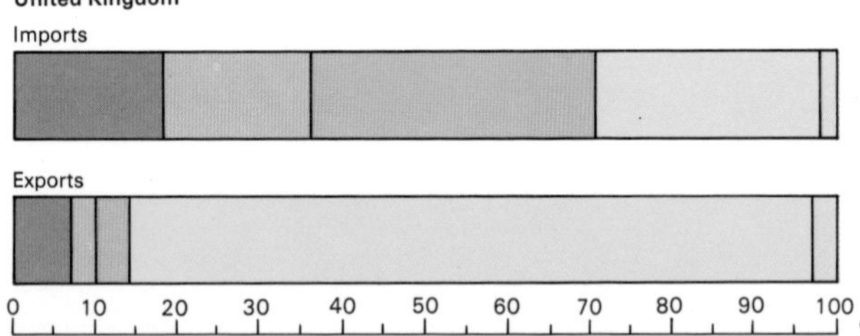

Fig. 200

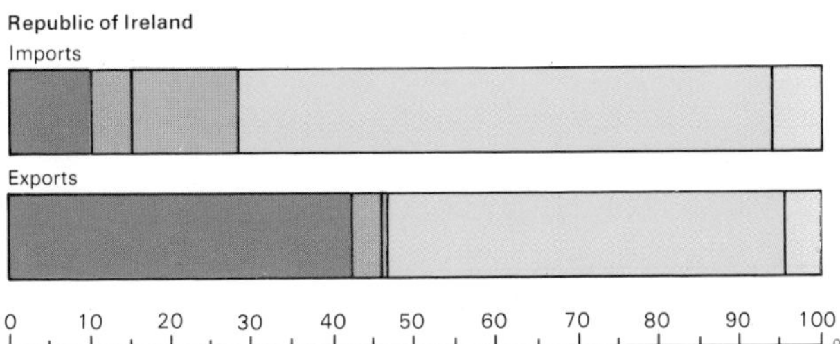

Fig. 201

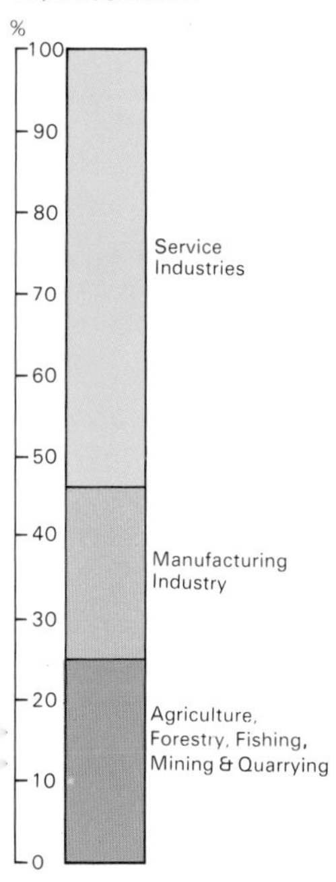

Change continues; new uses are found for new materials and new products drive old ones from the market place. Factories close and new ones are established – often in a different area; the *distribution* of industry, as well as its nature, is subject to change.

Today, industry is more widely distributed than ever before: a whisky distillery nestles in a Scottish glen; a rice-pudding factory rises from the soft rural landscape of South Devon; herrings are kippered in the Isle of Man. Wherever you live you are not far from a factory. Industry has, however, a most uneven distribution. Certain areas show great concentrations of manufacturing activity. These areas are indicated in a general way in Fig. 202.

Fig. 202

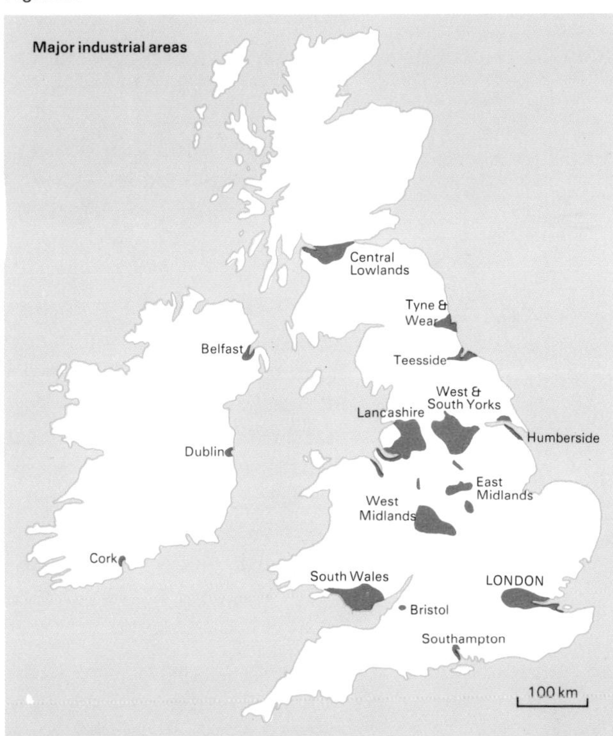

Ceramics

One of Britain's smaller industrial concentrations lies in North Staffordshire. It is mapped in Fig. 203. Study the employment figures given in Fig. 204. In Stoke-on-Trent, employment in manufacturing industry is 50 per cent of the work-force. This is above the national average. Note, too, the variety of manufacturing activity that is present. Virtually all occupational groups are represented. Here, as in industrial regions generally, a very wide range of goods is produced.

The many manufacturing groups represented are not of

Fig. 203

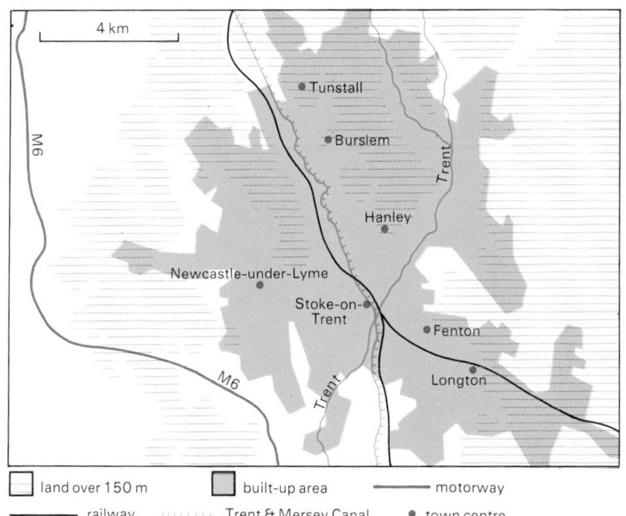

Occupational Group (Standard Industrial Classification)	*% of total employment in Great Britain* (1971 Census)		*% of total employment in Stoke-on-Trent* (1971 Census)	
I Agriculture, forestry and fishing	2.7		0.4	
II Mining and quarrying	1.7		4.8	
Total – Primary industry		4.4		5.2
III Food, drink and tobacco	3.1		1.9	
IV Coal and petroleum products	0.3		0.2	
V Chemicals and allied industries	1.9		0.8	
VI Metal manufacture	2.3		3.4	
VII Mechanical engineering	4.8		4.2	
VIII Instrument engineering	0.6		0.1	
IX Electrical engineering	3.6		0.4	
X Shipbuilding and marine engineering	0.8		—	
XI Vehicles	3.4		0.4	
XII Other metal goods	2.5		0.8	
XIII Textiles	2.5		0.3	
XIV Leather and fur	0.2		—	
XV Clothing and footwear	2.0		1.2	
XVI Bricks, pottery, glass, cement, etc.	1.3		27.5	
XVII Timber, furniture, etc.	1.3		0.9	
XVIII Paper, printing and publishing	2.6		1.8	
XIX Other manufacturing industries	1.4		6.3	
Total – Manufacturing industry		34.6		50.2
XX Construction	7.1		5.9	
XXI Gas, electricity and water	1.5		1.3	
XXII Transport and communication	6.6		5.7	
XXIII Distributive trades	12.8		10.8	
XXIV Insurance, banking, finance and business services	4.0		1.9	
XXV Professional and scientific services	12.3		9.4	
XXVI Miscellaneous services	10.0		6.7	
XXVII Public administration and defence	6.7		3.0	
Total – Services		61.0		44.7

Fig. 204

equal importance. Look again at Fig. 204. Groups X and XIV make an insignificant contribution. Several others are well below the national average. In contrast metal manufacturers (group VI) claim more than their fair share. Even more emphatic is group XVI, 'Bricks, pottery, glass and cement', for which the Stoke-on-Trent figure is more than twenty times the figure for the country as a whole. All but a tiny fraction of this employment is provided by the clay-based industries known collectively as ceramics. The main branches of this important industry are domestic tableware, tiles, electrical porcelain and sanitary ware. Ceramics have given Stoke-on-Trent its main claim to world renown, and the familiar nickname of 'the Potteries'.

Many industrial areas have their specialisations, often established in the early days of the Industrial Revolution. Cotton in Lancashire and wool in Yorkshire are familiar examples. In the twentieth century there has been a marked tendency for such specialisations to fade as old industries have declined, and new ones risen in stature. In Stoke-on-Trent, ceramics persist as Britain's most pronounced industrial specialisation. More than 75 per cent of the country's output comes from this one small area.

The reason for Stoke's profound interest in ceramics lies deep in history. In the seventeenth century, poor agricultural land offered little more than mere subsistence. Farmers turned to pottery as a sideline. Clay was dug in the fields and simple kilns were fired with brushwood or coal from nearby outcrops. Later, small factories were established in local villages. Burslem was the early leader. It sent butter-pots by pack-horse to be sold in market towns throughout midland England.

In its early interest in pottery, North Staffordshire was by no means unique. Many other parts of the country enjoyed similar opportunities and incentives. True, the long-flame coal from the local seams was of particular value in the kilns, but this is not sufficient to explain the dominance of Stoke. A factor of far greater importance was the technical skill and commercial enterprise of the Staffordshire potters. Several made outstanding contributions. The most famous was Josiah Wedgwood, who, in the 1760s, first used china clay to produce tableware of superior quality. He also encouraged the construction of the Trent and Mersey Canal which slashed the cost of raw materials and made easier the distribution of fragile finished products. Wedgwood ware was of high artistic merit. With aggressive salesmanship it found markets as far afield as Moscow.

The early factories were attracted to the outcrop of the most productive coal-seams which extended from Tunstall, through Burslem, Hanley, Stoke-on-Trent and

Fenton to Longton. These six busy towns prospered, expanded and merged with each other and with their neighbours into an urban strip some 10 kilometres long, for which the name of Stoke was adopted. Twentieth-century expansion has brought the old market town of Newcastle-under-Lyme within the urban complex. For the most part, the industry retains its original location, but much else has changed. Large modern factories feature efficient production methods. Ceramic goods are now fired as they travel slowly through tunnel kilns in which temperatures as high as 1200°C are maintained. Local resources are today of little significance; the clays which served the early potters are now largely ignored and electricity, oil or gas is the modern source of heat. Raw materials are assembled by road or rail; china clay and ball clay come in from south-west England, and flint from the southern chalklands. Imported animal bones, burnt to ash, form the basis of 'bone china'.

Fig. 205

In spite of the modernisation of production methods, individual skills are still highly prized in the industry. The worker gives each saucer and plate its final shape, and decoration is often applied by hand (Fig. 205). Stoke's dominant position in ceramics is due to a merited reputation for quality maintained by the availability of labour with the appropriate skills.

Iron and steel

The blast-furnace pictured in Fig. 206 has a hearth diameter of 9.45 metres and a working volume of 1875 cubic metres. It is ravenous for raw materials. Each day it swallows 38 500 tonnes of iron-ore, 11 000 tonnes of metallurgical coke and 2800 tonnes of limestone. The charged furnace is blasted by hot air to lift temperatures above 1800°C. At intervals, liquid pig-iron is drawn off, the furnace topped up with raw materials and so operation proceeds continuously. This single blast-furnace, one of five in the Port Talbot works, yields 23 000 tonnes of iron every week.

Fig. 206

The simplified flow-diagram (Fig. 207) shows that the production of pig-iron is but the first stage in a varied and complex sequence of processes. Apart from the small amount used for castings, iron moves on for conversion into steel. This may be accomplished in different ways. Until the late 1960s, the open-hearth furnace, effective but slow, dominated steel production. Now it is steadily giving way to basic oxygen converters which produce steel in a tenth of the time, and at greatly reduced cost. About a sixth of Britain's steel is made in closed furnaces, in which electric arcs give temperatures as high as 3400°C.

Steel furnace and converter receive more than just pig-iron. The charge usually includes ore, limestone and manganese in varying proportions. Scrap, too, is a common addition, and may be used exclusively in the production of steel, especially in electric furnaces. The significance of scrap is often overlooked. In an average year, over 11 million tonnes are used, and availability may influence the location of steelworks.

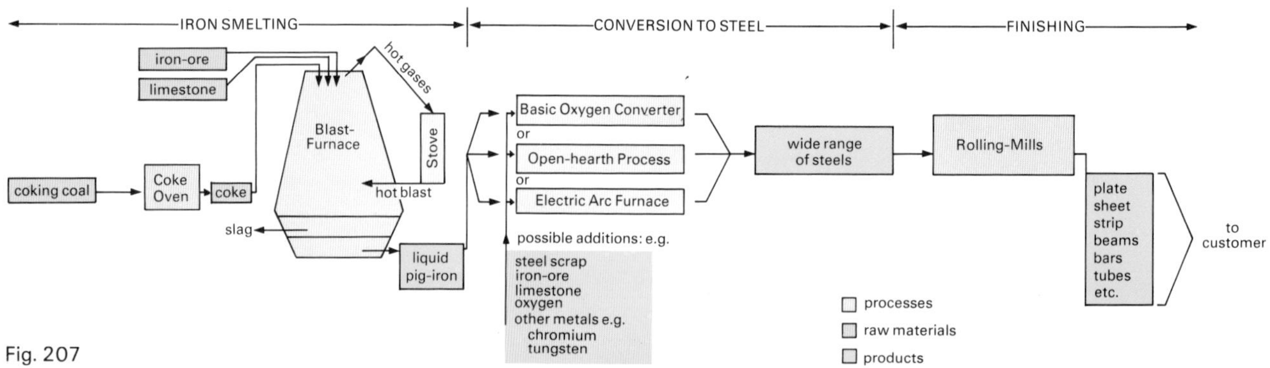

Fig. 207

Fig. 208

Steel production 1975 (thousand tonnes)

U.S.S.R.	141 156
U.S.A.	105 948
Japan	102 216
West Germany	40 404
Italy	21 852
France	21 516
United Kingdom	20 100
Poland	15 012
Czechoslovakia	14 196

By control of the carbon content, converter and furnace can be made to yield steel of diverse qualities. The addition of small amounts of other metals, such as nickel, chromium and molybdenum, gives a wide range of alloy steels suited to specific uses. Thus a great variety of steel moves to the finishing processes. Rolling-mills change hot steel ingots into the bars, beams, rails, plates and sheets needed by the industry's many customers. It is hard to think of an industry in which steel does not play a vital role. Steel is of such fundamental importance that output is often taken as an indication of a nation's economic strength. Britain's relative position is tabled in Fig. 208.

Blast-furnaces, steel making, and rolling-mills may exist alone or in varied combinations. Of greatest significance are works where the three processes share a common

Fig. 209

Fig. 210

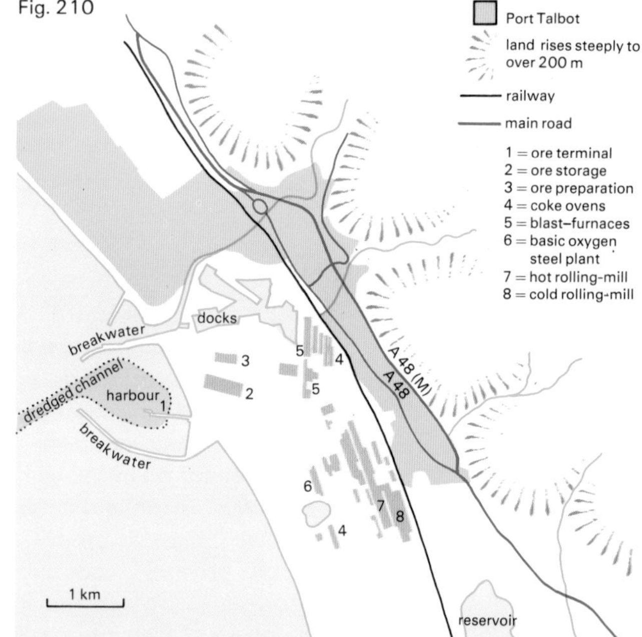

site. These *integrated* works claim great economies in manufacture. Transport costs are much reduced. The converter receives pig-iron in liquid form and so great savings of fuel are achieved. The large scale of operation further reduces the costs of production.

One of Britain's major integrated works is viewed from the air in Fig. 209 and mapped in Fig. 210. This is the British Steel Corporation's Margam and Abbey complex at Port Talbot. The sheer scale of the undertaking must be appreciated. It has a site area of 1093 hectares. It is nearly 5 kilometres from the most southerly unit marked on Fig. 210 to the tip of the northern breakwater. The hot-strip mill is 1.5 kilometres long. The various buildings and installations are stitched together by 64 kilometres of roadway and 164 kilometres of rail track.

Steel has been made at Port Talbot since the early years of this century. In 1923, the Margam works were opened just south of the docks. Great expansion followed the Second World War, and the completion, in 1951, of the Abbey unit created the basis of the great iron and steel complex that we see today. Further developments have since taken place, and more are planned for the future.

The development of steel production at Port Talbot reflects a most favourable location. On this large, level site, raw materials can be assembled easily and cheaply. The tidal harbour, opened in 1970, can accommodate bulk-carriers loaded with up to 100000 tonnes of rich iron-ore. After voyages from Canada, Brazil, Australia, Liberia and Norway, vessels berth at the ore terminal. Their cargoes are speedily discharged and moved to stockyards by high-capacity conveyor systems. In this way, the works receives its annual needs of 3.5 million tonnes of ore with an average iron content of 65 per cent. Port Talbot uses 2 million tonnes of prime coking coal each year. All but a small proportion is railed in from pits working the southern edge of the South Wales coalfield. The balance is imported from Virginia, U.S.A.

Fig. 211

Limestone is mainly derived from local resources. Quarries in South Wales make the major contribution to an annual total of 400000 tonnes, but some is brought in by rail from as far afield as Buxton in Derbyshire. 450 million litres of water are constantly in circulation within the works. Each day, mainly by evaporation, 77 million litres are lost and the replacement water is drawn from on-site reservoirs.

The Port Talbot steelworks employs over 13000 people. Modern techniques are used to produce about 3 million tonnes of steel each year. The old, slow, open-hearth capacity was scrapped in 1970, and replaced by two large basic oxygen converters which can produce 300 tonnes of steel in 45 minutes. In Fig. 211, one of these converters is being charged with liquid pig-iron from the blast-furnaces. In the rolling-mills, bulky slabs of steel are transformed into steel strips of varying thicknesses. 50 per cent of output finds large and accessible markets

Fig. 212

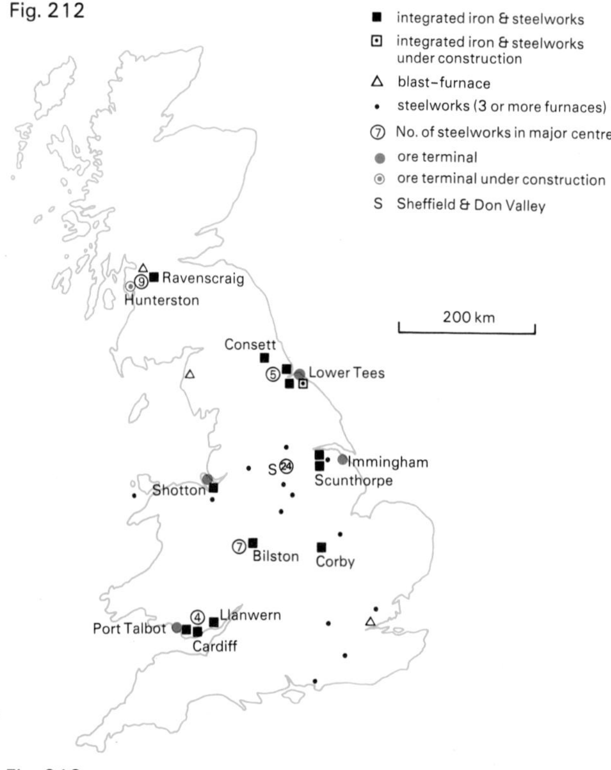

Fig. 213

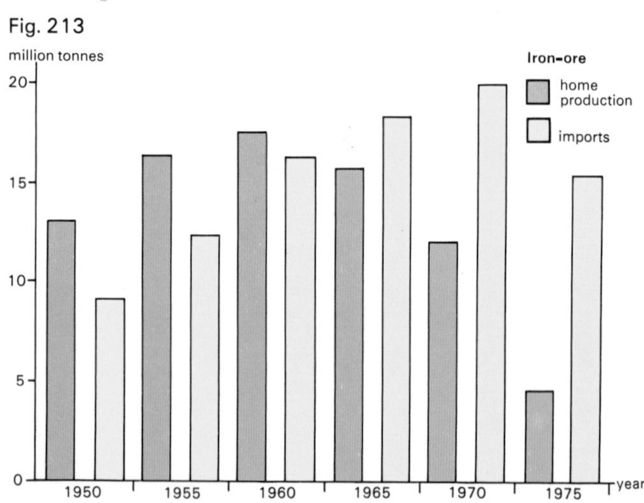

in the car, domestic appliance, office furniture and other manufacturing industries. 40 per cent moves north-west to the British Steel Corporation's tin-plate works at Velindre and Trostre, which are located on Fig. 248, page 129. The remainder is mainly alloy steel used in the electrical industry. Good road and rail facilities, which ease the assembly of raw materials, are also an asset in the distribution of the finished products.

In Fig. 212, Port Talbot takes its place in the general distribution of Britain's iron and steel industry. Sites where raw materials may be cheaply assembled dominate the distribution. The advantages enjoyed by Port Talbot (and coastal South Wales generally) are also to be found on Teesside. This area has ready access to the high-quality coking coals of South Durham, and a large new ore terminal welcomes vessels of up to 150 000 tonnes d.w.t. The Teesside plants feed the important engineering and shipbuilding industries of north-east England. The old-established steel industry in Scotland now makes great use of scrap, but supplementary supplies of iron-ore are imported through Glasgow. North Wales is similarly served by Birkenhead.

A coastal location is becoming increasingly attractive to the steel industry because of the lower relative cost of rich imported ores. Fig. 213 shows that the use of domestic ore is declining, and that Britain is becoming increasingly dependent on supplies from overseas. Nevertheless, Scunthorpe and Corby are located on ore fields within easy reach of coking coal. Even at Scunthorpe, however, increased use is being made of imported ores.

The areas mentioned above account for by far the greater part of Britain's crude steel output, but Fig. 212 reveals that the metal is also produced in other parts of the country. Often, these centres are relics of a distribution developed in former times when conditions were different. In the nineteenth century, for instance, the industry was located on the coalfields, for the rocks provided not only coal, but also 'blackband' ores (page 25). These ores have not been mined for many years, but the industry, in a reduced form, persists, usually with steelmaking rather than smelting.

Sheffield is a steel centre of distinctive character. As early as the twelfth century, coal-measure ores were smelted by the heat of glowing charcoal. Local sandstones made fine grindstones, and swift Pennine streams offered water-power. Specialisation in the manufacture of cutlery developed early, and, encouraged by the presence of skilled labour, expanded into the production of tools and intricate castings. Today, Sheffield boasts no blast-furnaces, but produces much high-quality steel to meet local and more general demand. Scrap and pig-iron are railed in to feed electric furnaces which yield alloy steels in great variety. Sheffield dominates this important branch of the steel industry.

In the course of its long history, the iron and steel industry has seen many changes. More may be expected in the near future. The British Steel Corporation plans to increase its steelmaking capacity to over 36 million tonnes by the mid 1980s. Development is to be concentrated on sites having access to cheap imported ores. At Port Talbot, for example, it is planned to double output in the next decade. At a cost of over £1000 million, South Teesside is to be developed into the largest steelmaking complex in Europe. Expansion in Scotland will be serviced by a large new ore terminal at Hunterston, where new technology for the direct reduction of iron-ore is to be established. In all areas, steel will be produced by the most modern and efficient methods. In less favoured areas, steelmaking is to be reduced or abandoned; several old-fashioned works, including those at Bilston and Shotton, face an uncertain future.

Aluminium

Aluminium's varied properties make it the most valued and versatile of the non-ferrous metals in common use. With low density, high conductivity and strong resistance to corrosion, the pure metal is made into excellent electricity transmission cables. When alloyed with small quantities of other metals, such as magnesium, manganese and copper, aluminium is tough as well as light. These qualities are appreciated in a range of products which includes cars and vans, pots and pans, barrels and cans, and, most important of all, components for the construction industry.

The production of aluminium demands large quantities of cheap electricity. 21 kWh are needed to liberate 1 kilo of aluminium from 2 kilos of alumina. This, the principal raw material, is produced at Newport and Burntisland from bauxite shipped in from overseas. Smelters produce aluminium in the form of ingots. These are taken to rolling-mills for conversion into many different shapes and sections, which usually move on to other factories for fabrication. The factories which use aluminium are far from the smelters. They are mainly found in traditional centres of the engineering industry, such as the West Midlands or south Lancashire. In the story of aluminium much transport is involved. In transit, as in use, the lightness of the metal is a great advantage.

Until the end of the 1960s, Britain's smelting capacity was restricted to small works at Fort William and Kinlochleven in the highlands of Scotland. Powered by cheap hydro-electricity, they have a combined annual capacity of 35 000 tonnes, a mere fraction of Britain's consumption. In recent years, three large new smelters have come into production. Today, more than two-thirds of Britain's increased needs are met from home production.

The new smelters are plotted on Fig. 214. They are widely separated but have much in common. All were built with government assistance, in areas in need of development. Their sites are close to port facilities. None of the new smelters uses hydro-electricity; Holyhead and Invergordon take power from the national

Fig. 214

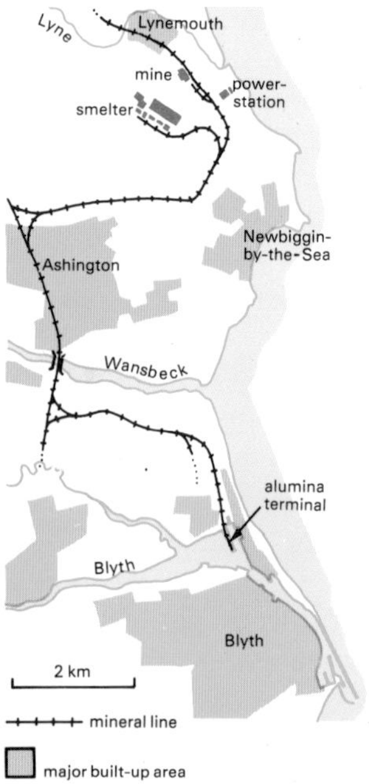

Lyne
Lynemouth
mine
power-station
smelter
Newbiggin-by-the-Sea
Ashington
Wansbeck
alumina terminal
Blyth
Blyth
2 km
mineral line
major built-up area

Fig. 215

grid, and Lynemouth has its own private power-station.

The Lynemouth smelter, and the undertakings on which it depends, are located on Fig. 215 and pictured in Fig. 216. 13 kilometres to the south lies the port of Blyth. Alumina is cheaply imported from Jamaica in large vessels which berth at a special quay on the north side of the harbour. Cargoes are conveyed first to storage silos and then to rail trucks for the short onward journey to the smelter. Britain's largest privately owned power-station provides electricity. It has a capacity of 390 MW. Fuel comes from the adjacent Lynemouth–Ellington colliery, which is one of the most efficient and highly mechanised in Europe. Low-cost coal is delivered directly to the power-station by a computer-controlled conveyor system. The sea is at hand to supply 545000 litres of cooling water every minute.

The Lynemouth site enjoys advantages which make for the efficient production of aluminium. Annual output is in the region of 120000 tonnes. Smelter and power-station together give employment to over 1000 people.

Fig. 216

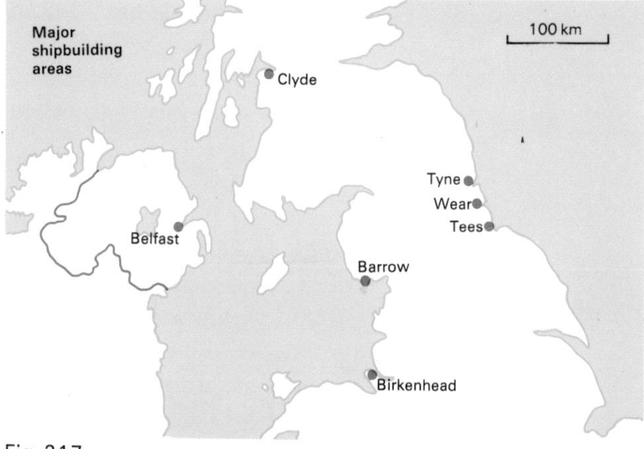

Fig. 217

Shipbuilding

A long and distinguished history of shipbuilding has left the U.K. with over 50 yards that have the capacity to launch vessels of more than 100 tonnes d.w.t. The main centres of the industry are indicated on Fig. 217, which emphasises the importance of the northern estuaries. Many shipbuilding yards claim a share of the allied industry of ship repair, which is located in greater degree in major ports such as London and Liverpool.

It was in the second half of the nineteenth century that the northern estuaries achieved their dominant position. Timber slowly gave way first to iron and then to steel as the main material of ship construction. The estuaries profited by ready access to plates and beams of the new materials. The Clyde, for instance, could call upon the growing output of Lanarkshire. Belfast, unsupported by a local iron and steel industry, could import supplies with ease. The banks of the estuaries afforded level sites for shipyards, from which completed hulls could slide smoothly into calm and sheltered waters. An adequate depth of water was available, or could be achieved by dredging. Shipbuilding was well served by the parallel growth of a host of supporting industries; the manufacture of marine engines is an important example.

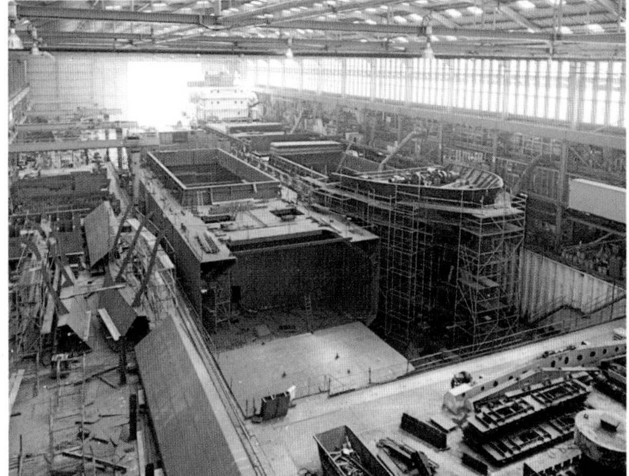

Fig. 218

Backed by these advantages, the U.K. became the world's leading shipbuilding nation. As recently as 1955, British yards completed more than 50 per cent of the world's new merchant shipping. Today, Britain's share of world production is less than 5 per cent.

Compared to her successful overseas competitors – Japan in particular – the U.K. shipbuilding industry has encountered serious difficulties. Shipyards are relatively small and have been slow to adapt to current conditions. Management has found it difficult to introduce the modern methods of construction used in other countries. Poor labour relations have been a further handicap. In addition, shipyard sites selected in the nineteenth century often fail to meet modern requirements. Few British yards have access to water that is deep and wide enough to receive the large vessels that are now in demand.

The U.K. industry is making vigorous efforts to overcome its difficulties. In recent years, with the aid of financial assistance from the government, considerable modernisation has taken place. Steel plates, for instance, are now commonly cut by computer-controlled flame-cutting techniques. Another example is seen in Fig. 218. In this fully enclosed shipyard, work can proceed whatever the weather. Problems posed by restricted sites have been overcome in ingenious ways. One yard builds large tankers in two halves which are welded together afloat.

Fig. 219

dock
major building
work area

1 = delivery wharf
2 = steel stockyard
3 = plate and section forming
4 = fabrication
5 = block assembly area
6 = electrical engineering
7 = woodwork
8 = blacksmith
9 = sheet metal
10 = paint
11 = engineering
12 = boilers
13 = marine engines
14 = computer
15 = stores
16 = transport
17 = offices

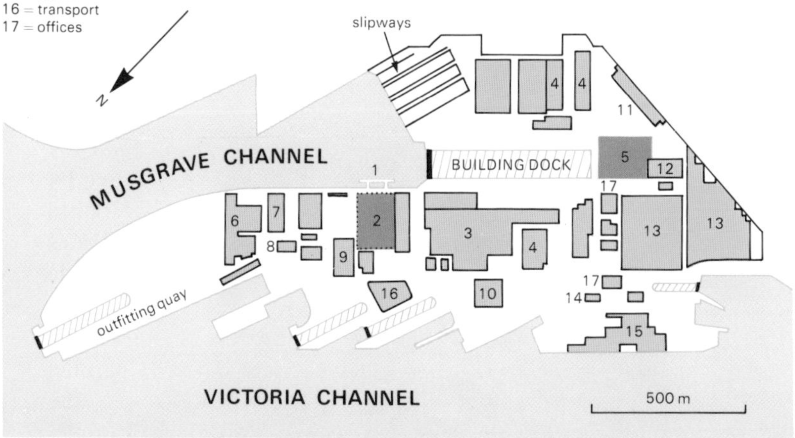

N
slipways
MUSGRAVE CHANNEL
BUILDING DOCK
outfitting quay
VICTORIA CHANNEL
500 m

Fig. 220

In the late 1960s, independent shipyards were merged into groups to bring about greater efficiency in production and marketing. With nationalisation, amalgamation is now complete.

One major yard that has been greatly modernised in recent years is that of Harland and Wolff. Its large, level site is viewed from the air in Fig. 220. The deep-water channels give access to Belfast Lough, and the built-up area of the Ulster capital can be glimpsed in the distance. The plan of the shipyard (Fig. 219) is keyed to indicate some of the facilities essential to modern shipbuilding.

Victoria Channel was once lined with busy slipways too small to hold the majority of ships now in demand. They have been abandoned, and the land converted to other uses. Four slipways remain on Musgrave Channel, but only two are now active. Today, the focus of shipbuilding operations is a massive building dock. It is 93 metres wide, 8.4 metres in depth and more than half a kilometre in length. It is large enough to permit the building of two 250000-tonne d.w.t. tankers at the same time. Should ever a vessel of a million tonnes d.w.t. be required, this dock gives Harland and Wolff the necessary construction capacity.

Ships bringing steel berth at the delivery wharf, and their cargoes are discharged into the adjoining stockyards. Girders and plates move on to the various processing shops. With the aid of modern techniques, they are speedily cut and shaped to the required dimensions. In the block assembly area, appropriate bits and pieces are joined together to make sections of considerable size. These are then moved to the dock where they are built up into hull and superstructure. The mobile bridge crane, seen in the background of Fig. 221, can lift sections of up to 840 tonnes and place them in position with absolute precision.

Ships are not launched in the traditional way, but are floated out into the Musgrave Channel. They are towed round to the outfitting quay. Here are added the diverse items which contribute to the finished vessel. Engines, boilers, and a wide range of other engineering products are made within the shipyard. An electrical engineering department provides such things as motors, generators and switchboards. Other necessary items are bought in from factories throughout the U.K.

If the shipbuilding industry has lost much of its former glory, it still makes a significant contribution to the national economy. Over 100000 people are directly employed in the building and repair of ships. A much larger number is indirectly supported, for shipbuilding is an *assembly* industry. It brings together the products of a whole range of other industries. The construction of a 250000-tonne d.w.t. tanker, for instance, needs 25000 tonnes of steel, 15000 litres of paint, and 100 kilometres of electric cable. The lengthy list of essential components ranges from radar to rope and from carpets to clocks. As many as 300 firms may contribute to the construction of a large modern vessel.

Fig. 221

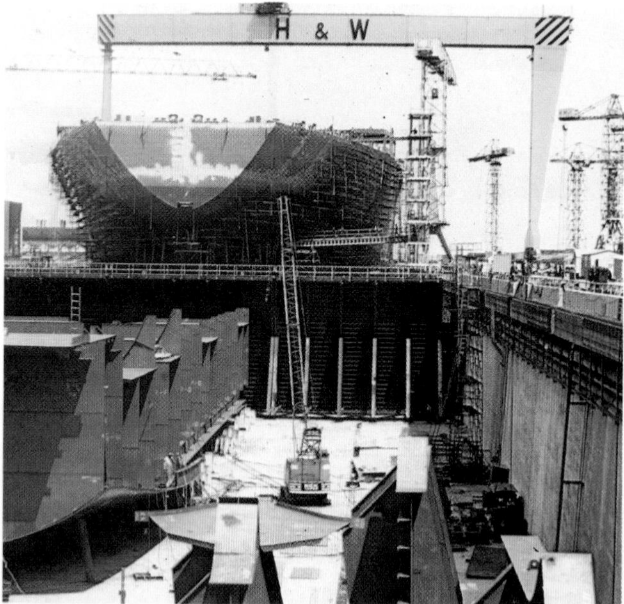

Motor vehicles

In 1861, James Starley, a self-taught inventor of genius, established a workshop in Coventry for the manufacture of his improved sewing-machine. The enterprise prospered. Later, with equal success, he turned to the manufacture of bicycles and tricycles. After the death of its founder, the family firm continued to develop. A nephew of the founder experimented with the new-fangled internal combustion engine. The trade name Rover, adopted for bicycles, was extended first to motor cycles and then, in 1904, to the motor car.

The Starley story is not unique. The motor vehicle industry owes much to its inventive pioneers. The names of many are still remembered through the firms they established: Hillman and Dennis rose from the ranks of the cycle manufacturers; Rolls-Royce and Austin had their origins in general engineering companies; and the familiar name of Leyland stems from the Lancashire town where, in the late nineteenth century, steam-powered goods vehicles were manufactured. Today, few of the pioneering firms retain their identity. Many have gone out of business. Others have merged into large, modern undertakings in order to gain the benefits of large-scale production. Leyland, for instance, Britain's largest manufacturer, produces vehicles bearing such famous names as Morris, Austin, Triumph, Jaguar, Rover and Daimler.

It was the West Midlands that nourished the industry's early development. In towns such as Birmingham and Coventry, skilled labour was available to man the workshops and small factories where the early cars were laboriously put together. Component parts in wide variety could readily be obtained in an area traditionally associated with metal-working industries. A central position within the country facilitated the distribution of completed vehicles.

Recent decades have seen the motor vehicle industry rise to a position of great importance in the industrial

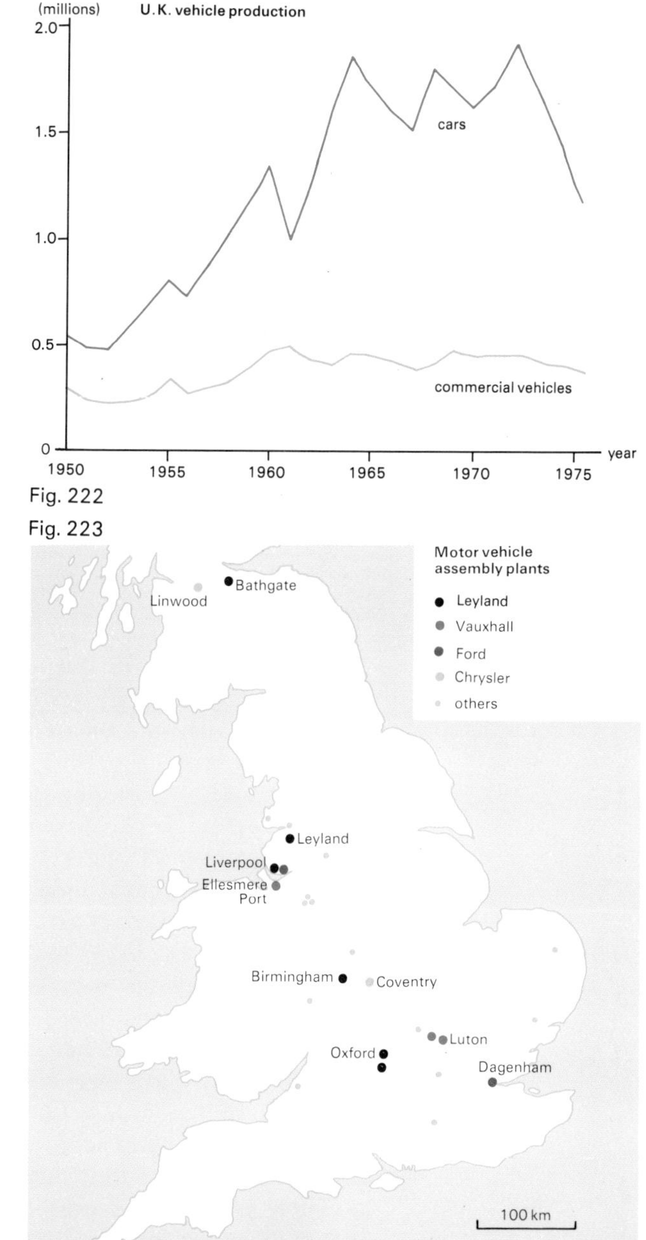

Fig. 222
Fig. 223

Fig. 224

life of the nation. Production figures for cars and commercial vehicles are graphed in Fig. 222. Annual output fluctuates in response to the economic climate, government taxation policies, and, more recently, the great increases in motoring costs. The 'big four' companies – Leyland, Ford, Chrysler and Vauxhall – together account for over 98 per cent of output. The industry makes a major contribution to Britain's balance of trade. In 1976, exports of cars, commercial vehicles and spare parts earned £1737 million in foreign currency. Like shipbuilding, the manufacture of motor vehicles is an assembly industry. Nearly half a million people are directly employed, but hundreds of thousands more work for firms who supply components. These include major enterprises, such as Lucas (electrical equipment) and Dunlop (tyres). In addition, more than 600 smaller firms deliver part of their output to the motor vehicle assembly plants. Their prosperity is closely linked to that of the motor industry.

Fig. 223 shows the distribution of motor vehicle assembly plants. The industry has expanded far beyond its important nucleus in the West Midlands. It has been attracted to south-east England by the presence of labour, a large market, and good facilities for export. Developments on Merseyside and in central Scotland date from the early 1960s, and were greatly influenced by government policy. Expansion was banned in the prosperous midlands and the south, but financial assistance was granted for the building and equipping of new factories in areas of high unemployment.

The Vauxhall company illustrates many characteristic features of the motor vehicle industry. In 1903, the first car to bear the familiar name rolled out of a little workshop in the Vauxhall district of London. After transfer to Luton in 1905, the firm prospered greatly, and in the 1930s branched out into truck manufacture at nearby Dunstable. Today, these two plants together employ nearly 20 000 people. Vauxhall's share of the 1960s expansion is viewed from the air in Fig. 224. This plant has a work force of 6000 and occupies a 160-hectare site near Ellesmere Port. In addition to motor vehicle production, it engineers a wide range of parts, many for delivery to Luton and Dunstable. As in all modern vehicle plants, production methods are highly mechanised and are becoming increasingly automated.

The average family car is made up of something like 25 000 separate parts. Ellesmere Port is where they are brought together and assembled into the finished product. Sheet steel is precisely pressed into the wide range of required shapes. Many mechanical components, engines and gearboxes, for instance, are made on the premises. Other parts are brought in from literally hundreds of other companies with factories in all parts of the country.

In putting together all the bits and pieces, intensive use is made of production-line techniques. In Fig. 225, engines sitting on a moving conveyor are nearing completion. A succession of workers have each made a

Fig. 225

Fig. 226

significant contribution. Similarly, it is on a conveyor that a jigsaw of pressings are welded together to form the rigid body shell. In Fig. 226, a car nears the end of the final assembly line. At various stations along the moving track, it has received engine, seats, headlamps, carpets and so on. Now it awaits its wheels. Soon it will roll off for testing and inspection. At two-minute intervals it will be followed by others.

Chemicals

The chemical industry has many faces. The more important may be identified with the aid of Fig. 227, which gives a glimpse of the varied interests of Imperial Chemical Industries Ltd. This company, familiar as I.C.I., dominates the British chemical industry. It operates nearly 150 factories and employs 132000 people. In the diagram, the red spots indicate the company's manufacturing divisions, blue its principal subsidiaries. Examples of the products of each are indicated. Some chemicals are familiar friends in home and garden. Others are the raw materials of manufactured products in wide variety. Still more play important roles in industrial processes. The products of the chemical industry make themselves useful in almost every walk of economic life.

Fig. 227 also illustrates the characteristic interdependence of the various sectors of the industry. The product of one plant is often the raw material of another. The Mond division, for instance, makes the dangerous paraquat, which is used in the herbicides manufactured by Plant Protection Ltd. The ammonia produced by the agricultural division is vital to four other divisions. When plants are far apart, the transport of these *intermediates* is often a complex undertaking. Chemicals are always on the move. Large quantities are shuttled about the country by road and rail. Pipelines are increasingly favoured for bulk supplies of liquids and gases. Links with foreign factories are forged by sea-going vessels.

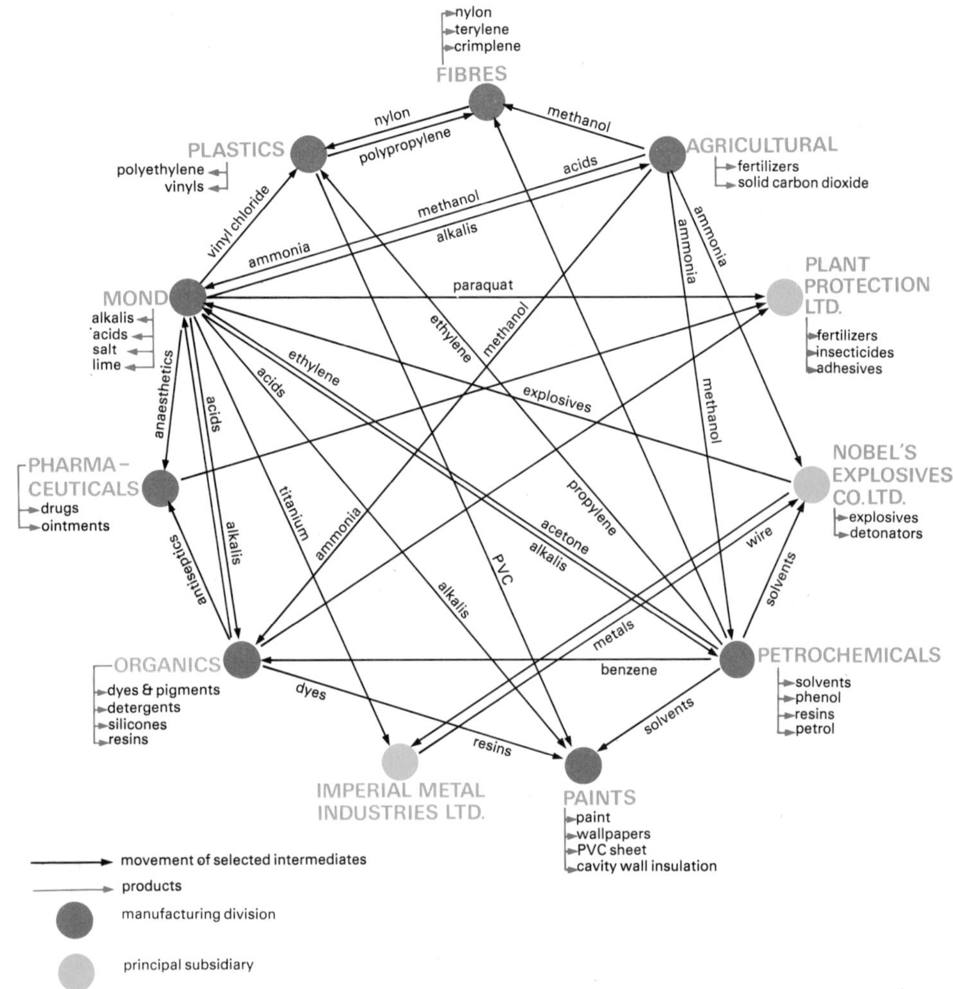

Fig. 227

The chemical industry has expanded greatly in the decades since the end of the Second World War. Discoveries made in research laboratories have been put into large-scale production. Many products now considered essential were unknown a few short years ago. The farmer, for instance, is much better equipped to nourish and protect his crops. The doctor and veterinary surgeon have the advantage of a much wider range of effective drugs. The petrochemical section of the industry has seen the greatest expansion. Chemicals obtained from petroleum are the basis of a host of new products, including plastics, detergents and synthetic fibres. Since the war, the chemical industry has expanded at a rate that is considerably higher than that of manufacturing industry. It is one of Britain's *growth* industries.

The industry is widely but unevenly distributed; northern industrial areas, the traditional centres of the industry, still show great concentrations. This is particularly true of north-west England, where Cheshire salt, Derbyshire limestone and the coal of south Lancashire may readily be assembled. The Mersey estuary is a convenient door for the import of other raw materials. Industries as varied as textiles, glass and soap provide a ready market for chemical products.

The distribution of the petrochemical sector of the industry reflects its source of raw material. Major plants are located close to oil refineries. In contrast, the pharmaceutical branch of the industry seeks the advantages of proximity to market and the availability of labour. Sites in south-east England are favoured for this reason.

The area mapped in Fig. 228 offers fine opportunities for chemical manufacture. Wide expanses of level land give suitable sites for large-scale enterprises. Road and rail communications are good, and a navigable estuary extends port facilities well inland. Some vital raw materials are close at hand. The southern edge of the Durham coalfield lies just a few kilometres north of the Tees. Salt and anhydrite are even nearer. Limestone can be quarried from the Pennines. Since 1973, potash has been available from Boulby mine (page 27). The pure water needed for many chemical processes can be obtained from reservoirs in the Pennines and Cleveland Hills, and the water for cooling purposes can be taken from the Tees.

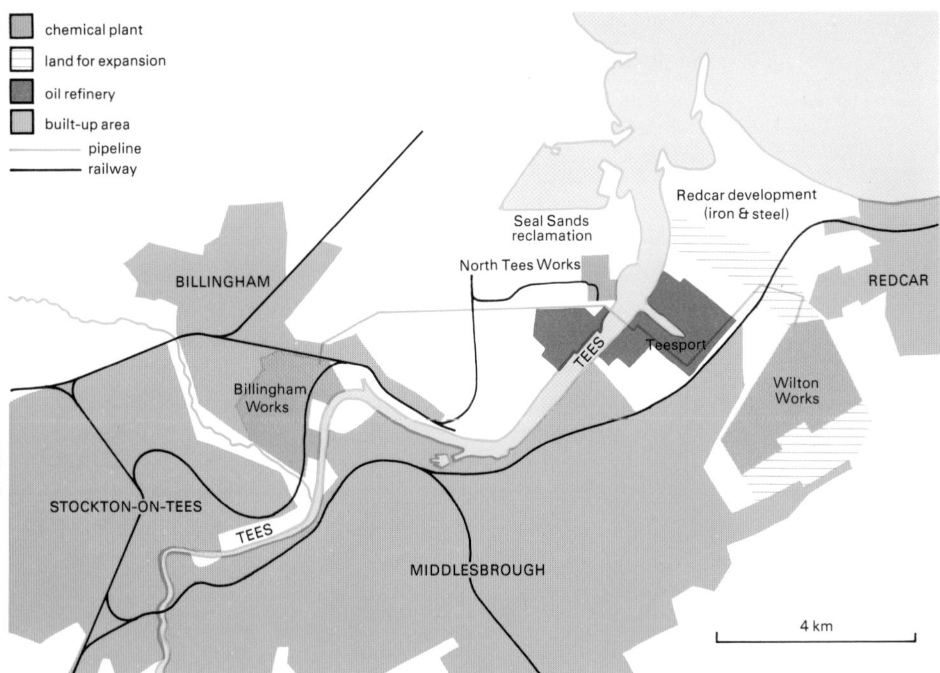

Fig. 228

These advantages have attracted many chemical plants to lower Teesside. The three largest, all part of I.C.I., are located and named on Fig. 228.

At Billingham, a plant established during the First World War for the manufacture of explosives was later converted to the production of sulphate of ammonia, which was much in demand as a fertilizer. For this the plant was well located; ammonia could be made by a process based on Durham coke, and sulphur could be derived from the anhydrite which lay deep in the rocks directly beneath the plant.

Billingham has grown enormously since the years of its modest start. It now occupies an area of over 400 hectares and employs 11 000 people. Early interests have been maintained and expanded. The plant is the world's largest producer of ammonia and dominates I.C.I.'s vast output of fertilizer. Frequent technical change is a feature of the chemical industry, and Billingham provides illustration. Ammonia is now made from natural gas. Sulphate of ammonia is no longer the basis of fertilizer production. Thus, coal and anhydrite, the availability of which stimulated early development, are now of no significance.

To its basic interests, Billingham has added a variety of other activities. It produces large quantities of such vital industrial chemicals as sulphuric and nitric acid, and contributes raw materials to the paint and dyestuffs industries. It also shares in the plastics industry. Much of its diverse output is used on site, but more is sold to other chemical plants at home and overseas. Export is eased by the opportunities offered by the navigable Tees. Billingham has private berths on the estuary, and additional facilities are available at Teesport. In similar fashion, the import of raw materials is made easier and cheaper.

The estuary also serves the other chemical plants on Teesside. Its waters are deep enough to accommodate loaded tankers of 80000 tonnes d.w.t. Crude oil is discharged into the Phillips-Imperial refinery and the North Tees works of I.C.I., where it is cracked into chemical feedstocks such as naphtha and benzene. These are passed on to the processing plants by pipeline.

In 1946, the Wilton site was agricultural land in close cultivation. Development has been rapid and Fig. 229 reveals a landscape of modern industry. 445 hectares of level land are swamped by fractionating columns, pipeways and buildings of all shapes and sizes. Wilton has its own 280 MW power-station fuelled by oil and waste industrial gases. Fig. 230 pictures just one tiny corner of the works. The intricate nature of modern chemical installations may readily be appreciated.

Five of I.C.I.'s manufacturing divisions operate plant within the Wilton site. The petrochemical division takes pride of place. It converts feedstocks received by pipeline into a wide range of chemicals. Ethylene is the most

Fig. 229

useful, being the basis of polyester fibres and plastics. Much of the ethylene is consumed at Wilton, which includes polythene and terylene among its manufactured output. A trans-Pennine pipeline takes ethylene gas to plastics factories in Lancashire, and in liquid form it is shipped to Rotterdam in refrigerated tankers.

Look again at Figs. 229 and 230. The construction of plant of this size and complexity involves the spending of vast amounts of money. The amount of capital invested is very large in relation to the number of people

Fig. 230

employed. Petrochemicals is an example of a *capital-intensive* industry.

Textiles

For centuries, man's basic need of cloth was met from local resources. Throughout Britain, in lonely farmhouse and urban workshop, spinning-wheels spun wool into the yarn which the hand-loom wove into cloth. By the eighteenth century, this domestic industry had achieved a degree of prominence in East Anglia, the Cotswolds and other areas where sheep rearing was important. As the Industrial Revolution brought mechanisation and power to manufacturing, textiles became highly localised on the flanks of the Pennines. Lancashire came to specialise in imported cotton while Yorkshire remained faithful and true to the traditional fibre, wool.

Lancashire

Rapid expansion of the Lancashire textile industry was nourished by a happy combination of favourable factors. The development of textile machinery was pioneered by Lancashire men. Their inventions found a convenient source of power in the swift streams which flowed in the youthful valleys of the Pennine fringe. The steam-engine liberated more abundant and more reliable power, and the need for fuel brought the industry down to the more open sites where coal could be cheaply obtained. Liverpool gave access to imported cotton, and man's ingenuity forged ever more efficient transport links between port and mill. The rain-soaked Pennines provided the large quantities of pure water needed by the finishing processes of bleaching, dyeing and printing. These processes also demanded bleach and dyestuffs which could be obtained from the chemical industry of the mid-Mersey area.

Industrial expansion brought rapid urban growth.

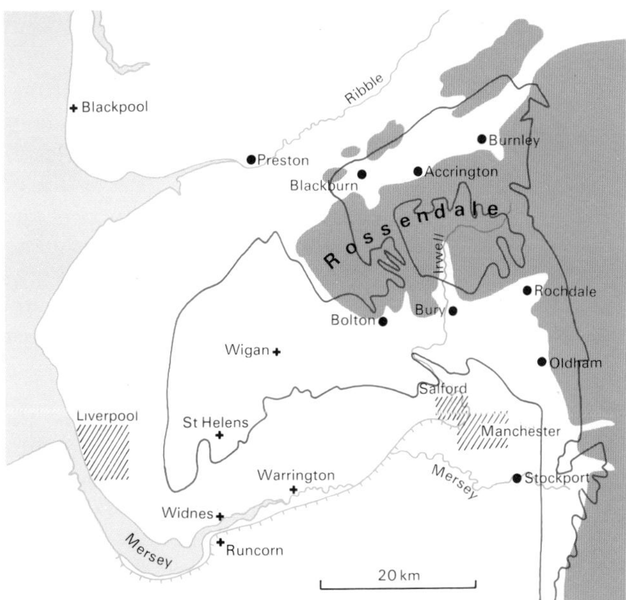

Fig. 231

Peaceful villages blossomed into thriving towns and many came to specialise in a particular process. In the arc of towns from Bolton to Stockport (Fig. 231), spinning was the dominant industry. North of Rossendale the weaving of cloth was more important. Finishing processes were concentrated in smaller towns in upland valleys where ample pure water was available. Manchester had little interest in manufacturing, but became important as the commercial and financial centre of the industry.

Fig. 232

Cotton textile industry: U.K.

	unit	1955	1960	1965	1970	1975
Looms	*thousands*	326.8	155.4	125.6	78.1	51.1
Cloth woven	*million metres*	2265.8	1746.6	1498.4	1218.5	909.3
Employment	*thousands*	281.6	213.6	158.9	109.6	79.4
Imports	*million m^2*	246.5	657.1	565.1	644.3	779.1
Exports	*million m^2*	576.8	316.5	254.9	256.1	252.3

The textile towns developed a characteristic urban landscape. Towns such as Bolton, Oldham and Rochdale were dominated by spinning-mills, often strung out along river or canal. Square, multi-storied buildings, with tall chimneys pointing skywards, the mills sat solidly amidst the close-packed rows of terraced houses which accommodated the workforce. Coal-mine winding-gear often rose above the roof-tops as a reminder of the industry's motive power. The towns north of Rossendale shared a similar landscape, but the long, low weaving 'sheds' were more common than the tall spinning-mill.

The industry continued to expand until the early years of this century. The peak of its prosperity came in 1912. Lancashire looms satisfied home demand and found wide overseas markets, especially in the hot climates of the Far East and Africa. British production of cotton cloth totalled 7358 million linear metres, which represented 25 per cent of world production. 1912 was a

Fibres used in Lancashire Circles proportional to cloth production

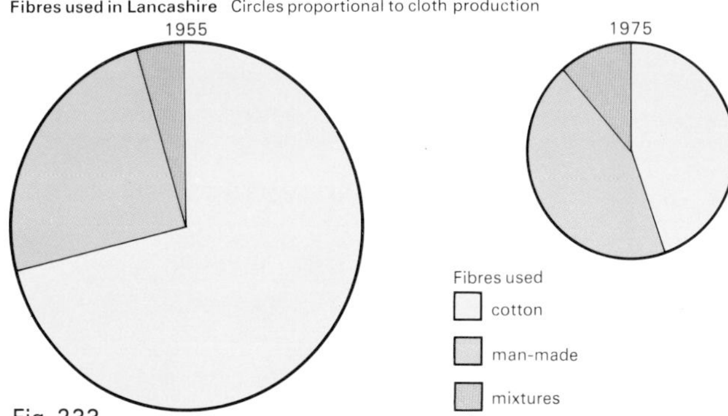

Fig. 233

watershed: the industry has since had its ups and downs, but the trend is one of steep decline. Exports were the first to suffer. One by one, foreign countries were able to meet their domestic requirements and the more successful were able to capture markets traditionally supplied from Lancashire. In recent years the position has become even more serious (Figs. 232 and 233). The home market is now under attack from cheaper foreign cloth

Fig. 234

and clothing. Imports of cloth are now three times greater than exports. Noisy mills and clattering sheds fall silent when no customers can be found for their output. Over the years hundreds of mills have been closed. Most of those that remain have been merged into large groups, such as that controlled by Courtaulds Ltd., in order to rationalise production. Much capital has been invested in new machinery. Examine, for instance, the modern loom pictured in Fig. 234. The yarn is drawn from the spool at the side of the loom and projected across by water jet, 380 times per minute. The cloth is drawn under the floor, heated to expel excess water, and wound into a roll.

In the Lancashire textile industry, cotton once was king. Today, it shares the throne with a variety of man-made fibres (Fig. 233). For many purposes cotton cloth has given way to fabrics woven wholly or in part from these new yarns. Shirts and sheets, for instance, are now commonly made from nylon or from terylene/cotton mixtures.

Man-made fibres are obtained from a variety of raw materials. Rayon, for instance, has its origin in wood-pulp. Terylene, derived from oil, is an example of the growing range of *synthetics* produced by the chemical industry. Fig. 235 illustrates the widespread distribution of man-made fibre production. It is clear that the traditional cotton districts have little attraction for this twentieth-century industry; the work-force does not need the skills of the cotton-spinner and a coalfield location has little attraction for an industry powered by electricity. Financial inducements offered by governments are significant locational factors.

Today, Lancashire retains only a faint shadow of its former textile glory. The contraction of the industry has brought serious human problems. Mill closures put the work-force out of work, and Lancashire towns have long known the hardships brought by a high level of unemployment. In recent years, however, the problem has been eased by the expansion of other industries.

Fig. 235

Some of these have long been established in the region. Engineering, which received an early stimulus with the need for textile and other machinery, has branched and blossomed. It is now Lancashire's most important industry. Paper and chemicals are other examples. In addition, a range of new industries has been established. Factors which have proved attractive include the availability of labour, and good communications. Governments, both local and national, extend financial assistance, and develop estates of new factories. Vacant mills and sheds have proved attractive to many firms; ready equipped with all necessary services, they make good cheap industrial accommodation. Today, once-silent mills echo to the noise of new occupants: engineering, clothing and plastics are common examples. Some mills serve as warehouses for mail-order firms. Others have been made into industrial 'flats' and meet the needs of a number of separate firms.

Urban landscapes are also changing. Many of the older mills have been demolished. The tall chimneys of those that remain no longer belch smoke into the atmosphere, for electricity is now the power employed. Superfluous canals and railways have been abandoned, and new roads and motorways built. Much nineteenth-century housing has been swept away and replaced by spacious new housing estates and tall towers of flats which often achieve vertical dominance in the urban landscape. In town centres, smoke-grimed buildings have been cleaned, or replaced by sparkling shopping precincts and blocks of offices. The Lancashire mill town is earning a new and more favourable image. Leigh is seen in Fig. 236.

Yorkshire

The Pennine watershed sends small, swift streams tumbling eastwards. These streams, like their westward-flowing counterparts, were significant in the early growth of textile industries. Rising on high moorlands of Millstone Grit, they provided the constant and abundant

Fig. 236

supply of pure, soft water needed to wash and scour away the dirt and grease from natural fleece. Moreover, when the new ideas of mechanised production spread over the Pennines and were adapted to the spinning and weaving of wool, these same streams provided the motive power. Wool ceased to be a domestic industry. It slowly moved from cottage and farmhouse to new mills on the banks of rivers such as the Calder and its tributaries. Later, when steam-power replaced stream-power, an ample supply of cheap fuel was available from the exposed Coal Measures.

The steady expansion of the industry brought a growing appetite for raw materials. Supplies available from the scattered flocks of hardy sheep that grazed the bleak Pennine moorlands soon became inadequate. Raw wool of superior quality was imported in increasing quantities from Australia, New Zealand and elsewhere, mainly through the port of London. Transport facilities were developed to meet the industrial needs of the area. Early canals were soon joined by an intricate network of railways and roads.

The rise and prosperity of wool and its associated industries prompted rapid urban growth which quickly turned small rural settlements into thriving towns.

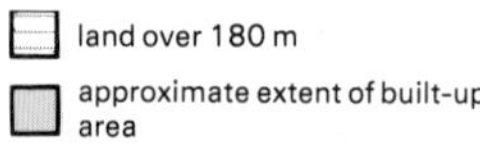

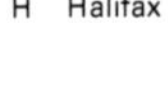

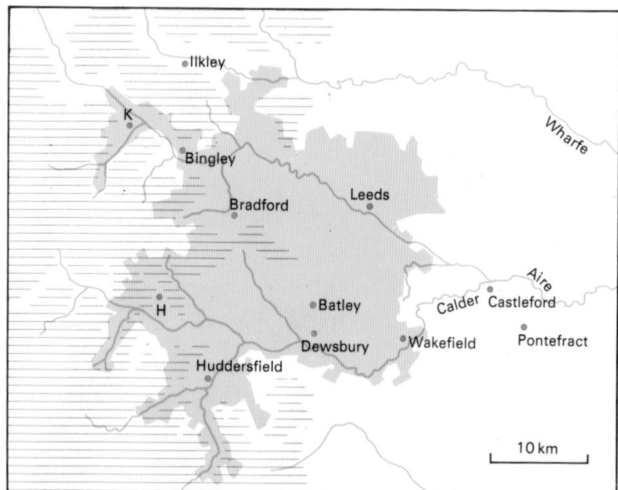

Fig. 237

Bradford, Huddersfield and Halifax are large examples, located on Fig. 237. Unlike the Lancashire textile centres, they show no specialisation by process; spinning, weaving, dyeing and finishing are often carried on in the same mill. There is, however, a certain degree of specialisation in the type of cloth produced. Towns in the north-west take pride in the conversion of long, silky fibres into high-quality worsteds. Elsewhere, woollen cloths of less distinguished qualities are relatively more important. The poorest fabrics, known as 'shoddy', are made principally in Batley and Dewsbury from waste wool and recycled clothing.

Other industries were encouraged by the growth of wool manufacture. Dyestuffs, and chemicals in general, are examples. So, too, is the engineering of textile and other machinery. Halifax branched out with carpets and the ready-made clothing industry became important in Leeds.

Urban growth spread along the valleys and linked town to town with thick ribbons of buildings. West Yorkshire, with a population of over 2 million, is one of Britain's conurbations. The extent of the built-up area is indicated in Fig. 237. Bradford assumed the commercial leadership of the wool textile industry, but Leeds, on the banks of the Aire, is the largest urban centre. The Aire drains large areas of limestone, and its waters, made hard by dissolved calcium carbonate, is unsuited to woollen manufacture. Hence, Leeds has played little part in the traditional industry. Well served by waterways, it developed its own wide range of industries and has established its position as the regional capital.

Fig. 238

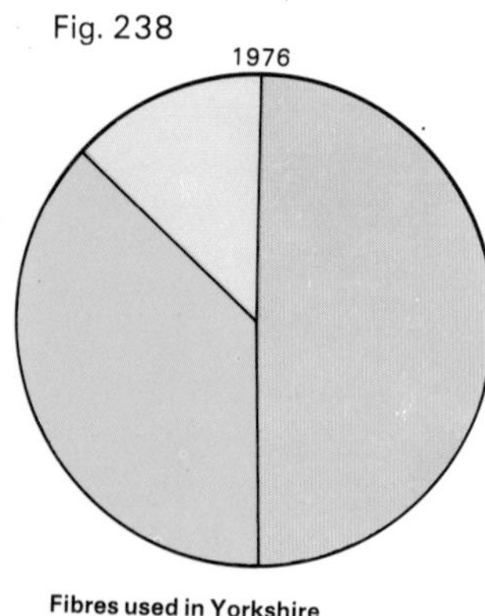

Fibres used in Yorkshire

- new wool
- man-made fibres
- others

In Yorkshire, as in Lancashire, the textile industry responds to changing circumstances. Chemical plants in the U.K., rather than sheep stations in the antipodes, are now the main source of raw material. Fig. 238 illustrates the impact of man-made fibres on the British wool textile industry. A decline in output and employment is revealed in Fig. 239. Many mills have been closed or converted to other uses (Fig. 240). Those remaining are now commonly merged into groups which allow individual mills to gain the economies of specialisation in a particular process or type of cloth.

Fig. 239
Wool textile industry: U.K.

	unit	*1950*	*1955*	*1960*	*1965*	*1970*	*1975*
Fabric woven	*million* m^2	376.5	342.8	306.9	269.9	215.2	151.4
Employment	*thousands*	169.3	159.6	152.6	126.3	92.4	57.4

In spite of its decline, wool is still an important part of the varied industrial structure of West Yorkshire. The factors which favoured its early growth are no longer of any significance: steam has given way to electricity; road vehicles meet present transport needs; and modern detergents have made natural soft water less vital. The traditional location now offers other advantages. These include a pool of skilled labour, proximity to markets such as the ready-made clothing industry, and the local presence of commercial and technical services. West Yorkshire continues to provide Britain with over 80 per cent of her wool and wool-mixture cloth.

Light industry

Fig. 240

Industry is responsible for the production of manufactured goods in immense variety. The majority are the concern of *light* industry. This important branch of manufacturing is exceedingly diverse. Generalisations are difficult but certain common characteristics may be recognised. Factories are normally of modest size and served by road transport. Raw materials are usually obtained from other factories, and used in limited quantities. Finished products are small in volume and easily and cheaply transported. They may be consumer goods for the general public or may be delivered to other firms for inclusion in more complex products. For light industry, the availability of labour and proximity to market are the chief factors influencing location. It is therefore attracted to sites in or near large urban areas.

Fig. 241

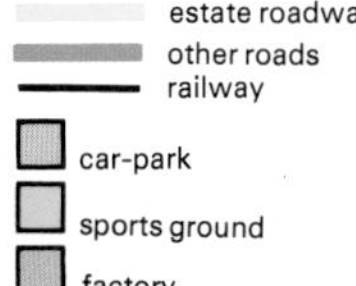

Fig. 242

Light industry may be carried on in all manner of buildings, but is increasingly housed in smart new factories of attractive design. Power is by electricity and there are no waste products to pollute the atmosphere or mar the landscape, and so light industry is often permitted in predominately residential areas. Increasingly it is gathered together in *industrial estates*, examples of which may now be found in or near most urban centres.

Fig. 243

Hartlepool Industrial Estate Company	*Floor area (m^2)*	*Product*
Addressograph/Multigraph Ltd.	2557	office machinery
Agresin Ltd.	2445	concrete products
Ambrose Shardlow & Co. Ltd.	3432	engine crankshafts
Automotive Products Ltd.	5085	car components
Blair Knitwear Ltd.	4864	knitwear
Clo-Far Ltd.	2679	fireplace surrounds
Decoflex Ltd.	4790	lithography and printing
Expanded Metal Co. Ltd.	3739	steel reinforcement
G.E.C./A.E.I. Ltd.	43 388	telephone exchange equipment
Kismet Ltd.	8680	lubricating equipment
Marbourn Ltd.	3965	lighting equipment
Polypac (Hartlepool) Ltd.	2241	hydraulic sealing systems
R.W. Instrumentation & Controls Ltd.	1245	control panels
Reed Corrugated Cases Ltd.	25 965	cardboard boxes and packaging
Remploy Ltd.	2925	light assembly work
Rydgeway Group Ltd.	1373	plastic mouldings
United Drapery Stores Ltd.	11 749	multiple tailoring

Hartlepool Industrial Estate–employment by industry

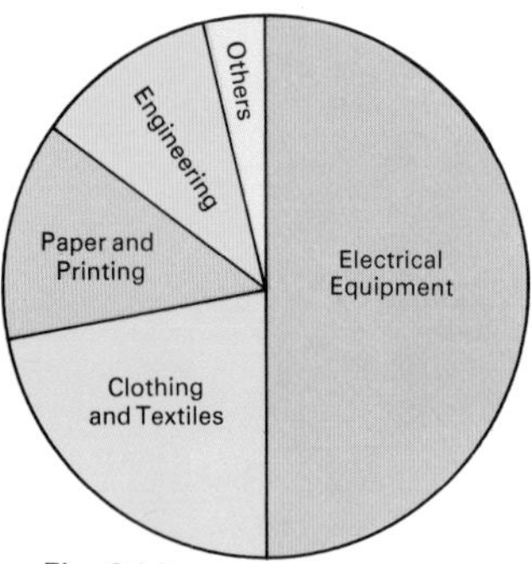

Fig. 244

The example illustrated by Figs. 241 and 242 is located at Hartlepool in Cleveland. Development began in 1945 on a site of 40 hectares close to docks and railway and within easy reach of the A1 route from London to Edinburgh. Today, 17 firms, some in multiple premises, occupy a total of 131 000 square metres of factory space. Fig. 243 illustrates the variation in factory size and the diversity of product that are characteristic features of industrial estates. Total employment afforded by the estate is approximately 7000. Fig. 244 shows how this figure is distributed among major industrial groups.

Shifting industrial distribution

In recent decades the rate of industrial expansion has been uneven. North-east England, central Scotland and other coalfield areas, which prospered in the nineteenth and early twentieth centuries, record lower than average growth. Their coal and railways are less of an advantage in an age of electricity and road transport. Old established industries such as coal-mining, shipbuilding and cotton are in decline. The industrial landscapes which developed in the nineteenth century are often congested and unattractive. Access to markets and labour are now the factors which have the greatest influence on the location of industry. Today, it is a lowland triangle widening south-eastwards from Manchester, through the English midlands to the Channel coast, that offers the greatest attractions. This area enjoys a rate of industrial growth that is above the national average. It has provided sites for many of the industries which have been born or expanded since the end of the Second World War. Important examples are pharmaceuticals, electronics, scientific instruments and business machines. London and the south-east have proved particularly attractive. The computer industry, for instance, is heavily concentrated in the vicinity of the capital.

Fig. 245

Fig. 245 shows the 'standard regions' into which the country is divided for purposes of economic planning. West Midlands, East Midlands and South-East regions generally offer superior employment opportunities and attract migrants from other parts of Britain. Industrialists find greater opportunities for investments in these favoured regions. This slow concentration of capital and population is often described as the 'drift to the south'. It has contributed to problems commonly found in these relatively prosperous regions. Examples include traffic congestion, urban sprawl, increased pressure on housing, and difficulty in maintaining public services such as transport and waste disposal.

Peripheral regions – the North, Wales and Scotland, for instance – suffer a relative loss of population through migration, and it is often the skilled who move away. In spite of this migration, unemployment often remains stubbornly high. With lower than average prosperity, these regions are ill equipped to cope with the problems of sub-standard housing, damaged landscapes, and other legacies of nineteenth-century growth.

The role of Government

Regional contrasts in prosperity first became apparent in the period between the First and Second World Wars. It was painfully demonstrated in the economically difficult years of the 1930s when, in some coalfield areas, more than 40 per cent of the working population was unemployed for long periods. In parts of north-east England, the figure was as high as 80 per cent. Governments have since tried to achieve a more even spread of prosperity in order to avoid the social hardships and wastage of manpower that are the result of high levels of unemployment.

Fig. 246

One of the main ways in which governments have endeavoured to achieve this aim is by influencing the location of new industry. In this, financial inducements have proved effective. Examine Fig. 246. In the 'assisted areas', which cover the whole country except for the midlands and the south, new enterprises may qualify for financial assistance. This is greatest in the 'special development areas', and least in the 'intermediate areas'. The Government of Northern Ireland has separate powers to attract industry, and offers special incentives.

Government support takes various forms. Consider the case of a company wishing to establish a factory in a development area. Part of the costs of construction may be claimed from the government. Loans at low rates of interest are available for the purchase of essential machinery. By its presence in a development area, the company will enjoy lower labour costs, for the government pays a premium for each worker employed. Extra assistance is granted if the company is transferring its operations from a prosperous region. Together, these inducements are very attractive, and many firms have taken advantage of them.

Through the English Industrial Estates Corporation, and its Scottish and Welsh equivalents, the government exerts further influence on industrial location. Efforts are concentrated in areas of greatest need, such as north-east England. Team Valley, Gateshead, established in 1936, was the first government-financed industrial estate and now accommodates over 100 firms giving employment to more than 19000 people. Other estates, Hartlepool, for instance (page 126), are of more recent foundation and on a smaller scale. Often, new factories stand in groups of two or three, or even on individual sites. These estates and sites offer the financial advantages mentioned in the previous paragraph. In addition, factory premises may be available rent free for two years. The corporation builds factories of standard designs in advance of requirements. These 'advance' factories, ready for immediate occupation, prove most attractive when a firm is preparing to set up or expand its business.

It must be stressed that not all industrial estates have been inspired by central government. Local authorities have been active in this field, and many estates, in all parts of the country, have been developed by private enterprise.

The motor vehicle industry (page 115) and aluminium smelting (page 111) have already been quoted as examples of the influence of government policy on the location of industry. The small factory pictured in Fig. 247 provides more homely illustration.

In 1966, Coutant Electronics Ltd. were denied permission to expand their works in Reading, and the establishment of a branch factory became necessary. Ilfracombe, on the north coast of Devon, was the site eventually chosen. It lay in the assisted area closest to Reading, and qualified for the financial assistance offered by the government. A suitable 'advance' factory with a floor area of 450 square metres was ready and waiting. Ilfracombe and district offered labour of the type required. Electronics is a good example of modern light industry. Apart from small quantities of sheet metal, aluminium extrusions and copper wire, the raw materials used in the factory are manufactured components. Finished products, mainly power supply units and transformers for the computer and telecommunications industries, are distributed to all parts of the home market, and some are exported, mainly to France and Germany. Transport costs are only a tiny fraction of total costs, and so Ilfracombe's rather remote situation has not proved to be a disadvantage of any significance. The factory has prospered. It has been extended to more than five times its original floor area, and now gives employment to 240 people.

Efforts to improve employment prospects in the regions are not restricted to manufacturing. Service industries may qualify for financial aid if they bring new jobs to an assisted area. The government practises what it preaches; branches of the Civil Service and government agencies are transferred to, or established in these areas. National Giro, for instance, has its home in Bootle (Merseyside) and Premium Bond prizes are distributed from Lytham St. Annes on the coast of Lancashire.

Government efforts have met with considerable success. It is estimated that well over a million jobs have been steered to areas of economic difficulty. South Wales is one of the areas to benefit. Once, the region's prosperity was largely dependent on coal and steel. Both were sensitive to economic conditions. Times of depression brought high levels of unemployment. This problem has been eased by the post-war creation of a new and more diverse industrial structure. A handful of examples, located on Fig. 248 will serve as illustration. Pontypool is now an important producer of nylon. Hoover Ltd. make washing machines at Merthyr Tydfil and Dowlais. Oil refining has expanded at Llandarcy, and components for the motor car industry are manufactured on a large scale at Cardiff, Llanelli and Bargoed. The new Royal Mint is at Llantrisant, and the Department of the Environment's Driver and Vehicle Licensing Centre

Fig. 247

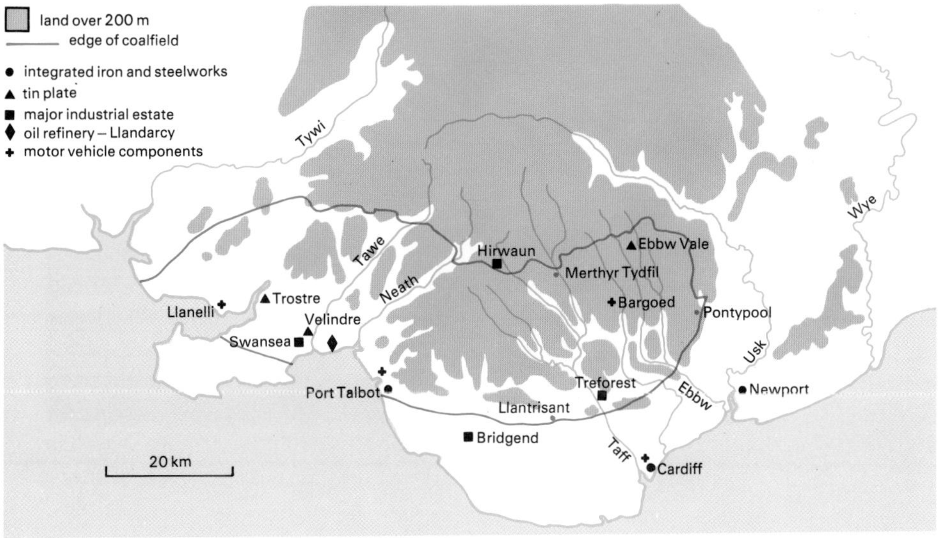

Fig. 248

is at Swansea. Large modern industrial estates have been established at Bridgend, Treforest, Hirwaun and Fforestfach (Swansea). These and many smaller estates have given South Wales an interest in such diverse industries as light engineering, plastics, clothing, toys and pharmaceuticals.

8 Urban Britain

Chapter 8

Loppington

By no stretch of the imagination may Loppington be described as a town, but it is a useful starting-point nevertheless. Strung out along the B4397, 4 kilometres west of Wem (Fig. 249) in rural north Salop, the village has a population of approximately 300. Its buildings are of varied age and architecture. This may be appreciated from Fig. 250, which looks towards the weathered tower of the parish church. Loppington now has its quota of residents who work in urban settlements that lie within daily travelling distance, but the link with the land is still strong. Farms are included in the main string of buildings. A firm of agricultural contractors has its base in the village. Fig. 251 emphasises the farming connection.

Fig. 249

land over 750 m

national boundary

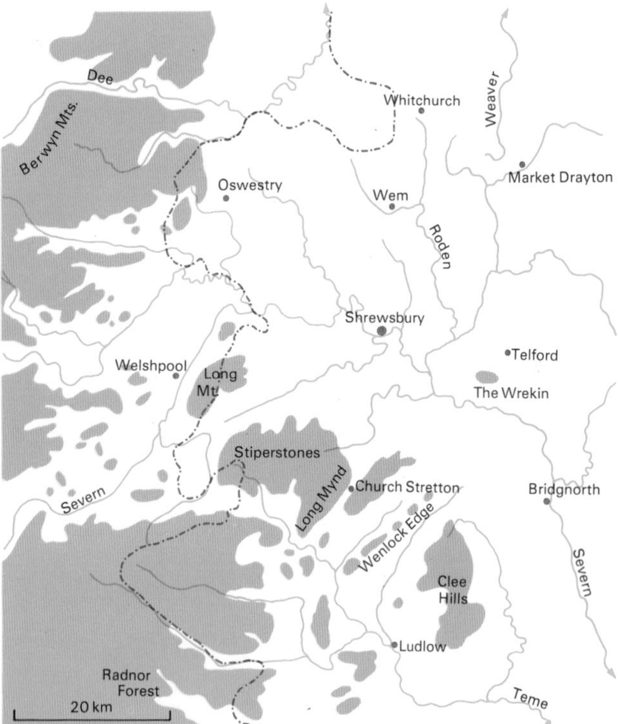

Fig. 250

Loppington provides services for its own inhabitants and those of nearby hamlets and farms. It is a *central place* but one of lowly rank. The population of the area it serves is too small to support more than a very limited number of services. They are quickly listed. The village school has about 40 pupils of primary age. They buy their sweets and ice lollies at the village store, which is also the sub post-office. More adult refreshment is available at two public houses. A garage repairs motor cars and agricultural machinery, but sells no petrol. For

Fig. 251

other needs, the population of Loppington must look beyond their village to larger settlements. It is to the town of Wem that they journey most often.

Wem

Wem is a small town of considerable antiquity. It merited a substantial mention in the Domesday Book of 1086. An earthen mound behind the parish church marks the site of a twelfth-century castle, and an inconvenient kink in the High Street reflects the line of the former moat. The privilege of a weekly market was granted by King John in 1205. The site of the mill has been in continuous occupation for more than 800 years. Over the centuries, Wem has slowly expanded beyond its original nucleus on the north bank of the placid River Roden. The present extent of the built-up area is indicated in Fig. 252.

Fig. 252

approximate extent of built-up area
school
church or chapel
1 Fire Station
2 Town Hall
3 Post Office
4 Library
5 District Council offices
principal thoroughfare
High Street
railway
site of castle

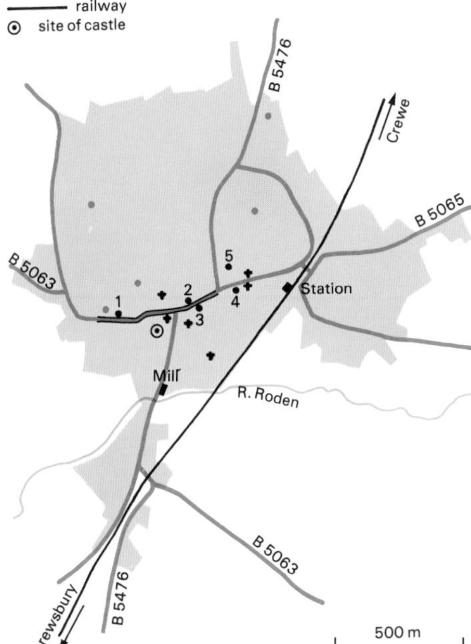

Fig. 253

Wem has a population of 3400. To this may be added the people who live in the surrounding area. The total gives Wem considerable importance as a central place. The town is able to support a wide range of services. Most are to be found in the High Street (Fig. 253) which is the town's short commercial artery. A quick walk along this ancient thoroughfare gives a count of seven shops that specialise in clothing. There are six butchers and five grocers. Tobacconists, antiques, shoes, greengrocers, electrical equipment and chemists each have two representatives. There are also shops for the sale of fish, ironmongery, flowers, stationery, soft furnishing, paint and wallpaper, fancy goods, and fish and chips. To this list may be added three public houses, two garages, a café, a snack bar, a dry-cleaners, two barbers and two hairdressing salons. Professional services are also well represented on the High Street. They include branches of two banks and the offices of insurance brokers, solicitors, estate agents, opticians and accountants. Other professional services are more widely distributed around the town. Examples include doctors, dentists and veterinary surgeons. Showing a similar distribution are plumbers, electricians, decorators and joiners.

Wem is not large enough to support a cinema but films are screened every Monday in the Town Hall, which is also available for various social functions. The town has a swimming-pool, and active sports and social clubs.

The North Shropshire District Council, which has major responsibilities for housing, planning and public health, has its headquarters in Wem. Its offices are also used for sittings of the Magistrates' Court, meetings of Wem Town Council and registrations of matrimony. Local government gives employment to nearly 300 people.

Wem's role as an agricultural market is no longer of any significance. With improvements in transport, this function has been lost to neighbouring towns which enjoy a better command of important routes. The site of the livestock market is now a car-park. The traditional retail market has shrunk to the handful of stalls which are assembled each Thursday in the Town Hall.

Manufacturing, a function of virtually all towns, is weakly represented in Wem. Industry had its origins in the produce and needs of the surrounding farmland, but these links have faded. Tanning, malting and cheese making have died out, the last as recently as 1976. The brewery, with a history that goes back more than 400 years, now looks far afield for its raw materials. Spent grain, however, is sold to local farmers as cattle food. The old mill is one of two small enterprises which manufacture a range of animal feeding stuffs. Locally grown grain is included in a long list of raw materials. Baking materials and farm buildings are other items produced in the town, but the largest undertaking is concerned with saw-milling and timber products. The site and buildings of a wartime ordnance depot to the north-east of the town are slowly being converted into an industrial estate. A handful of modest enterprises has been established. Their interests include seed preparation, joinery, scrap-metal and tyre remoulds.

Fig. 254

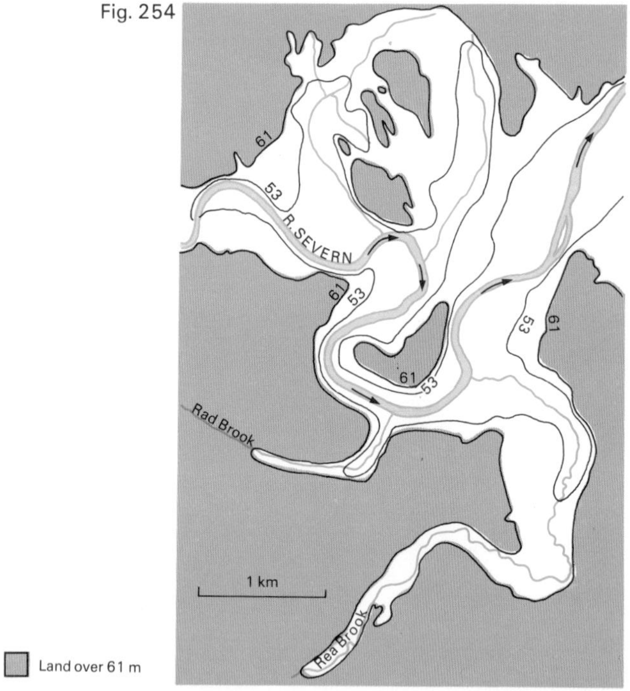

Land over 61 m

Industry plays a minor role in the life of the town. It gives employment to fewer people than local government. Wem's importance lies in the services it provides. These are available in variety, and basic needs are adequately catered for. There are, however, services which Wem does not provide. There is no hospital. You will look in vain for a Job Centre, a branch of F. W. Woolworth, an Electricity Board showroom, or a specialist bookshop. You will be unable to commission an architect or hire a private detective. Services such as these have a large *threshold*. They need the support of a population greater than that which Wem can command. They are available in central places of higher rank. Shrewsbury is 20 kilometres to the south.

Shrewsbury

After leaving the hills of Wales, the River Severn loops eastwards in a series of wide meanders. One of these has proved to be of great significance. It nurtured the growth of Shrewsbury.

The site is mapped in Fig. 254. Within the tight-necked meander, the ground rises more than 20 metres above the level of the river. Steep on the east, the land falls more gently to the south and west, where the lowest levels suffer the risk of flooding. The Severn, here joined by minor streams, is deep, but fords, then bridges, gave access to the meander core which offered obvious defensive advantages. In former times, the river also offered modest opportunities for fishing and transport.

In occupation of this site, Celts gave way to Saxons before control passed to the Normans in the eleventh century. It was the Normans who reinforced the defensive opportunities by sealing off the neck of the meander

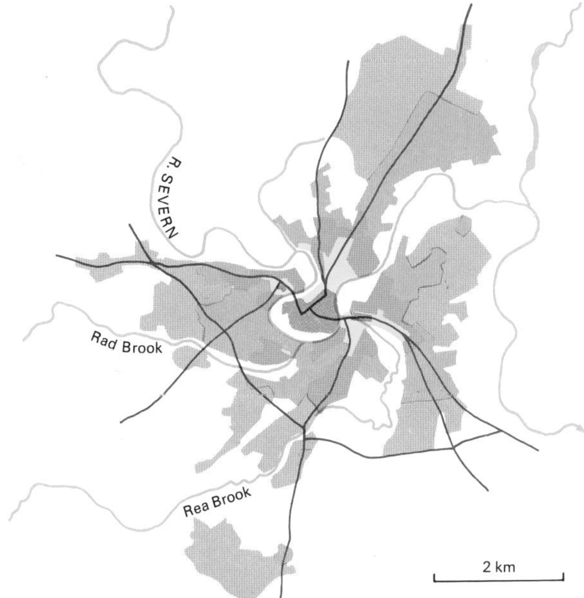

Fig. 255

with a stout castle. In the thirteenth century, the town was encircled by a tall wall. Defence was a vital consideration in view of proximity of the turbulent border with Wales. In later and more peaceful times, Shrewsbury's situation (Fig. 249, page 130) became an advantage rather than a liability. Encouraged by a focus of land routes on bridges over the navigable Severn, the town developed into a market centre for a wide area of productive farmland. In particular, the medieval trade in Welsh cloth brought wealth and prosperity. This trade declined and died, but with social and administrative leadership of the county of Shropshire (now Salop), and the later development of industry, the town has retained its importance.

At its heart, Shrewsbury retains many reminders of its long history. Remnants exist of castle and walls. Ancient parish churches and fine examples of sixteenth-century domestic architecture rise from an intricate pattern of narrow thoroughfares and passages. Even the street names have an air of antiquity. Shoplatch, Mardol, Wyle Cop and Dogpole are intriguing examples. Market Square, Fish Street, and Butcher Row speak of medieval business activities.

From its small nucleus, Shrewsbury was slow to expand. With the exception of tiny suburbs which developed over the bridges, the town was for centuries confined within the embracing arms of its meander. Stages of growth are indicated in Fig. 255, and the importance of the twentieth century will be appreciated. Outward expansion was influenced by the nature of the site. The flood-prone meadows of the Severn were avoided by housing and adapted for recreational purposes. Tributary streams imposed similar restrictions but on a smaller scale. The main routes were favoured arteries of expansion and the undulating land to the south and west was steadily colonised by high-quality housing, and old villages were engulfed in the process. The route to the north, unhampered by bridges, had a further incentive to growth. Factories were established along the line of canal, railway and road, and this is now Shrewsbury's main industrial district. Engineering is particularly well represented, and the largest enterprise is the Rolls-Royce plant for the manufacture of diesel engines. Industry and associated housing have taken Shrewsbury almost to the site of the 1403 battle where Henry IV was victor.

Shrewsbury, with a population of 83 900, is a central place of high station. Aided by the lines of communication seen in Fig. 256, it is well placed to serve a wide area. The services available in Wem are here represented in greater abundance and variety. There are others which thrive on Shrewsbury's larger and more populous sphere of influence. Shopping facilities are an obvious example. The population served by Shrewsbury is large enough to support department and chain stores which need a large threshold in order to survive. The same is true of specialist shops dealing in such things as books, jewellery, sewing-machines and sports equipment.

Selected services

- ■ hospital
- ▲ tertiary education
- ● 1 livestock market
  - 2 agricultural show ground
  - 3 fire station
  - 4 Divisional H.Q. West Mercia police
  - 5 Shrewsbury Town F.C.
  - 6 government offices
  - 7 ambulance station
  - 8 Shirehall
  - 9 Guildhall
- railway station
- bus station
- built-up area
- A road
- B road
- railway

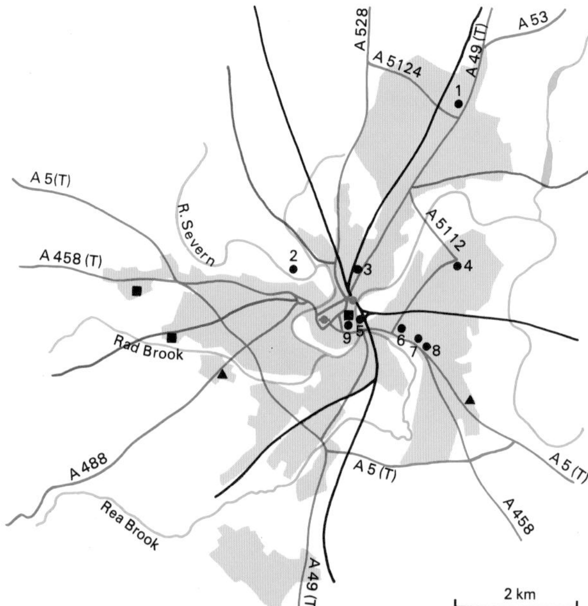

Fig. 256

Administration is an important function of Shrewsbury. District and County Councils have headquarters in the old Guildhall and new Shirehall respectively. Branches of central government departments and agencies, including Inland Revenue, Customs and Excise, and Ordnance Survey, have offices in the town. Administration in the private sector is represented by the regional headquarters of banks, building societies and insurance companies.

Other examples from a long list of available services may be briefly mentioned. Town and district are well served by hospitals, and Shrewsbury is the seat of Crown, County and Magistrates' Courts. Tertiary education is represented by technical, art and domestic science colleges. Shrewsbury maintains its long-established links with agriculture; the Tuesday cattle market is now held on the northern edge of the town in a new complex complete with abattoir, and Shrewsbury is the annual host to the Shropshire and West Midlands agricultural show. Entertainment facilities include a cinema, bingo hall, and the old music hall, which now stages such diverse attractions as orchestral concerts, variety shows and all-in wrestling.

Services are to be found throughout the town. Those meeting daily needs are dispersed in residential districts. Examples of some others with wider appeal are located on Fig. 256. The great majority, however, are concentrated within the meander. Old Shrewsbury, the focus of routes, has largely lost its residential function and become the *central business district*, where shops and offices are predominant. Ireland's Mansion (Fig. 257) which dates from about 1580, is now occupied by the

Fig. 257

Fig. 258

Westminster Bank. Form as well as function is subject to change. Redevelopment brings new architectural styles to an ancient city. Modern stores, shops and offices occupy the site of the old cattle market. Multi-storey car-parks relieve congestion in medieval streets ill-suited to modern needs. New jostles with old in Fig. 258.

In Shrewsbury, in Wem, in virtually every town, services and manufacturing are the main sources of employment. These two functions often differ in relative importance. In Shrewsbury, services are dominant, and manufacturing is of secondary importance (Fig. 259). The situation is reversed in industrial towns such as Stoke-on-Trent (Fig. 204, page 106). A range of urban contrasts is revealed in Fig. 260.

The list of services available in Shrewsbury is long and impressive, but not complete. The town falls under the influence of larger towns in the *hierarchy* of urban settlement. Shrewsbury lies in the West Midlands standard region (Fig. 245, page 126) of which Birmingham is the capital. Birmingham provides services on a scale in keeping with its status. Central government departments and agencies, for instance, are well represented. So, too, are wide-ranging commercial enterprises. Two examples may be quoted in illustration. The Midland Red Bus Company operates Shrewsbury's public transport and the town watches A.T.V. commercial television. Both have their headquarters in Birmingham.

Even Birmingham is not self-sufficient. It is part of the United Kingdom and, like every settlement, is dependent on the national capital in ways that will be suggested in a later section.

Fig. 259

Occupational Group (Standard Industrial Classification)	*% of total employment in Shrewsbury (1971 Census)*	
I Agriculture, forestry and fishing	0.5	
II Mining and quarrying	0.2	
Total – Primary industry		0.7
III Food, drink and tobacco	1.2	
IV Coal and petroleum products	0.5	
V Chemicals and allied industries	0.2	
VI Metal manufacture	0.2	
VII Mechanical engineering	12.2	
VIII Instrument engineering	—	
IX Electrical engineering	2.0	
X Shipbuilding and marine engineering	—	
XI Vehicles	0.9	
XII Other metal goods	1.9	
XIII Textiles	—	
XIV Leather and fur	—	
XV Clothing and footwear	2.2	
XVI Bricks, pottery, glass, cement, etc.	0.1	
XVII Timber, furniture, etc.	0.3	
XVIII Paper, printing and publishing	1.0	
XIX Other manufacturing industries	—	
Total – Manufacturing industry		22.7
XX Construction	6.5	
XXI Gas, electricity and water	2.1	
XXII Transport and communication	8.4	
XXIII Distributive trades	15.0	
XXIV Insurance, banking, finance and business services	5.0	
XXV Professional and scientific services	17.0	
XXVI Miscellaneous services	11.8	
XXVII Public administration and defence	10.7	
Total – Services		76.5

Occupational Group (Standard Industrial Classification)	*% of total employment in Cheltenham*	*% of total employment in Blackpool*	*% of total employment in Blackburn*	*% of total employment in St. Helens*
		(1971 Census)		
I Agriculture, forestry and fishing	0.1	0.6	0.3	0.3
II Mining and quarrying	—	—	—	5.0
Total – Primary industry	0.1	0.6	0.3	5.3
III Food, drink and tobacco	2.1	6.5	3.8	1.8
IV Coal and petroleum products	—	—	—	—
V Chemicals and allied industries	0.4	0.5	0.8	3.9
VI Metal manufacture	0.7	0.6	0.3	1.9
VII Mechanical engineering	7.3	1.4	12.6	2.6
VIII Instrument engineering	0.7	0.6	0.1	0.1
IX Electrical engineering	0.7	0.7	10.0	1.4
X Shipbuilding and marine engineering	—	—	—	—
XI Vehicles	3.7	3.6	1.1	0.4
XII Other metal goods	1.3	1.9	2.0	1.5
XIII Textiles	0.1	0.2	11.0	0.7
XIV Leather and fur	0.2	—	0.5	—
XV Clothing and footwear	0.1	0.9	3.3	2.7
XVI Bricks, pottery, glass, cement, etc.	0.1	0.5	0.3	33.3
XVII Timber, furniture, etc.	0.9	1.3	0.8	0.4
XVIII Paper, printing and publishing	2.0	1.5	2.3	1.0
XIX Other manufacturing industries	1.1	1.2	0.7	0.1
Total – Manufacturing industry	21.4	21.4	49.6	51.8
XX Construction	6.4	7.2	5.2	5.2
XXI Gas, electricity and water	1.3	2.1	2.8	2.4
XXII Transport and communication	4.6	6.5	5.4	4.4
XXIII Distributive trades	17.5	18.9	12.8	10.5
XXIV Insurance, banking, finance and business services	7.4	3.5	2.3	1.6
XXV Professional and scientific services	14.8	11.2	10.8	9.2
XXVI Miscellaneous services	12.0	22.8	7.0	5.7
XXVII Public administration and defence	14.6	5.9	3.7	3.8
Total – Services	78.6	78.1	50.0	42.8

Fig. 260

Merseyside – the growth of a conurbation

The Mersey Estuary bulges westwards from Widnes but narrows north-west before joining the Irish Sea. Its lower reaches are flanked by the undulating lowlands of south-west Lancashire and the Wirral peninsula. In the early nineteenth century, this area was thinly peopled; an agricultural landscape was dotted with small villages and hamlets, often sited where outcrops of Triassic sandstone peeped through a broken blanket of boulder clay. There was one exceptional settlement. Liverpool, with a population of less than 10000, contained the seeds of the spectacular growth that converted this rural area into one of Britain's major conurbations.

A small stream, now lost beneath the concrete and bricks of central Liverpool, flowed down to the Mersey. Its sheltered tidal waters offered facilities for the safe beaching of the small sailing vessels of the period. This tiny creek, or 'pool', was the foundation stone of the commercial success of Merseyside. Growth was favoured by several factors. Chester, an early rival, was silted up by the rapid infilling of the Dee estuary. Liverpool prospered with the growth of Atlantic trade. It did, for instance, indulge in and profit from the slave trade. Then, with the coming of the Industrial Revolution, the port found itself well placed to serve the growing industries of the midlands and the north of England.

The expansion of trade demanded the development of port facilities. The estuary was not an unmixed blessing. Deep water penetrates far inland, and the strong tidal outflow from the inner estuary keeps the narrows relatively free from silt. But a tidal range as high as 10 metres is most inconvenient and the approach to the estuary is marred by shifting sandbanks. In addition, the links with the port's hinterland were made difficult, not only by the estuary itself, but also by the presence of ill-drained peatlands on the plain of Lancashire. Progress depended on man's conquest of these natural disadvantages.

As early as 1715, the pool of Liverpool was converted into a dock, which made cargo handling independent of the state of the tide. As trade and the size of ships steadily increased, more and larger docks were developed on both sides of the estuary. The opening in 1973 of the massive Royal Seaforth Dock (Fig. 261) completed the complex pattern mapped in Fig. 262. Access to the port is assured via the Crosby Channel which is now virtually man-made. Confined between submarine training walls, it is constantly dredged to maintain an adequate depth of water. The port's land links have been steadily improved. The Leeds and Liverpool Canal, completed in 1816, brought West

Fig. 261

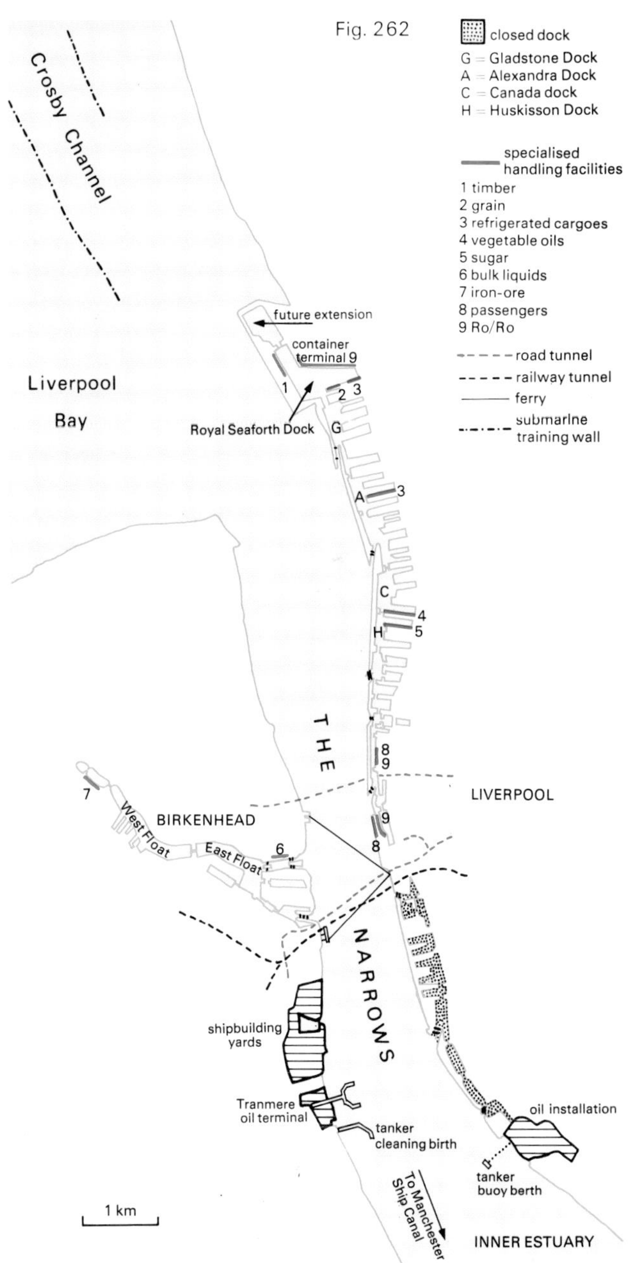

Fig. 262

Yorkshire within range of the Mersey. After 1830, railways forged iron ties with the hinterland. Merseyside was connected to the motorway system in 1974.

The expansion of Merseyside was hastened by the development of large-scale industries typical of major ports. The building and repair of ships is one example, now mainly represented by the Birkenhead yards of Cammell Laird. Others depend on raw materials imported through the docks. The north side of the East Float is lined by flour-mills. Major sugar refineries are located adjacent to the docks on the Liverpool shore. Imported vegetable oils are the basis of the soap and margarine made at Port Sunlight.

Population, and the built-up area, mirrored the rise of commerce and the growth of industry. Liverpool, and other centres of growth, notably Bootle and Birkenhead,

Fig. 263

(Scale – 1:10 000)

Fig. 263

expanded along and away from the river. Agricultural villages were swallowed up in a flowing tide of new building. Their names are often retained to describe districts within the conurbation; Anfield and Everton may be familiar examples. Old village sites are today often marked by local shopping centres. Continued growth depended on the development of communications. The introduction of reliable steam-ferry services opened up the attractive Wirral shore to water-borne commuters. The railway greatly extended the range of suburban settlement. Crosby, Formby, and even the holiday resort of Southport, came to contribute their daily train loads of city workers. Similarly, in Wirral, after the completion of the rail tunnel under the Mersey in 1886, Hoylake and West Kirby expanded as dormitory settlements. The greater flexibility that came with the bus and the motor car brought further extension of the built-up area.

In post-war years, the rate of urban expansion has accelerated. Population has continued to increase. The tight-packed terraced housing of the congested inner districts is being redeveloped at densities lower than those tolerated in the nineteenth century. Large new housing estates are pushing the edge of the built-up area even further from the Mersey and filling many of the gaps between existing towns and villages. St. Helens, for instance, is now linked to Liverpool by a wide ribbon of building.

Fig. 264 (Scale – 1:10650) © Crown Copyright 1967

Fig. 265 (Scale – 1:10650) © Crown Copyright 1968

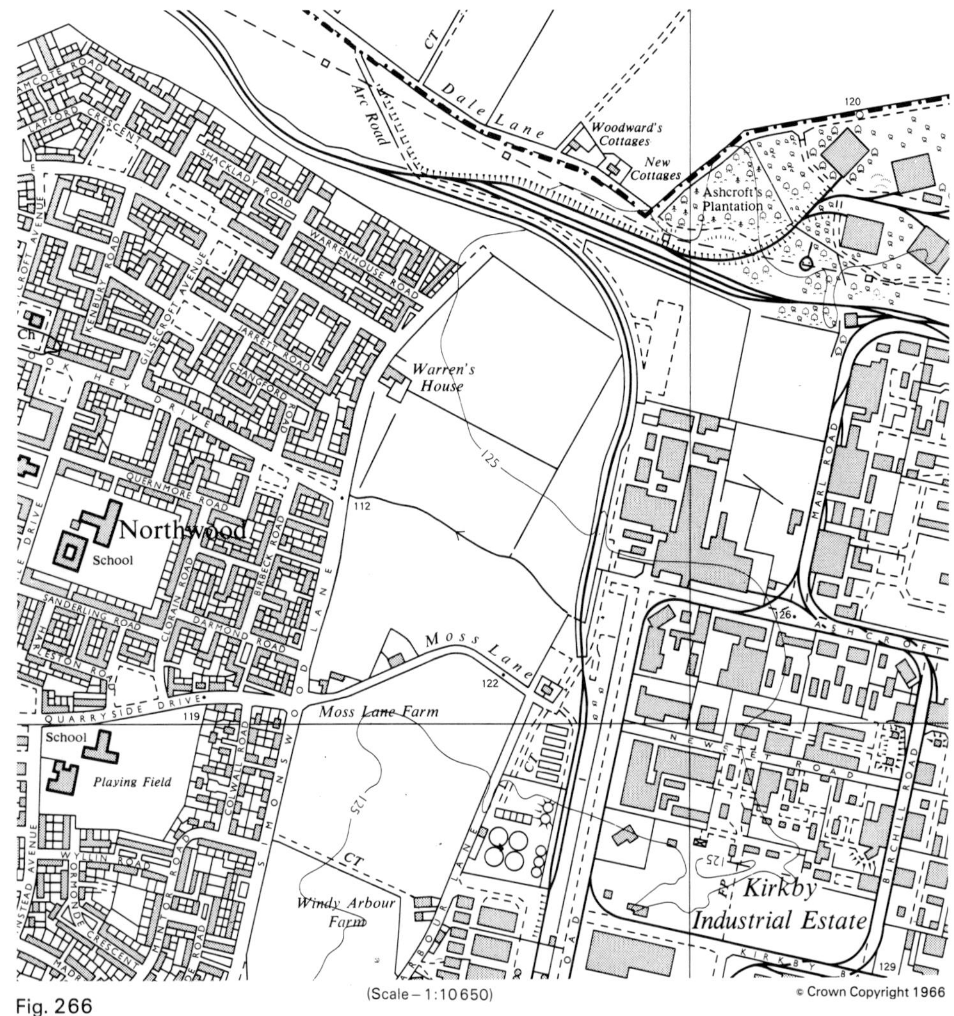

Fig. 266

Successive stages of growth have left their distinctive imprint on the urban landscape. These may readily be recognised on the map.

In the south-east corner of Fig. 263 the old nucleus of Liverpool has lost its residential function. Dominated by offices, shops and public buildings, it is now the central business district of the conurbation. Enclosed docks point northwards along the Mersey. Behind them, and astride the railway, lies a belt of warehouses and industrial premises. To the north-east of the map, the urban landscape is in the process of renewal. Prompted by the need for easier circulation and improved living conditions, the tight-packed terraces of the innermost residential districts are swept away. They are replaced by broad roadways and new housing in a variety of forms, including tower blocks of flats.

East of this zone of urban renewal lies a broad belt of Victorian housing, the distinctive pattern of which is illustrated by Fig. 264. On the northern edge of the map, factory premises lie close to a radiating rail route. Public parks or, as here, a cemetery, represent the only breaks in the heavily built-up landscape.

Still further east, newer residential areas are built to lower densities and planned with more imagination. The geometrical example mapped in Fig. 265 is a council estate built in the immediate pre-war years, and more recent development is seen in Fig. 266.

New factories make a significant contribution to the extension of the built-up area (Fig. 266). Sited away from the docks they have little in common with traditional port industries. Kirkby and Speke, for example, have major industrial estates. The motor vehicle industry is represented by large plants at Halewood and Speke (Fig. 267).

Post-war development has greatly widened the range of manufacturing on Merseyside. In Liverpool, for instance, it has helped to produce the diverse employment structure revealed in Fig. 268. Refer to Fig. 204 (page 106) and compare Liverpool with the country as a whole. Note the above average significance of the service industries. This reflects Liverpool's leadership of the Merseyside conurbation, for which it offers many central place functions. In some instances, its influence radiates even further. Port, insurance, local radio and two cathedrals may be cited in illustration.

So, over the years, settlements close to the Mersey have slowly expanded and merged to create a conurbation with a population of over a million and a half. Towns of varied character share a unity based on the commercial opportunities of the estuary. They are locked together by a complex web of communications at the heart of which are the road and rail links which tunnel under the river. Separate towns retained their political independence until 1974. In that year, local government was reorganised, and the creation of the Metropolitan County of Merseyside gave administrative recognition to the unity of the conurbation (Fig. 267).

Fig. 267

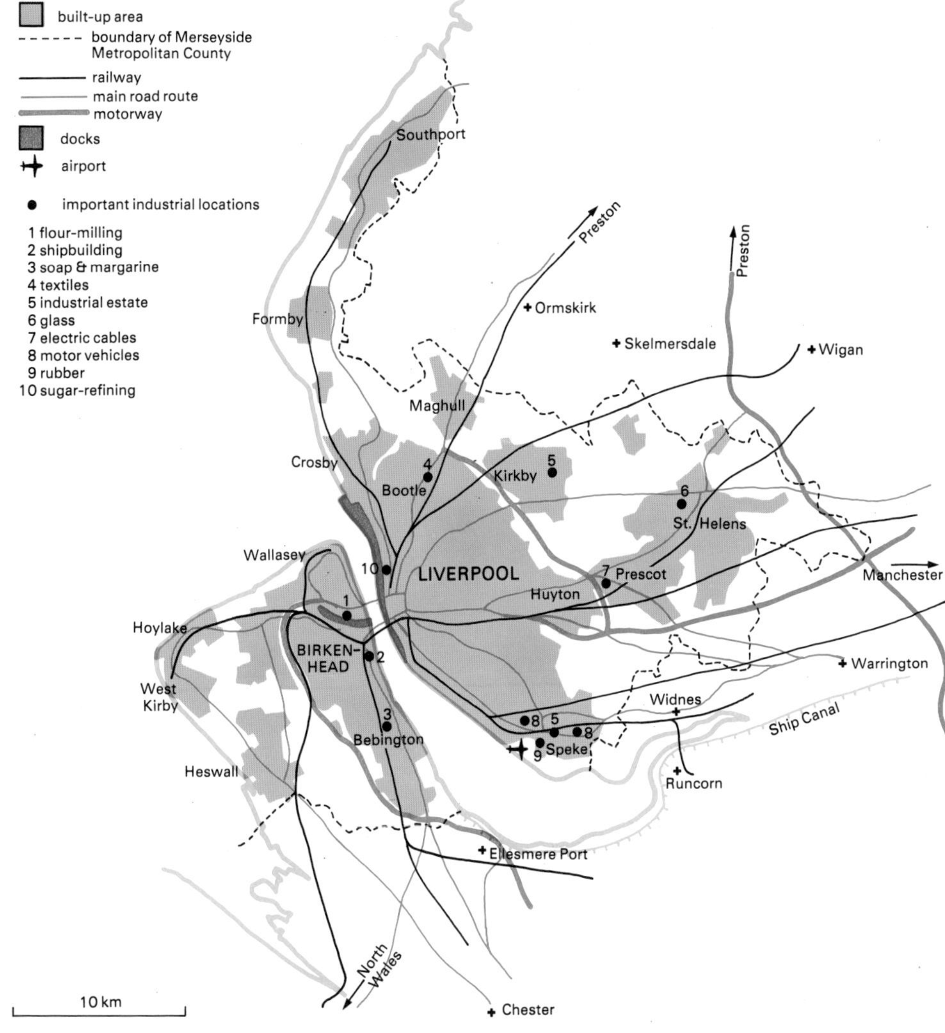

Merseyside is one of Britain's seven major conurbations. They are located on Fig. 269. Together they house 30 per cent of the country's population.

Fig. 268

Occupational Group (Standard Industrial Classification)	*% of total employment in Liverpool (1971 Census)*	
I Agriculture, forestry and fishing	0.05	
II Mining and quarrying	0.04	
Total – Primary industry		0.09
III Food, drink and tobacco	8.4	
IV Coal and petroleum products	0.05	
V Chemicals and allied industries	1.9	
VI Metal manufacture	0.1	
VII Mechanical engineering	1.7	
VIII Instrument engineering	0.2	
IX Electrical engineering	5.8	
X Shipbuilding and marine engineering	0.9	
XI Vehicles	2.4	
XII Other metal goods	1.5	
XIII Textiles	0.8	
XIV Leather and fur	0.1	
XV Clothing and footwear	1.4	
XVI Bricks, pottery, glass, cement, etc.	0.2	
XVII Timber, furniture, etc.	0.8	
XVIII Paper, printing and publishing	2.7	
XIX Other manufacturing industries	1.8	
Total – Manufacturing industry		30.8
XX Construction	5.5	
XXI Gas, electricity and water	1.1	
XXII Transport and communication	14.3	
XXIII Distributive trades	15.2	
XXIV Insurance, banking, finance and business services	4.7	
XXV Professional and scientific services	13.7	
XXVI Miscellaneous services	8.9	
XXVII Public administration and defence	5.7	
Total – Services		69.1

Fig. 269

The capital

London grows

The Thames collects its headwaters from the dip-slope of the Cotswolds. It snakes its way over the Oxford clay and cuts through the chalk at Goring. Below Reading, it begins its looping course over the gentle plains of the London Basin. The Thames receives its first salty taste of the sea at Teddington, and settlement crowds to the banks of the now tidal river. Winding and widening, it flows between western suburbs to the cities of Westminster and London, the twin hearts of the capital. Here, tightly confined between strong embankments and spanned by many bridges, it flows past landmarks as famous as the Houses of Parliament and the Tower of London. Downstream of the Tower, the river serves London's dwindling dockland, and its banks are studded with industrial enterprises. Eventually, the ever-widening estuary merges with the waters of the North Sea which give access to the Baltic, Rhine and, via the English Channel, to the sea lanes of the world.

London's river, described in song as 'Old Father Thames', is parent to a mighty offspring; Britain's capital, with a population of over 7 million, is one of the world's major urban centres. It had a distant and modest origin.

The Roman legions approached the Thames along the chalk of the North Downs. This gave a dry and open line of movement between the forested Wealden clays and marshy coastal lowlands. The character of the valley as seen by the Romans may be appreciated with the help of Fig. 270. Low gravel terraces rose above an ill-drained flood-plain. At one point on the north bank, the Thames was joined by a small tributary – the Walbrook. On either side, the gravel was heaped into two small hills which rose about 15 metres above the level of the Thames. It was around these two hills that the Romans built the walls of their town Londinium.

It was a happy choice. The gravel was dry and free from the risk of flooding. Pure water could be obtained from shallow wells. Since the town was founded, sea-level has risen by several metres, and the Thames at Roman London could be conveniently forded, and later bridged.

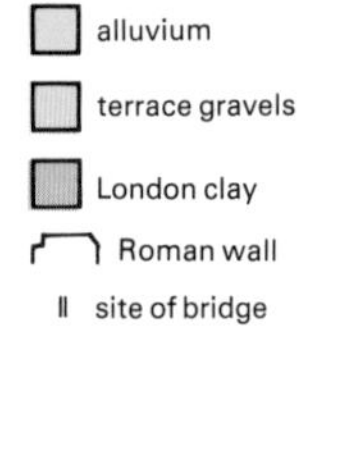

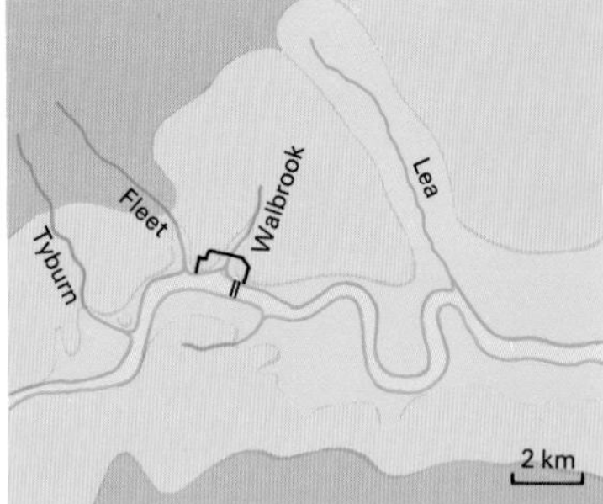

Fig. 270

London was then at the limit of tides and the effective head of navigation. With Londinium the centre for Roman occupation of Britain, roads radiated outwards like the spokes of a wheel. Bridging-point, route focus and port, these functions persisted, but in the eleventh century, capital status was surrendered to a point about 4 kilometres upstream. On a patch of gravel close by a convenient ford, Edward the Confessor built an abbey and palace. Westminster came to be the centre of government and administration that it is today.

The site of the Roman town was re-walled in medieval times and buttressed by the Tower. Trade and commerce brought prosperity to this small area which corresponds closely to the present City of London. For centuries, settlement was closely confined, but eventually houses appeared outside the walls and over the bridge in Southwark. At Westminster, the presence of king and court encouraged urban growth. Expansion of both centres was slow, and the two were not firmly linked until the seventeenth century. Later development took place piecemeal as the need arose. Differences in age, architecture and street plan have left rich local contrasts within the inner built-up area. The Georgian squares and terraces of Bloomsbury are the setting of the British Museum and London University. Mayfair, Kensington and Soho are other well-known districts of distinctive character.

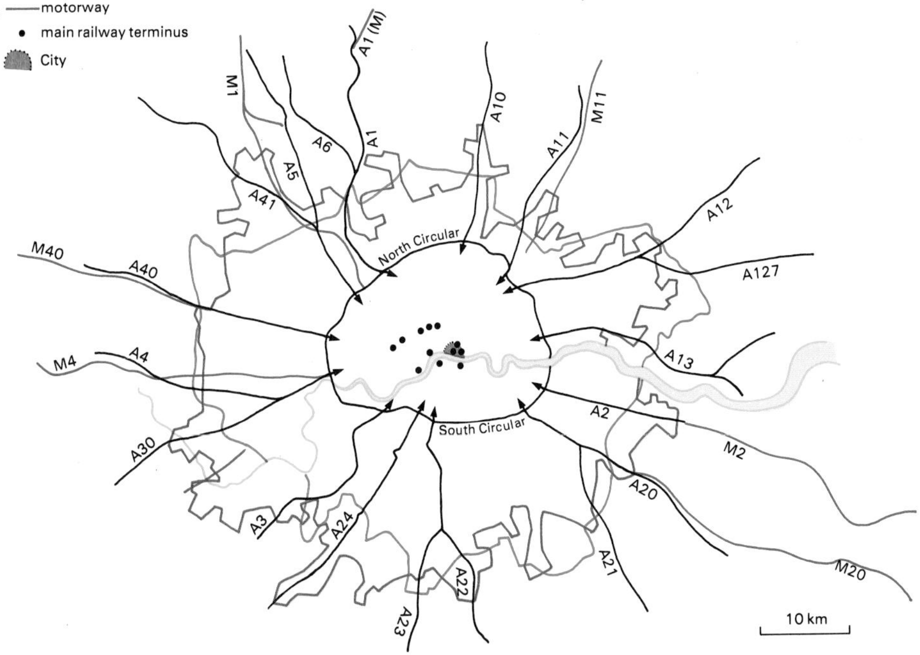

By the middle of the nineteenth century, the edge of the built-up area corresponded roughly to the ring of main-line railway terminii (Fig. 271). Prompted by growing population and prosperity, and progressive improvements in transport, expansion has since been rapid. London captured many surrounding villages and converted them into suburbs. Post-war redevelopment of old, congested residential districts has reinforced the outward tide of settlement. The present extent of the built-up area is indicated in Fig. 271.

London, and the south-east generally, is still a magnet for industry and people. Further expansion of the conurbation is restricted by London's tight green belt (page 157). Growth is to be more widely dispersed. New towns (page 148), which draw many Londoners away from the conurbation, continue to grow and prosper. It is planned that future development will be largely concentrated in radiating wedges, the most important extending as far as Southampton, Northampton and Ipswich.

Local government had difficulty in keeping pace with the capital's outward explosion. The County of London, created in 1888 to serve a population of over 4 million, corresponded closely to the built-up area of that time. Subsequent expansion left the new County far behind. The Greater London Council, set up in 1965, administers an area which approximates to the extent of the modern conurbation. The City of London, with an area slightly larger than that of the old walled town, retains its administrative independence and has its own Lord Mayor and corporation.

Fig. 271

Greater London boundary
approx. edge of built-up area
main road
motorway
• main railway terminus
City

M1 A1(M) A10 M11 A6 A1 A5 A11 A41 A12 North Circular M40 A40 A127 M4 A4 A13 A2 A30 South Circular M2 A20 A3 A24 A21 A22 M20 A23 10 km

London functions

This chapter's journey has taken us through sample settlements of increasing size. They differ greatly but share one important characteristic; they are all *central places*. They provide services to their inhabitants and to the population of surrounding districts. The larger the central place, the wider the range of services. As size increases, the number of examples grow less. More may be compared to Loppington than to Wem. Less common are those of Shrewsbury's size and Liverpool has few equivalents. Thus we speak of a *hierarchy* of central places.

Fig. 272

Occupational Group (Standard Industrial Classification)	*% of total employment in Greater London (1971 Census)*	
I Agriculture, forestry and fishing	0.1	
II Mining and quarrying	0.1	
Total – Primary industry		0.2
III Food, drink and tobacco	2.6	
IV Coal and petroleum products	0.2	
V Chemicals and allied industries	1.8	
VI Metal manufacture	0.5	
VII Mechanical engineering	3.2	
VIII Instrument engineering	0.9	
IX Electrical engineering	4.1	
X Shipbuilding and marine engineering	0.1	
XI Vehicles	1.6	
XII Other metal goods	1.8	
XIII Textiles	0.4	
XIV Leather and fur	0.3	
XV Clothing and footwear	2.2	
XVI Bricks, pottery, glass, cement, etc.	0.6	
XVII Timber, furniture, etc.	1.3	
XVIII Paper, printing and publishing	4.0	
XIX Other manufacturing industries	1.3	
Total – Manufacturing industry		26.9
XX Construction	6.3	
XXI Gas, electricity and water	1.5	
XXII Transport and communication	10.5	
XXIII Distributive trades	13.6	
XXIV Insurance, banking, finance and business services	9.4	
XXV Professional and scientific services	12.6	
XXVI Miscellaneous services	11.1	
XXVII Public administration and defence	7.9	
Total – Services		72.9

Fig. 273

Fig. 274

London is the peak of the pyramid. The population of Greater London is more than twice the figure for the West Midlands, its nearest rival. 72.9 per cent of the capital's employed population is engaged in service occupations (Fig. 272). Hardly surprising, perhaps, in view of the fact that the needs of a huge population must be catered for. The corner shop and public house play their part. Many basic services are provided by neighbourhood shopping centres. Suburbs have developed central business districts of their own. In some cases, these are of considerable size, and have more than a local significance. Croydon, Ealing and Ilford are examples. They offer shopping and other facilities that would be a credit to many large independent towns, and draw customers from far afield. In Fig. 273, we look down on the centre of Croydon. Tall, modern office blocks rise to meet us. Office development in suburban centres has been encouraged by lower rentals and stimulated by government policies aimed at reducing congestion in central London.

London as a central place does more than cater for its own inhabitants. It provides services for the whole of the United Kingdom. Often, these services are concentrated in restricted areas. The City of London is a case in point. With an area of 274 hectares, the City is the financial and commercial capital of the country. Within its bounds are found familiar institutions such as the Bank of England, the Stock Exchange, and Lloyds. Clustered around are the offices of companies with interests in banking, insurance, shipping and trade. The City is pictured in Fig. 274. The almost complete domination of office accommodation will be appreciated. Some of the modern tower blocks, developed on land devastated by war-time bombing, are higher than St. Paul's Cathedral, which is seen left of centre of the photograph. Some modern development includes dwelling accommodation, but less than 6000 people have homes in the City, which is the weekday destination of nearly half a million commuters.

With the help of Fig. 275, climb Ludgate Hill, with St.

Fig. 275

Paul's on your right. The route out of the City follows Fleet Street, along which newspaper offices have congregated. This illustrates another way in which London serves the nation as a whole. Temple Bar marks the City boundary and is set in a zone of buildings with legal functions. The Royal Courts of Justice, Lincoln's Inn and The Temple are examples. Progress along The Strand leads to that small part of the conurbation which most visitors think of as 'London'. Here are the buildings and amenities which help to make London a tourist centre of major importance. There are further examples of important functional specialisation. A world-famous shopping centre is bounded by Regent Street, Oxford Street and Bond Street. Standing in Leicester Square, one is within easy walking distance of the majority of the capital's many theatres.

A symbol of one of London's major functions may readily be identified on Fig. 276. The Houses of Parliament, sited between Westminster Abbey and the Thames, are a reminder that London is the seat of national government and the centre of political life. The administrative arm of government extends northwards along Whitehall. This famous thoroughfare is lined by imposing office buildings which house important government departments and their staffs of civil servants. London's administrative function has other aspects. Large industrial companies, trade associations, nationalised industries, societies and institutions, whose interests extend over the whole country, generally choose to establish their headquarters close to the centres of government and finance. Most aspects of national life are represented. Miscellaneous examples include Imperial Chemical Industries Ltd., The British Quarrying and Slag Federation, the National Coal Board, and the Trades Union Congress. A further example is pictured in Fig. 277. This is the Shell Centre, which overlooks the Thames. It is the workplace of 4700 people.

Fig. 276

London performs its varied functions with the essential help of a complex web of communications. Over 420 000 are employed in this branch of the service industries. Many, of course, are concerned with moving people and goods from place to place within the conurbation. Others derive their employment from London's national and international links. Chapter 6 describes how road, rail, and domestic air traffic focus on the capital. Heathrow (page 93) is an airport of supreme international significance. The port of London has sea links with all parts of the world. The Post Office Tower (Fig. 278) represents London's command of telecommunications.

Manufacturing also depends on efficient communications for its well-being. London is Britain's principal industrial region. Manufacturing, which gives employment to 26.9 per cent of the working population, is highly varied in nature and widely scattered throughout the conurbation. Fig. 279 shows its general distribution. It must be stressed that the shaded areas are not devoted

Fig. 277

Fig. 278

exclusively to industry. They all share residential and other functions, but within their bounds works and factories are common landscape elements.

Sheer size is London's main industrial advantage, for this implies a large market for the full range of manufactured products and a rich reservoir of labour. The oldest industrial districts are clustered around the City,

Fig. 279

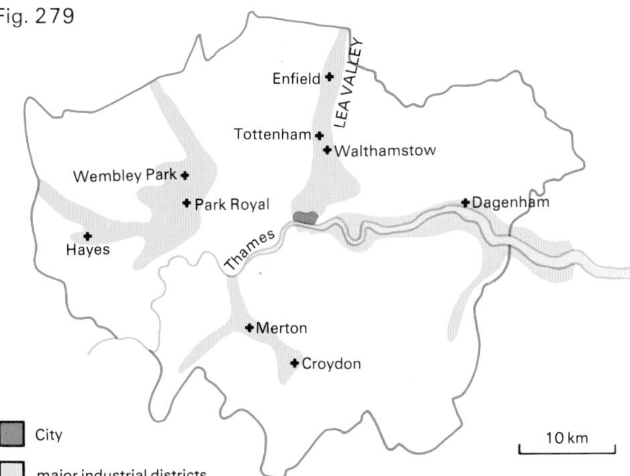

especially to north and east. Printing, clothing, furniture and leather goods are important specialisations. There are few modern factories; industrial units are generally small, and set in areas of congested Victorian development. Workshops can be found in converted shops, houses and other buildings. These inner manufacturing regions are declining in relative importance, for, with redevelopment, industry and workers are moving out to new premises in other parts of the conurbation or in the new towns.

An earlier northwards migration has long been received by the southern end of the Lea Valley industrial zone (Fig. 279). Thus, furniture and clothing are important in Tottenham and Walthamstow. Further north, engineering and electronics assume greater importance.

The Lea Valley is an illustration of the tendency for industry within the conurbation to develop along radial lines of communication. The River Thames provides another example. Its banks are punctuated with establishments dependent upon imported raw materials. Typical Thames-side industries include sugar refining, flour-milling and saw-milling. The Ford Motor Company at Dagenham uses the river to import raw materials for its blast-furnaces. Downstream, beyond the Greater London boundary, the story is continued with paper-mills and achieves a fitting climax with the huge oil refineries at the mouth of the estuary.

Lacking coal, London could claim little share of the industries commonly associated with the Industrial Revolution. In the present century, the development of electricity and road transport has reinforced the attractions of London, and the capital has experienced great industrial expansion. The greater part has been located in new areas, especially the north-west which has easy access to markets in the midlands and north as well as in London itself. Sites along major road routes, such as the A4 and the North Circular, have proved highly popular. In addition, large industrial estates have been established. Park Royal and Wembley Park are two major examples. Output is highly diverse. The light engineering and electrical industries are well represented. So, too, are foodstuffs, pharmaceuticals, precision instruments and a vast range of consumer goods.

New towns

The major problems of Britain's conurbations are the legacy of more than a century of uncontrolled development. Rapid unplanned growth brought congestion and poor housing conditions in inner districts, urban sprawl on the outskirts and, for many, a tedious daily journey to work. The establishment of new towns has been an important part of post-war efforts to repair the damage and improve the quality of urban life.

Fig. 280

New towns: U.K.	*Year of designation*	*Area designated (hectares)*	*Population*		
			At designation	*(Estimate) 31st December 1975*	*Ultimate*
Great Britain:					
Stevenage	1946	2530	7000	76000	105000
Crawley	1947	2450	10000	73000	79000
Hemel Hempstead	1947	2420	21000	76000	80000
Harlow	1947	2560	4500	83500	90000
Aycliffe	1947	1000	60	26000	45000
East Kilbride	1947	4140	2500	73800	100000
Peterlee	1948	1080	200	26500	30000
Hatfield	1948	950	8500	26000	30000
Welwyn Garden City	1948	1750	18500	40000	50000
Glenrothes	1948	2300	1100	32000	70000
Basildon	1949	3120	25000	88000	140000
Bracknell	1949	1900	5000	42600	55/60000
Cwmbran	1949	1260	12000	45000	55000
Corby	1950	1770	15700	53500	83000
Cumbernauld	1955	3150	3500	43000	100000
Skelmersdale	1961	1670	10000	40700	80000
Livingston	1962	2700	2100	24860	100000
Telford (formerly Dawley)	1963/8	7790	70000	96700	220000
Redditch	1964	2910	32000	51800	90000
Runcorn	1964	2930	28500	51698	100000
Washington	1964	2120	20000	41000	80000
Irvine	1966	5040	40000	52600	120000
Milton Keynes	1967	8800	40000	70000	250000
Peterborough	1967	6400	80500	102500	185000
Newtown	1967	600	5500	7200	13000
Northampton	1968	8000	131000	151000	230000
Warrington	1968	7460	124000	133400	230000
Central Lancashire	1970	14250	235000	243900	430000
Northern Ireland:					
Craigavon	1965	25900	40000	75700	180000
Antrim	1965	} 113680	7000	38000	50000
Ballymena	1967		21000	54000	80000
Londonderry	1969	34700	72000	87000	100000

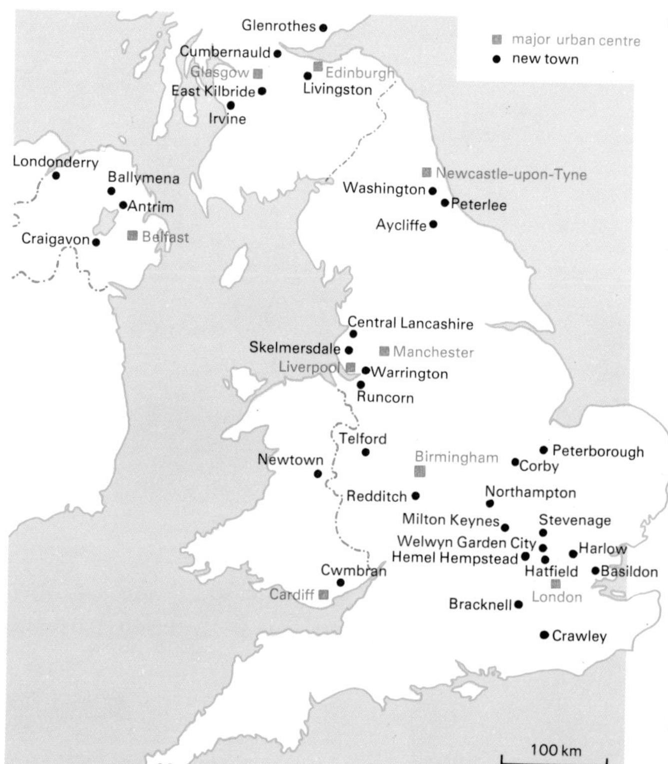

Fig. 281

In 1946, an area of 2530 hectares was designated as the site of Britain's first new town. It had as its nucleus the old Hertfordshire market centre of Stevenage. Under the guidance of a development corporation, a detailed plan was drawn up and steadily translated into reality. Finance for capital investment was made available by the government. Old Stevenage had 7000 inhabitants. The present town houses more than ten times as many, and an ultimate population of 105000 is anticipated.

Stevenage was the first of many. Today, there are 32 new towns, distributed as indicated in Fig. 281. Many, like Stevenage, are now well-established. Others are at an early stage of growth. Progress of all is charted in Fig. 280.

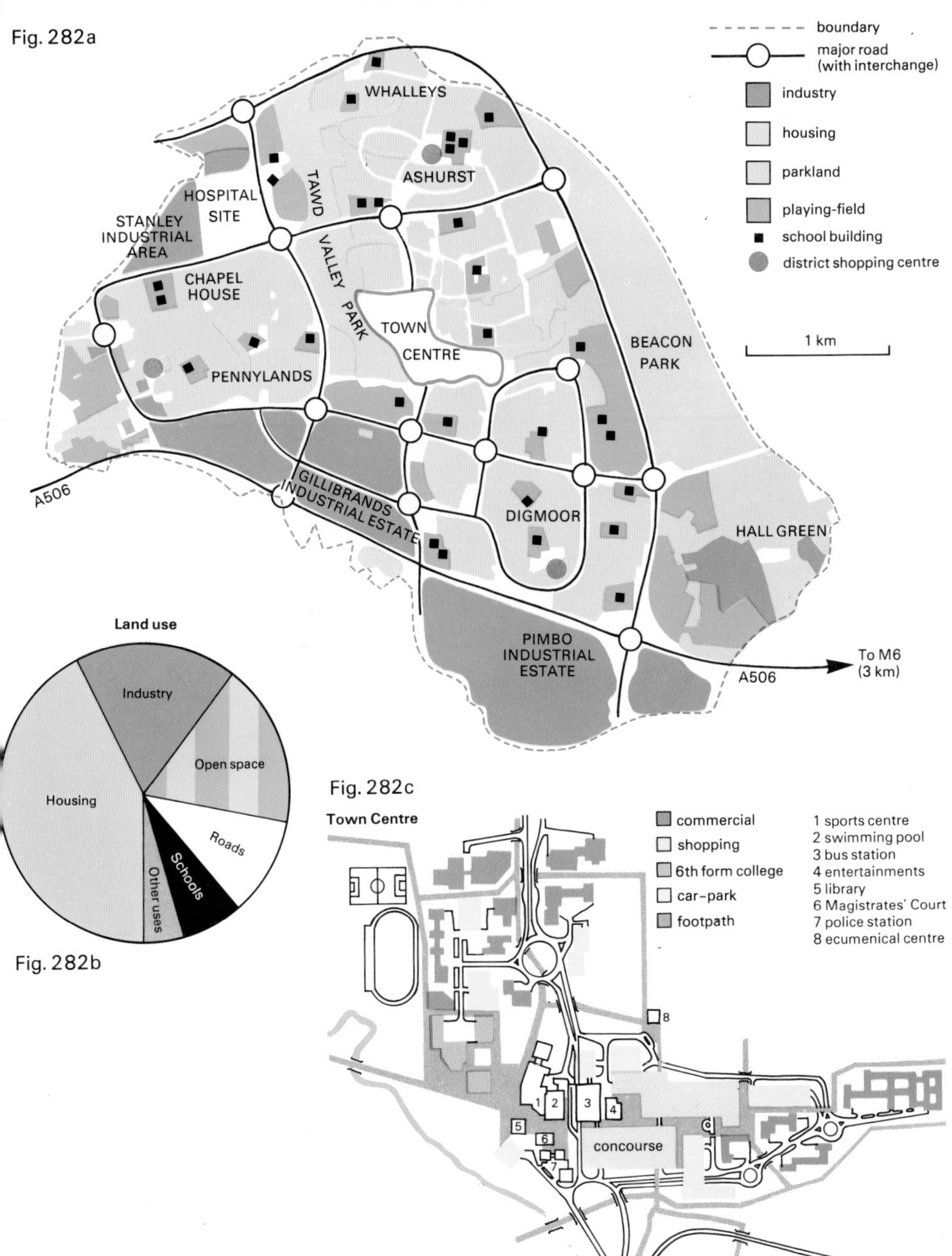

New towns share a name and an origin, but are far from being carbon copies of each other. Differences in the nature of the sites present planners with differing problems and opportunities. Accumulated experience and changing circumstances have modified planning consideration. Younger new towns, for instance, must take into consideration the growth of car ownership. Increased national concern over the loss of valuable farmland is another consideration. It prompts higher housing densities.

New towns show some variation in aims. The majority are designed to relieve the pressures on the conurbations with which they are associated. The provision of employment and homes draws people out of congested districts which can then be redeveloped at lower densities and hence higher standards of amenity. There are exceptions to this general picture. Peterlee, for example, was designed to provide new jobs and housing in an area seriously affected by the decline of the coal-mining industry. The new town of Newtown was established to encourage growth in an area of declining population.

Size introduces another element of contrast. The earliest new towns had a target population of less than 100 000. Some recent plans are on a much larger scale. Milton Keynes, for instance, is expected to have a population of 200 000 by the end of the century. Peterborough illustrates another recent trend – the designation of large existing centres located far from the conurbations. This has the advantages that necessary services are already available, and greater and more varied industrial growth is encouraged.

Although differing in detail, new towns are united by an important guiding principle. They plan to create an urban settlement which offers good living and working conditions for its inhabitants.

A brief study of Skelmersdale will illustrate distinctive new town characteristics. Sited on 1600 hectares between Wigan and Ormskirk, its purpose is to accommodate

Fig. 283

Fig. 284

50 000 people from central Merseyside, which lies some 30 kilometres to the south-west. The site has a varied relief. From the bold Ashurst Ridge, which rises to over 150 metres, the land undulates westwards to the old town which gave its name to the new. The northward flowing River Tawd bisects the site and collects a handful of small tributaries in the process. At the date of designation, Skelmersdale had a population of approximately 10 000. By mid 1976, the total had swollen to 41 500. A compact, clearly defined urban settlement of 80 000 is the ultimate target.

The basic plan is seen in Fig. 282. In drawing it up, the need to cater for a high density of road traffic was a prime consideration. The road system is designed to facilitate safe and easy movement. Cars and pedestrians are kept apart. There are no traffic lights in Skelmersdale. A grid of major roads gives uninterrupted flow to all parts of the town. Secondary roads lead to individual districts, where all premises are served by access roads.

The needs of the pedestrian are by no means forgotten. Town footpaths radiate from the town centre. Roads are crossed by bridges and underpasses.

Every effort is made to create a pleasing urban landscape. Dwellings are built in a wide range of styles and sizes, but high-rise accommodation is avoided. Units are combined in different ways to create further variety. The planting of trees and shrubs is an integral part of development. Fig. 283 gives a representative picture.

Primary schools are set in residential districts and are easily and safely reached on little legs. Public houses and corner shops meet more mature daily requirements. Minor shopping centres are found in outlying districts, but the compact size of the town enables the bulk of essential urban services to be located in the town centre. The facilities already available are indicated in Fig. 282, and their visual quality may be appreciated from Fig. 284.

The development plan makes ample provision for open-air leisure facilities. Of particular interest is the use made of natural features. The western slopes of the Ashurst Ridge are now public parkland, and the Tawd valley will slowly be transformed into a linear park. Tributary valleys are left in woodland to break up the built-up area.

The main industrial zones are situated on the southern outskirts of the town. Skelmersdale has been most successful in attracting new manufacturing enterprises. It can offer all the advantages of a development area (page 127) and, in addition, is well served by road communication, for the M6 motorway lies a mere 13 kilometres to the east. By 1976, over 100 companies had been established. The range of output is extremely diverse. Groups that are particularly well represented include engineering, electronics, clothing and plastics.

9 Leisure and Amenity

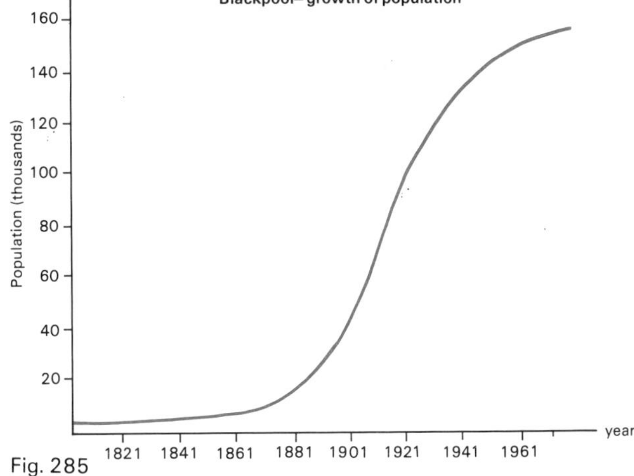

Fig. 285

'Oh! I do like to be beside the seaside'

In the second half of the eighteenth century, doctors discovered a new 'cure' for many troublesome ailments. They commonly prescribed a course of daily bathing in the sea. An optimistic prescription, perhaps, but one that was less dangerous than many that were popular at the time. Many followed their doctor's advice. By carriage and coach they journeyed to recommended coastal settlements. These grew with the influx of visitors. Hotels and boarding-houses increased in number. Facilities were provided for balls, concerts and other entertainment. Attractive gardens were laid out. Small, simple villages grew into fashionable 'watering places', which came to attract the healthy as well as the sick. Thus was born the traditional British seaside holiday.

The development of cheap and speedy rail transport enabled holidaymakers to flock to the coast in ever-increasing numbers. In the second half of the nineteenth century, quiet watering places expanded into the large holiday resorts which now punctuate our coastline. Sea and sand were obvious requirements for growth. Proximity to large urban centres was also important. Southend, Margate, Eastbourne and Brighton, for instance, are close to London, and Scarborough is not far from Leeds and Bradford. Summer climate is another important factor. South coast resorts claim the longest hours of sunshine (Fig. 67, page 39). Llandudno and Rhyl, which nestle in the rain-shadow of the Welsh Highlands, have the additional advantage of attractive inland scenery.

In 1846, the railway arrived at Blackpool, then a small collection of hotels, houses and fishermen's cottages. The subsequent growth of population is graphed in Fig. 285. The steep rise after 1881 reflects Blackpool's growing popularity in a period when rising standards of living enabled increasing numbers of working folk to take an annual holiday. To natural attractions of sea and sand were added a wide range of entertainments. Powerful publicity ensured that Blackpool's charms were widely known. Visitors were attracted not only from nearby Lancashire mill towns, but also from Yorkshire, the midlands, Clydeside and even further afield. The first two weeks of August are still known locally as 'Scottish fortnight'.

From its original tiny nucleus, the built-up area expanded north and south along the coast to merge with the minor resorts of Cleveleys and St. Annes. The linear form, revealed in Fig. 286, is common to most major holiday resorts. It is also a feature of urban land use. Look at Fig. 287. A wide beach is traversed by two of Blackpool's three Victorian piers. It is flanked by a wide promenade which accommodates road, tram-lines and, during the season, flocks of strolling holidaymakers. To the right is found a 'golden mile' of minor attractions such as amusement arcades, bingo halls and stalls for candy-floss. Next comes a belt of hotels, boarding-houses, and, increasingly, self-catering flats, which merges into the town's residential districts. The photograph also shows the famous Blackpool Tower. This prominent landmark rises from a base which houses a circus, a ballroom and bars. It is a reminder of

Fig. 286

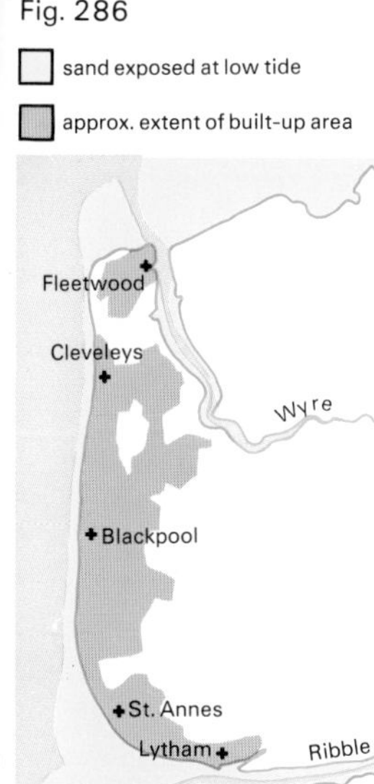

Fig. 287

the importance of entertainments in the modern resort. Each year Blackpool welcomes 6 million visitors. Many never set foot in the sea.

Catering for the needs of the holidaymaker is a highly seasonal occupation. 65 per cent of annual holidays are taken in July and August. School holidays are obviously a factor in this. So, too, is the belief, often belied by the statistics, that these months hold the least risk of inclement weather. Resorts attempt to extend the length of the holiday season: Blackpool's elaborate and expensive illuminations attract visitors as late as the end of October; and out-of-season conferences, such as those of the political parties, also fill vacant hotel accommodation. Unemployment in the winter months is high. Industry is being attracted in an attempt to build a more balanced employment structure. Examples from Blackpool include the motor industry, confectionery and clothing.

New trends can be recognised in the pattern of annual holidays. Traditional resorts retain their attraction, but increased mobility has brought a considerable dispersion of the holiday industry. Many small, once remote, coastal settlements now thrive on the tourist trade. Devon and Cornwall contain many examples, including the former fishing village of Mousehole which is pictured in Fig. 288. The south-west peninsula now rivals the resort-studded south-east coasts as Britain's most popular area. Private transport prompts many to seek the peace and tranquillity of a country holiday. In Scotland, Wales and other scenic upland areas, this brings increased income to accommodating inns, cottages and farmhouses. Alternatively, the motorist may tow his holiday home behind him. More and more holidaymakers are journeying abroad. Dependable sunshine and the economy of packaged air tours have helped to make Spain the most popular destination. The attractions of Ireland, until recently the second most popular destination, are quite different. The coolness and uncertainty of the summer climate are tolerated by those who appreciate the Republic's scenic charm and uncluttered roads.

Fig. 288

Time on our hands

In recent years, the great majority of the working population has enjoyed an increase in personal leisure. A reduction in the average working week to 40 hours or less has liberated the weekend. Virtually all workers are now entitled to three weeks' holiday with pay. Modern labour-saving machines have lightened the housewife's burden. The trend will doubtless continue; wage negotiations commonly involve further reductions in hours of work. Greater affluence enables many to make full use of their increased leisure, and the mobility brought by car ownership widens the scope of their activities.

Much of the increased leisure is, of course, absorbed in and about the home. The average adult watches television for more than 17 hours each week. House maintenance and improvement is increasingly a matter of do-it-yourself. Bingo and betting grow in popularity. Local authorities build elaborate sports centres. There, is, however, a growing tendency for leisure to be spent out-of-doors and away from the home. Fishing, sailing, water-skiing, hiking, climbing and camping claim greater devotion. Outings by car and coach are more frequent and historic houses and safari parks are developed as suitable destinations.

The increased popularity of outdoor recreation makes great demands on the environment; the yachtsman needs water on which to sail and the hiker needs open land on which to wander. In summer months, the pressure on available resources is often excessive: climbers must queue at the foot of popular rock faces; cabin cruisers wait their turn to pass through locks on inland waterways; and popular field-study areas are often littered with abandoned worksheets.

As leisure increases, so, too, does public awareness of the damage man can do to his environment. Derelict land and polluted rivers are common reminders of his destructive power. Natural beauty is easily destroyed: a quarry can make an ugly hole in a fine rural landscape; a belching chimney can ruin the view and pollute the atmosphere; and an ill-sited caravan park may impair the landscape that the tourist comes to enjoy.

There is a growing tendency for natural amenities to be conserved and for damaged land to be reclaimed. Conservation ensures that attractive landscapes are preserved for the pleasure of future generations. Reclamation puts derelict land to profitable use. Both have a part to play in the provision of greater opportunities for recreation.

Conservation

Defence against harmful development is strongest in the ten *national parks* which together occupy about 10 per cent of the total land area of England and Wales. Fig. 289 gives locations and names. National parks are found mainly in highland and upland areas where attractive natural landscapes have suffered little at the hands of man. They are rich in contrast. Snowdonia and the Lake District feature rugged ice-carved highlands. Dramatic coastal scenery is enclosed in the Pembrokeshire Park. Wild open moorlands cut by steep-sided valleys are a feature of North Yorkshire.

National parks are not all owned by the nation; the bulk of the land is in private ownership and productive use. Agriculture is usually the main support of the resident population. The park authorities have wide powers to protect the natural amenities and to prevent any harmful changes of land use. Steps are taken to ensure that any essential development is in harmony with the landscape. The use of traditional building materials is encouraged.

Park authorities have a further responsibility. They must promote access to, and enjoyment of, the amenities they conserve. Increased recreational use may, however, be in conflict with the interests of local people. Visitors are often careless and inconsiderate: a flowering hedgerow is less beautiful when seen against a background of

national park
area of outstanding natural beauty
green belt (approved)
green belt (under consideration)
▲ forest park
——— heritage coast

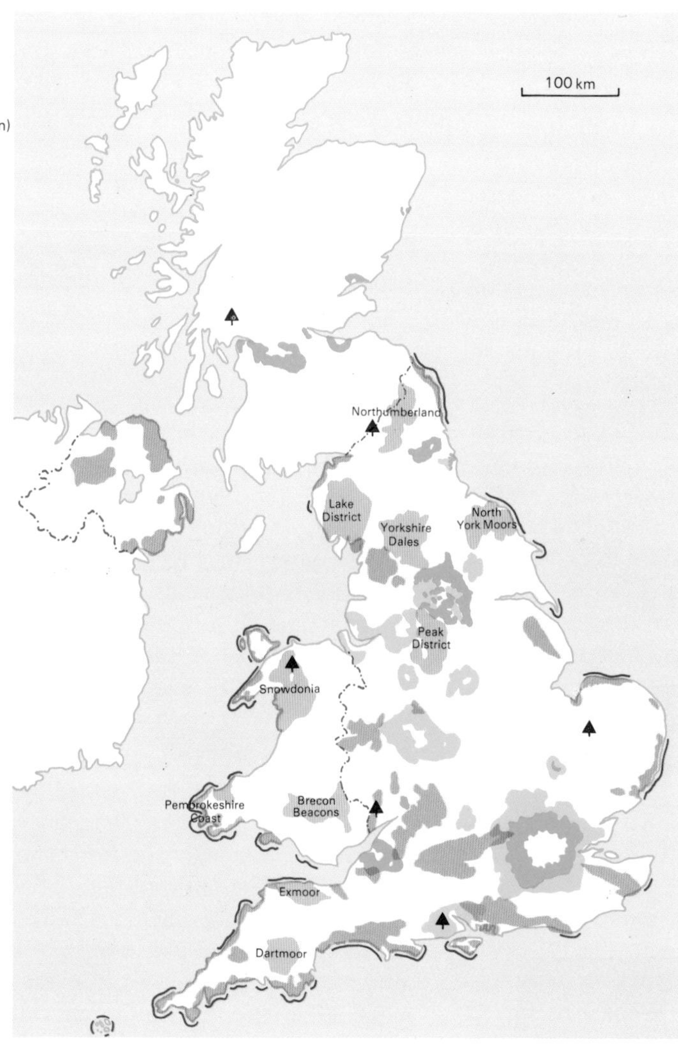

Fig. 289

empty bottles and plastic bags; growing crops can be flattened by hiking feet. These and other dangers are highlighted in the *Country Code*, which all visitors to the national parks, or, indeed, to any rural area, should follow religiously. The ten-point code is printed for reference in Fig. 290.

Economic considerations lead to further conflict of interest. National parks are not without resources, but their development poses problems. A new quarry may create jobs in an area of poor employment prospects. A new power-station may offer a cheap source of much needed electricity. But such developments would doubtless damage landscapes that the parks are designed to conserve. The interests of development and amenity are often delicately balanced, and each case must be judged on its merits. Boulby mine (page 27) is a recent development in the North York Moors National Park. It does nothing to enhance the beauty of its surroundings, but it exploits a resource of national importance, and creates employment for local people. The nuclear power-station at Trawsfynydd (page 82) is another example. Ironically, perhaps, it has become a tourist attraction of considerable popularity.

The Peak District National Park, the first to be established, is mapped in Fig. 291. Neighbouring industrial towns, Glossop, for instance, are carefully excluded. So, too, is the area of large quarries centred on Buxton. The park boundaries enclose 1400 square kilometres of varied Pennine landscapes. In the north, rocks of the Millstone Grit series give high barren moorlands cut by a multitude of small youthful valleys. In the heart of the park, limestone is dominant, and pastoral farming is practised on rolling plateau surfaces gashed by gorge-like dales. On either flank, tilted strata of differing resistances have been eroded into sharp-edged, inward-facing cuestas (Fig. 13, page 11).

Public use and enjoyment of this attractive area is actively promoted by the Peak Park Planning Board, which is financed by local rates and government funds. Recreational facilities available within the park include walking, climbing, fishing, sailing, gliding, caving, bird-watching, skiing, shooting, camping and caravanning. In addition, there are historic houses and archaeological sites to visit.

COUNTRY CODE

Fig. 290

The Peak Park rises like an island from an urban sea. It separates Greater Manchester from West and South Yorkshire. Nottingham, Derby and Stoke-on-Trent fringe its southern borders. Merseyside and the West Midlands are close at hand. Lying as it does within easy reach of such great centres of population, the park is well placed to serve as a recreational area. Each year it welcomes an estimated 10 million visitors.

The Peak Park faces the problems that result from increased use of leisure opportunities. Not all visitors follow the Country Code, and the dangers of litter, fire and trespass are ever present. Some areas suffer actual physical damage. Fig. 292 was taken at the foot of Mam Tor, a noted view-point. Grazing land is deeply scarred by multiple paths carved out by the boots of passing hikers. In some places, popular paths across patches of peat must be protected by strips of plastic

Fig. 291

Fig. 292

(Fig. 293). The motor car is the biggest problem; it opens up the park to millions of visitors, but endangers the qualities they seek. It brings noise and fumes when in motion, and occupies space when at rest. Fig. 294 shows The Winnats, a beauty spot near Castleton, on a Sunday afternoon in summer.

In one small part of the park, an attempt is made to reduce the damaging effects of the motor car. The Goyt Valley, mapped in Fig. 295, lies within 30 kilometres of the heart of Greater Manchester. This accessible valley of

Fig. 293

Fig. 294

considerable natural charm attracts many day visitors from the nearby conurbation. Congestion at peak periods caused the authorities to introduce the scheme outlined on the map. On summer Sundays, part of the road that follows the Goyt is closed to private vehicles.

Fig. 295

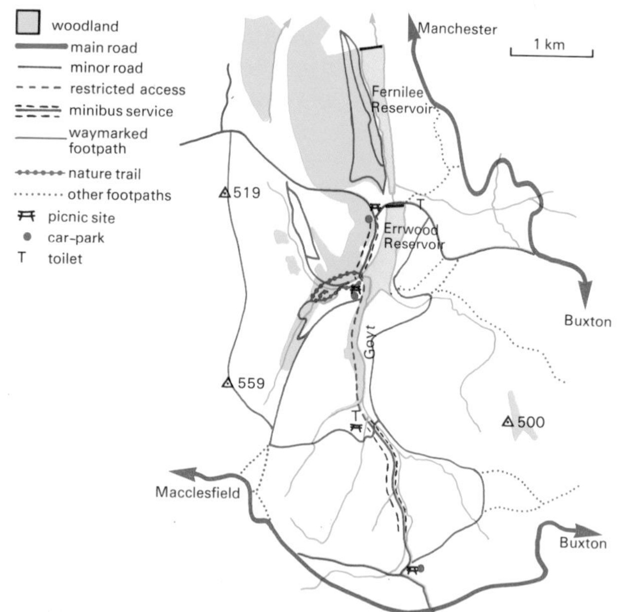

Cars are left in discreet car-parks, and a mini-bus service shuttles visitors into the valley, where rural peace is undisturbed by the bustle of traffic. The map gives examples of other steps that have been taken to encourage public use and enjoyment of the area.

Recreational facilities in attractive surroundings are also available in the growing number of *country parks*. Much smaller than national parks, they range in area from 7 to 1500 hectares, and offer richly varied opportunities. Many have been developed around country estates or ancient monuments. Others incorporate stretches of attractive coastline. In some areas, country parks have been created by the repair of damaged landscapes. In the Wirral, for instance, a disused railway line now forms a rural track for walking and horse riding.

The majority of country parks have been established by local authorities and receive financial support from the Countryside Commission. Amenities appropriate to the surroundings are provided. Fishing, boating, camping and nature trails are common examples. All have car-parks, toilets and litter removal services.

There are now well over 100 country parks in England and Wales. Their distribution is mapped in Fig. 296. The concentrations near major conurbations reflect the desire to provide leisure facilities within easy reach of the centres of population.

Elvaston Castle, an early nineteenth-century hall and landscaped estate, formed the basis of the first country park to be officially opened (1970). Situated 10 kilometres south-east of Derby, it is also within easy reach of Nottingham, Leicester and other towns of the east midlands. Of the estate's 158 hectares, 32 are now open to the public, the remainder being in agricultural use. Fig. 297 indicates some of its attractions. In addition, the 'castle' and its outbuildings have been adapted to house a museum of rural life, a field-study centre, and a café. Each year, the park receives approximately 75,000 visitors.

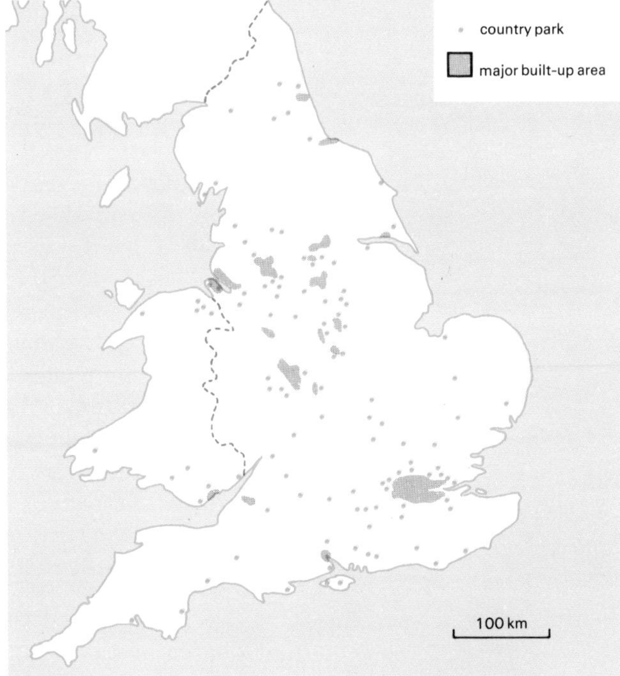

Fig. 296

Fig. 297

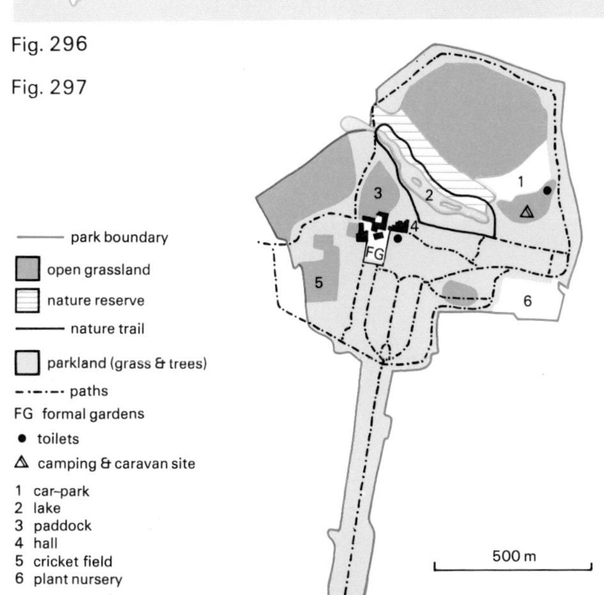

National and country parks are not the only areas subject to planning control in the cause of conservation and amenity. Fig. 289 (page 154) locates *'areas of outstanding natural beauty'*. The chalklands of south-east England provide prominent examples. So, too, do the coasts of Devon and Cornwall. Although these areas lack the status of national parks, much is done to preserve natural landscapes and to improve public access.

Fig. 289 also locates areas designated as *heritage coasts*. These include the finest unspoilt lengths of the coastlines of England and Wales. Strict planning control will ensure that they remain unspoilt.

Large urban areas are, or will be, ringed by *green belts*, where building is severely restricted. This is done to limit the sprawl of the built-up areas and to retain, within easy reach, the amenity of open country. A green belt may stop two large towns merging into one. It is hoped that Liverpool and Manchester, Birmingham and Coventry, Nottingham and Derby can be kept apart in this way.

Many small patches of land are preserved for posterity by the National Trust. Numerous nature reserves have been established to protect plant and animal life. In total, about one-fifth of the land surface of England and Wales is now strongly protected against harmful development. Public access to our scenic heritage is steadily improved. An example of this is the unbroken rights of way which make up the long-distance footpaths marked in Fig. 298.

One important way in which leisure facilities are increased is by the multi-purpose use of scarce resources. This is by no means restricted to recognised conservation areas. A reservoir, for instance, may store water and be a convenient centre for water sports. Forested land can yield more than trees; until recently, plantations were closed to the public for fear of fire, but now they are being opened up for recreation. This is particularly true of the *forest parks* which have been established by

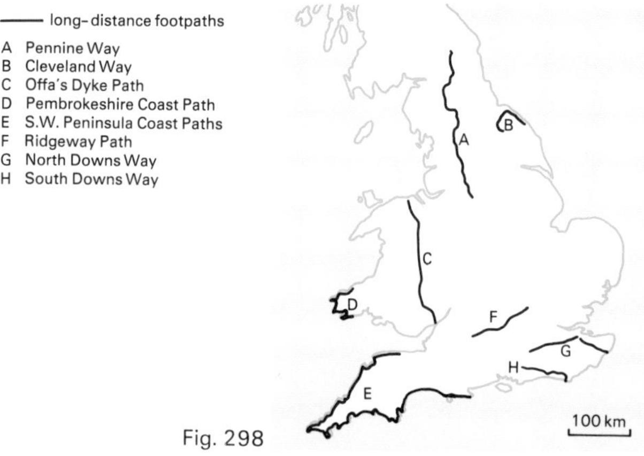

Fig. 298

the Forestry Commission (Fig. 289, page 154). All are in areas of great natural beauty. An example is sketched in Fig. 299.

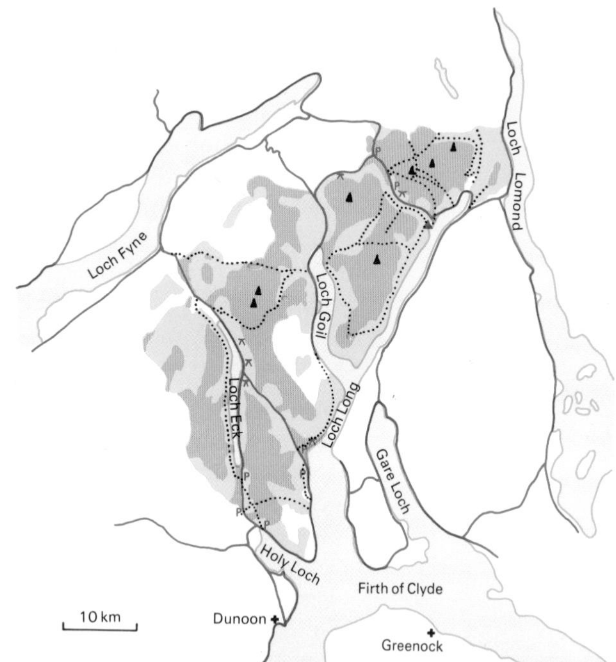

Fig. 299

Argyll Forest Park

- plantation
- open moorland and farm land
- ▲ peak > 750 m
- —— road
- ········ path & track
- P car-park
- picnic site
- camp site
- C caravan site

Reclamation

In Britain today, more than 1000 square kilometres of land are classified as 'derelict'. Examples are numerous: the mining of kaolin leaves an imprint of deep craters and tall conical spoil heaps (page 29); the extraction of sand and gravel creates large shallow water-filled pits (page 24); and there are hillsides in north Wales which have been eaten away by the quarrying of slate (page 9). Unsightly man-made landscapes can be found in most parts of the country. The great majority are the legacy of nineteenth and early twentieth-century industrial activity. They become more offensive as our concern for the quality of the environment increases. They offend in another way; derelict land is waste land, and land is in short supply. As population increases and standards of living rise, space is needed for new houses, new factories, new roads and new recreational facilities. These are essential and are provided often at the expense of good farm land. Thus, prompted by considerations of amenity and economics, efforts are made to convert derelict land to more productive use. Reclamation takes much time and money, and progress is slow. In many areas, coal-mining is the main cause of devastation. This is true of the area sketched in Fig. 300, which lies just south of Wigan on the western edge of Greater Manchester. The map illustrates land use in the 1960s when evidence of dereliction was livid on the landscape (Fig. 301). There were extensive spreads of pit waste which, in the central area, was piled into three large conical spoil heaps. These prominent features, known locally as the 'Three Sisters', rose 60 metres or more above the gentle plain of south Lancashire. The area was dotted with patches of standing water. Some of these were abandoned reservoirs, but most were the result of mining subsidence, which had also interfered with natural drainage to create marshland. Opencast mining operations had left their imprint on the landscape. Unsightly groups of decayed surface installations marked the sites of the mines that had done the damage.

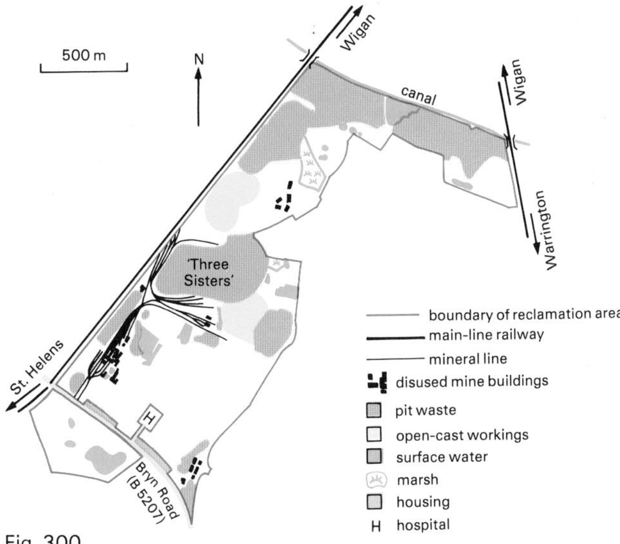

Fig. 300

Fig. 302

Reclamation, now virtually complete, has been long and expensive. Essential civil engineering work has included the excavation and redistribution of more than 3.5 million tonnes of material, and the construction of more than 16 kilometres of ditches, drains and sewers. The present land use is shown on Fig. 302. To the south of Bryn Road, which lends its name to the whole reclamation scheme, 15 hectares are now shared by housing, schools and public open space. The road also borders an area of 57 hectares which is the site of a growing number of industrial premises. In the north, pit waste has been levelled, mixed with clay and topsoil, and put down to

Fig. 301

Fig. 303

Fig. 304

pasture for the support of dairy cattle. It was the central area which posed the greatest problems of reclamation. The 'Three Sisters' were too huge to move. They have been sculpted into an arena, seen under construction in Fig. 303, which is large enough to accommodate a variety of motor sports. Nearby, a newly created lake nearly 2 hectares in area offers opportunities for fishing and sailing. It is intended that the 'Three Sisters' complex will eventually develop into a recreational centre of regional importance.

Fig. 305

On a smaller scale, local successes are widely recorded. The Olympic-standard rowing course at Holme Pierrepont near Nottingham was, not long ago, an unsightly water-filled gravel-pit. Also, look at Fig. 304. This small corner of the home of the Eccles cake was once overshadowed by a railway station perched on a bridge and embankment. The bridge has been swept away and its site has been landscaped. The former embankment is now a pleasant, tree-lined footway. Adjacent waste land has been converted into a miniature golf-course.

Present-day industrial activity adds to the total of land in need of reclamation, and may have other harmful effects on the environment. Minerals are still needed, and must be mined. Chemical plants must still dispose of waste products. Factory processes still demand the emission of fumes. Cables are needed to transport electricity. Happily, the dangers are now more closely appreciated and great efforts are made to minimise their effects. Marshland is reclaimed with coal-mine waste (page 72) and power-station ash (page 79). Dust is filtered from factory chimneys and the air we breathe is cleaner. With greater control over the disposal of effluent, rivers become less polluted; fish may now be caught in the shadow of London Bridge. In areas of great beauty, electricity transmission cables are laid underground, although this is sixteen times more expensive than hanging them on pylons.

Fig. 305 provides a happy footnote. Industry makes use of its own derelict land. The new factory of the London Brick Company at Whittlesey, near Peterborough, is built 30 metres below ground level on the floor of an abandoned clay-pit.

Population

Growth

Population statistics are tabled in Fig. 306 and the growth of the population of Great Britain is graphed in Fig. 307. In 1801, the year of the first official census, 10500965 people were counted. By 1901, population had risen to almost 37 million. Throughout the nineteenth century, the birth rate remained fairly steady. The tremendous increase in population was due mainly to a dramatic fall in the death rate, to which greater medical knowledge, improved sanitation and a rising standard of living made major contributions. Population would have risen even higher, but for the effects of migration. During the century, many millions of people left Great Britain to make new homes for themselves in other parts of the world, especially the U.S.A. and Empire territories. This movement was much greater than the influx of people from overseas.

In the present century, the death rate has continued its decline, but the birth rate has fallen more steeply. Except for wartime fluctuations, the two rates have come closer together. The excess of births over deaths has become progressively smaller. The curve in Fig. 307 rises less steeply after 1901. The effect of migration has been less pronounced in this century than it was in the last. Emigration, mainly to the traditional areas such as Australia, Canada and New Zealand, has continued, but at a reduced rate. In return, Britain has gained population from various overseas countries. There was, for

Fig. 306

British Isles – area and population *1975*

	Estimated population (thousands)	*Area (km²)*	*Population density per km²*
England	46453.7	130375	356
Scotland	5206.2	78774	66
Wales	2765.0	20766	133
Total – Great Britain	54424.9	229915	237
Northern Ireland	1537.2	14120	109
Total – United Kingdom	55962.1	244035	229
Republic of Ireland	3127.0	70282	45

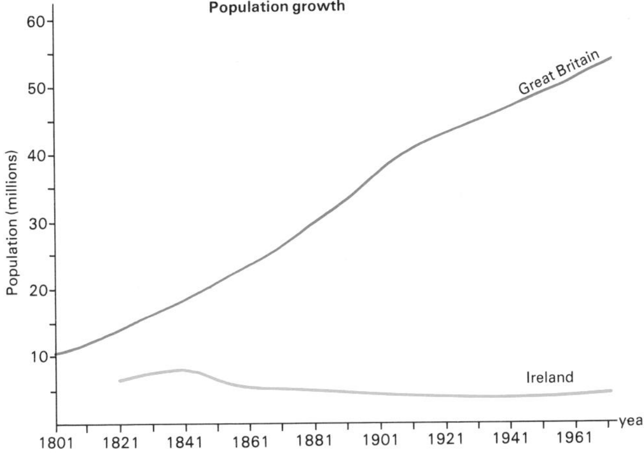

Fig. 307

instance, considerable immigration from Europe in the troubled years before and after the Second World War. More recently, Britain has been a popular destination for migrants from the West Indies, Pakistan, India and other parts of the New Commonwealth. Movement in 1975 is recorded in Fig. 308. In that year, the net loss of population through migration exceeded the excess of births over deaths, to give Britain its first peace-time fall in population since records were kept.

The lower graph in Fig. 307 tells a contrasting story. In 1801, the population of Ireland was estimated to be in the region of 5 million – roughly half the figure for Great Britain. For the first four decades of the century, population rose steadily. The increase was largely accommodated in rural areas where the pressure of population on the soil became intense. The high-yielding potato was the staple food. In 1845, the failure of the crop brought famine to the land. Hundreds of thousands of people died of starvation. For an even larger number, emigration was the only means of survival. In the decade following 1841, the population of Ireland declined from more than 8 million to less than 4 million. It has never recovered. Large-scale emigration has persisted as people have sought an escape from rural poverty or a

U.K. migration – 1975

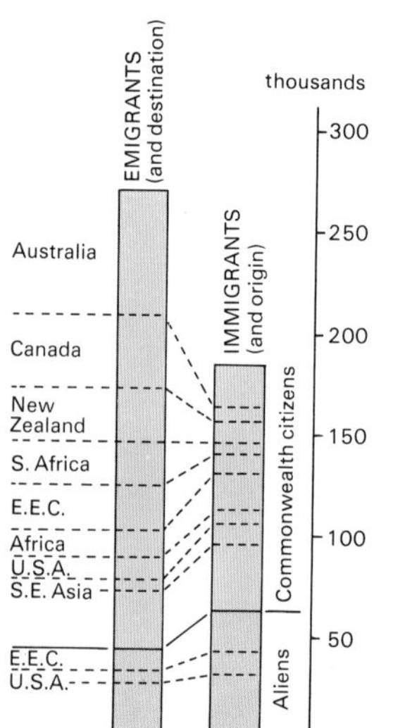

Fig. 308

gateway to greater opportunities. The losses have been greater in the south, for in Ulster the growth of industry brought some slight relief. Since its political creation in 1921, the north has experienced a slow but steady growth of population. In the Republic, however, it is only in the last few years that the persistent downward trend has been checked.

Density and distribution

Further examination of Fig. 306 (page 161) reveals that the population of the British Isles is unevenly shared among the constituent countries. England is obviously the dominant partner in terms of numbers. An equal division of land would give each inhabitant less than 4 hectares. England's population density of 356 per square kilometre is only exceeded by a handful of other countries. For the rest of the British Isles, much lower figures are recorded.

Within national boundaries there are even greater contrasts in density. The appropriate map in a good atlas will paint a varied and intricate picture. Complex areas of great congestion may readily be identified. So, too, may areas which are virtually devoid of residents. The gradient between the two is often steep. Fig. 309 is a highly simplified map of population density, and claims to do no more than highlight the major contrasts.

In England, the pattern is dominated by a broad but broken belt of high density which stretches from Lancashire and Yorkshire, via the midland counties to Greater London and the Channel coast. Similar densities are found in Northumberland and Durham, Avon, and other smaller patches, especially around the coasts. Elsewhere, densities are seldom less than moderate. Only in Cumbria, the Pennines and the moorlands of the south-west peninsula does shading indicate the map's lowest classification. Scotland has but one area of concentrated settlement; population density is high throughout the central lowlands, but thins rapidly to the highland areas which lie to north and south. In Wales, a core of sparse population is bordered by peripheral areas of much higher density. Ireland, too, shows contrasts; they are particularly pronounced between gateway areas such as Dublin and Belfast, and the scattered blocks of the broken upland rim.

Population density is a reflection of the opportunities offered by the environment and the extent to which man has accepted them.

The figures quoted in population maps, '25 per km^2', for instance, have a pleasing air of precision, but are often hard to visualise in terms of landscape. Perhaps another look at photographs considered earlier in different contexts may help our appreciation. Take Fig. 90, page 51, for example. It covers many square kilometres but houses are few and scattered. It is clear that in this area, residents are not overblessed with neighbours. The photograph was taken in Snowdonia, an area shaded yellow in Fig. 309. It is not hard to understand the low population density in areas such as this. Man clings close to his livelihood. Here there are few opportunities. Industry is denied its vital requirements such as power, raw materials, market and labour. Agriculture is hampered by high, steep relief, thin, poor soils and a bleak, wet climate. The land supports little but sheep. Extensive sheep-rearing needs much land but little labour. Farms are far apart. The density of population is low.

The area seen in Fig. 91 (page 52) offers greater opportunity for the support of man. Industry is again absent, but the land is more fruitful. Lowland relief gives cultivable farm land and soils are deeper and more fertile. Climate imposes few restraints. The farmer uses his land intensively. Dairy farms are relatively small in area. The land supports more people, both directly in farming and indirectly in providing the services needed by farming and farmers. Density of population is notably higher than in Snowdonia.

Fig. 309

Little green is seen in Fig. 273 (page 144). There are no farmers in the middle of Croydon. The soil sprouts bricks and concrete. Factories and offices occupy little space but give employment to many. Housing is clustered close at hand to accommodate urban residents at very high densities. In Britain's towns and cities, average population densities commonly range between 2500 and 5000 per square kilometre. Locally they are even higher.

Movement

People are mobile. They have the freedom to move in search of new and better opportunities. A factory closes and the work-force seeks new employment – sometimes in distant districts. A new enterprise may attract its workers from far afield. Perhaps, by moving home, you and your family have made a small contribution to the changes in density and distribution that are constantly taking place. The pattern of population portrayed by the map in your atlas was not achieved overnight. It has been built up over the centuries as a result of changes prompted by social and economic circumstances. A map of population in 1801, for instance, would present a very different picture from the one of today. Outside London, towns were small and few. Agriculture was the support of the great majority. Density closely reflected the fertility of the land, and the intensity of its cultivation. The rich plains of southern England offered the greatest opportunities and supported the highest densities.

The picture was soon to change. New developments were taking place on the coalfields. Mills and factories demanded an ever-increasing supply of labour. Factory villages grew into towns as surplus rural populations arrived in search of employment. In spite of the great national increase in population, rural densities remained steady, or even declined, as the towns expanded. Britain became steadily more urbanised. In 1801, 33 per cent of the population lived in urban areas. In 1901, the figure was 80 per cent. During this century, although London expanded greatly, southern England lost its dominance to areas further north, where towns such as Birmingham, Leeds, Manchester and Glasgow rose to prominence.

The northward emphasis in population growth which developed in the nineteenth century has been reversed in the twentieth. Declining coalfield industries have less demand for labour. People must often move in search of employment. It is mainly the young, skilled and vigorous who move, and this reduces the level of natural increase in the towns they forsake. Some areas have suffered particularly badly. South Wales mining towns and Lancashire mill towns commonly have lower

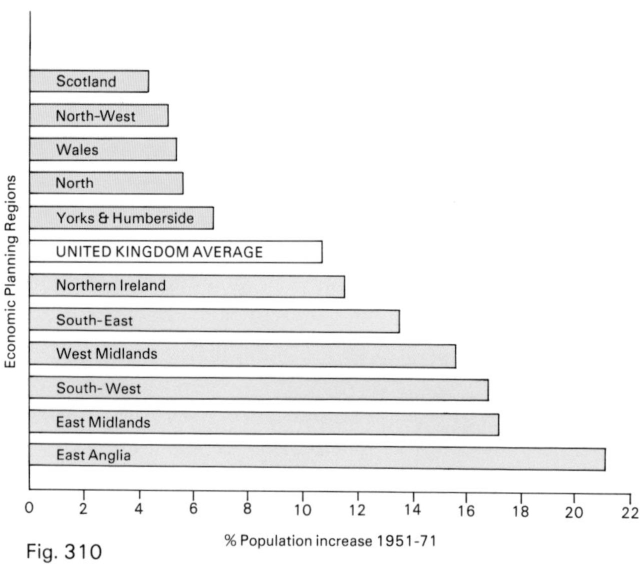

Fig. 310

populations than they did in the heyday of their local industries. These, however, are exceptions. More typically, population totals have not fallen, but the rate of increase is below the national average. Illustration on a regional basis is provided by Fig. 310. This shows the areas which have gained. Clearly, the 'drift' has been 'to the south' (page 126).

Britain retains its high level of urbanisation. Large urban areas, especially the more prosperous, have great powers of attraction. They offer unrivalled opportunities for rewarding employment, and the full range of services and amenities. The great majority of overseas immigrants make their new homes in the cities. In addition, the inward movement of people from rural areas continues. Encouraged by the reduction of farm employment due to mechanisation, it is of varying significance. In some areas it accounts for less than the excess of births over deaths, and so density continues to rise. Hardest hit are the areas of lowest density. In hostile upland environments, the loss through migration is often greater than natural increase, and so population declines.

The area mapped in Fig. 311 is one area where the problem of depopulation gives cause for concern. As population falls, it becomes increasingly difficult to maintain essential services such as health and education. Again, it is generally the younger, more active sections of the community that move away, and this makes for an unbalanced population structure. Efforts are made to halt the damaging outflow of population illustrated in Fig. 312. The Highlands and Islands Development Board shoulders much of the burden, but difficulties are great: settlements are small and remote; transport links are often tenuous; and natural resources are limited. Agriculture (page 57) offers little scope for improvement. Fishing (page 66) and forestry (page 64) give employment to relatively few. The requirements of large-scale industry are seldom available. Nevertheless, prompted by grants, loans and advice made available by the Highlands and Islands Development Board, fuller use is being made of resources and labour, and the opportunities for employment are increasing. Of necessity, most of the new enterprises are small in scale. Improved facilities for tourism is one example and support for the fishing industry is another. Employment in manufacturing increases steadily. Newly established factories produce such diverse items as alginate (from seaweed), toys, frozen crab, blue-veined cheese, electronics equipment and fudge. Examples of large-scale undertakings are pulp and paper at Corpach (page 64) and nuclear power at Dounreay (page 81). North Sea oil creates employment mainly in east coast districts and in Orkney and Shetland. Over much of the Highlands and Islands, the steady decline in population has been checked, and in some districts, appreciable increases are recorded. Illustrative statistics are included in Fig. 311b.

Movement of population is a current trend in Britain's major urban areas. Movement is outwards. Crowded central districts, built in the nineteenth century, are in the process of redevelopment. Some residential land is lost

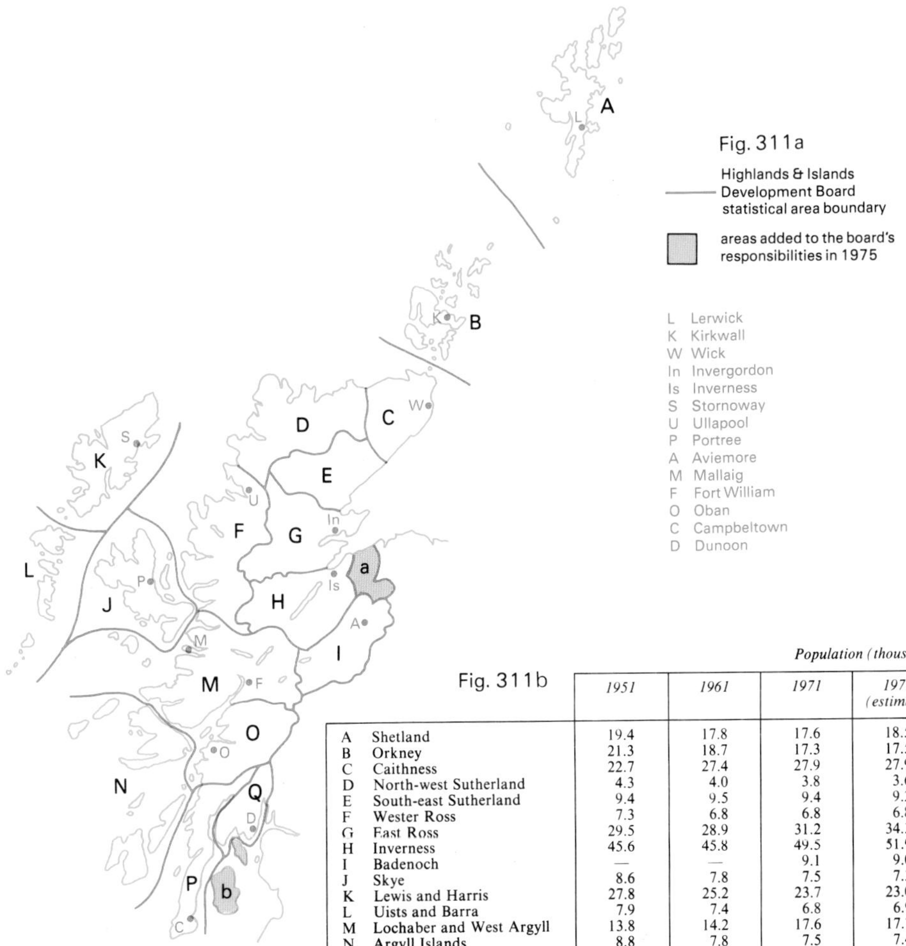

Fig. 311a
Highlands & Islands Development Board statistical area boundary
areas added to the board's responsibilities in 1975
L Lerwick
K Kirkwall
W Wick
In Invergordon
Is Inverness
S Stornoway
U Ullapool
P Portree
A Aviemore
M Mallaig
F Fort William
O Oban
C Campbeltown
D Dunoon
A
B
C
D
E
F
G
H
I
J
K
L
M
N
O
P
Q
a
b

Fig. 311b

		Population (thousands) 1951	1961	1971	1977 (estimate)
A	Shetland	19.4	17.8	17.6	18.5
B	Orkney	21.3	18.7	17.3	17.5
C	Caithness	22.7	27.4	27.9	27.9
D	North-west Sutherland	4.3	4.0	3.8	3.6
E	South-east Sutherland	9.4	9.5	9.4	9.2
F	Wester Ross	7.3	6.8	6.8	6.8
G	East Ross	29.5	28.9	31.2	34.3
H	Inverness	45.6	45.8	49.5	51.9
I	Badenoch	—	—	9.1	9.0
J	Skye	8.6	7.8	7.5	7.3
K	Lewis and Harris	27.8	25.2	23.7	23.0
L	Uists and Barra	7.9	7.4	6.8	6.9
M	Lochaber and West Argyll	13.8	14.2	17.6	17.7
N	Argyll Islands	8.8	7.8	7.5	7.4
O	Oban and Lorne	14.6	15.2	15.1	15.1
P	Mid Argyll and Kintyre	20.2	18.8	18.6	18.6
Q	Dunoon and Cowal	17.9	16.2	16.8	17.3
a	Nairn	—	—	8.3	8.9
b	Clyde Islands	—	—	12.0	11.5

to commerce and industry, and new housing is built at lower densities. Displaced population is often housed in large, new estates on the outskirts. In central districts, the density of population is much reduced. Suburban growth extends the built-up area. Many are daily faced with an extended journey to work. The pressure of population on urban space is often eased by the creation of new towns, discussed in Chapter 8.

Highlands & Islands Development Board Area
Population (thousands)
400
300
200
100
1841
1861
1881
1901
1921
1941
1961
71
year

Fig. 312

This outward movement has been extended into the rural fringe. Many urban workers now have homes in country districts. Modern transport, especially the private car, enables them to commute to their jobs in the city. Agricultural villages within range of the town expand into dormitory settlements. The division between town and country becomes increasingly blurred. In rural areas close to the cities, fewer work the land, but the density of population often increases.

Finally, before we reach the last full stop, look again at Fig. 309, page 163, or, better still, at your atlas map of population density. In a sense, this map is a summary of much that has gone before in earlier chapters. It speaks of man's response to the many and varied environments to be found within the limited compass of the British Isles. The questions it provokes require answers that are fundamental to geography.

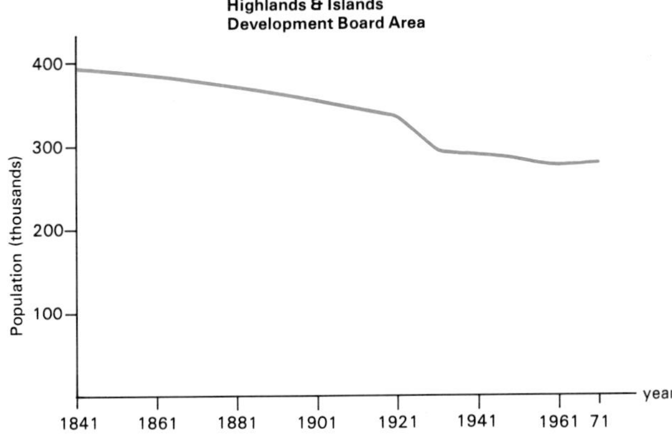

Index